The Hermeneutics of Participation

Studies in Missional Hermeneutics, Theology, and Praxis

The volumes in this series explore the significance of the so-called "missional turn" for Christian hermeneutics, theological reflection, and praxis. This entails both a critical reconstruction of mission in more holistic and decolonizing terms, as well as the ways in which this renewed conception of mission reorients biblical interpretation, theological reflection, and Christian praxis. In so doing, the series seeks to explore and reimagine texts and themes, hermeneutical dynamics, theological issues, and faithful, located engagement for a post-Christendom church in the contemporary world.

Series Editors

Michael Barram, St Mary's College of California (mbarram@stmarys-ca.edu)

John R. Franke, Fuller Theological Seminary (johnrfranke@gmail.com)

Editorial Board

Sarah Bixler, Eastern Mennonite University
Lisa Bowens, Princeton Theological Seminary
Dennis Edwards, North Park Seminary
Michael J. Gorman, Saint Mary's Seminary & University
Drew Hart, Messiah University
Greg McKenzie, Abilene Christian University
Amanda Pittman, Abilene Christian University
Charlene Han Powell, First Presbyterian Church, Berkeley, CA
Al Tizon, Grace Fellowship Community Church, San Francisco, CA
Colin Yuckman, Duke Divinity School

The editors welcome proposals on topics related to the series from scholars at all stages of academic development working in both the academy and the church. Proposals may be submitted to either of the series editors at the email addresses listed above.

"This is the book I for which I have been waiting! McKinzie explores why theological hermeneutics needs the discipline of missional hermeneutics lest theological interpretation fall short of its own goals. Readerly formation must include missional participation. Healthy theological interpretation is saturated and driven by the *missio Dei* or else it becomes merely an extra-ecclesial activity. This, in turn, misses the message and practices of the narrative itself. Both disciplines need each other. Missional hermeneutics recasts theological interpretation toward participating in the mission of God. McKinzie offers what is generally lacking in the literature. He defines missional participation through the lens of theological, missiological, and ecclesial formation. Participation in the *missio Dei*, the book cogently argues, forms better readers of Scripture. This is a primary virtue of missional hermeneutics."

—**John Mark Hicks**, Retired Professor of Theology, Lipscomb University

"Christians have long realized that ecclesial practices shape faithful readers of Scripture. But is mission one of these practices? In *The Hermeneutics of Participation*, Greg McKinzie responds with a resounding 'yes.' Substantive, deeply researched, and engaging, this book offers the most thorough argument available that participation in God's mission is hermeneutically foundational for the church. McKinzie's case is convincing: mission constitutes the eyes of faith necessary to read Scripture well. The arguments this book offers, if taken seriously, will strengthen the church's hermeneutical imagination."

—**Derek W. Taylor**, Director, Emmaus Program, Whitworth University

"Greg McKinzie has provided an invaluable contribution to the urgent need for the church to be at heart a missional church participating in the trinitarian mission of God to the world. From his own missional experience and theological immersion, he has woven together an impressive number of sometimes disparate threads, especially missional theology, the theological interpretation of Scripture, and the philosophical hermeneutics of Paul Ricoeur. All readers will be more properly formed through his work."

—**Dan Stiver**, President, Fletcher Seminary, Texas

"In this sophisticated and significant book, Greg McKinzie argues for a missional hermeneutic of transformative, cruciform, embodied participation in the life and mission of the Triune God—or 'works seeking understanding.' Building on, but also challenging, previous work in missional hermeneutics and in theological interpretation, McKinzie reconfigures the landscape of both as he creatively brings them together. A landmark volume."

—**Michael J. Gorman**, Raymond E. Brown Professor of Biblical and Theological Studies, St. Mary's Seminary's University, Baltimore

The Hermeneutics of Participation

Missional Interpretation of Scripture and Readerly Formation

BY Greg McKinzie

FOREWORD BY
Joel B. Green

CASCADE *Books* • Eugene, Oregon

THE HERMENEUTICS OF PARTICIPATION
Missional Interpretation of Scripture and Readerly Formation

Copyright © 2025 Greg McKinzie. All rights reserved. Except for brief quotations in critical publications or reviews, no part of this book may be reproduced in any manner without prior written permission from the publisher. Write: Permissions, Wipf and Stock Publishers, 199 W. 8th Ave., Suite 3, Eugene, OR 97401.

Cascade Books
An Imprint of Wipf and Stock Publishers
199 W. 8th Ave., Suite 3
Eugene, OR 97401

www.wipfandstock.com

PAPERBACK ISBN: 979-8-3852-1306-1
HARDCOVER ISBN: 979-8-3852-1307-8
EBOOK ISBN: 979-8-3852-1308-5

Cataloguing-in-Publication data:

Names: McKinzie, Greg [author]. | Green, Joel B., 1956– [foreword writer].

Title: The hermeneutics of participation : missional interpretation of scripture and readerly formation / by Greg McKinzie ; foreword by Joel B. Green.

Description: Eugene, OR: Cascade Books, 2025 | Series: Studies in Missional Hermeneutics, Theology, and Praxis | Includes bibliographical references.

Identifiers: ISBN 979-8-3852-1306-1 (paperback) | ISBN 979-8-3852-1307-8 (hardcover) | ISBN 979-8-3852-1308-5 (ebook)

Subjects: LCSH: Missions—Biblical teaching. | Bible—Hermeneutics. | Missions—Theory. | Hermeneutics—Religious aspects—Christianity.

Classification: BV2073 M355 2025 (paperback) | BV2073 (ebook)

VERSION NUMBER 07/14/25

Scripture quotations are from New Revised Standard Version Bible, copyright © 1989 National Council of the Churches of Christ in the United States of America. Used by permission. All rights reserved worldwide.

To my companions
in God's mission

Contents

List of Illustrations | viii
Foreword by Joel B. Green | ix
Preface | xi
Acknowledgments | xiii
Abbreviations | xv

1. Introduction: Participation as Readerly Formation | 1
2. Participation in Missional Theology | 26
3. Participation in God's Mission as *Theōsis* | 59
4. Participation as Embodied Narrativity | 97
5. Participation as Solidarity | 140
6. The Hermeneutics of Participation | 177
7. Conclusion: The Formation of Missional Readers | 219

Bibliography | 233

List of Illustrations

Figure 1: The Selfhood-Sameness Dialectic | 126

Figure 2: The Ethics-Practice Circle | 196

Figure 3: The Bad Infinite of Disembodied Hermeneutical Reflection | 197

Figure 4: The Good Infinite of the Incarnate Hermeneutic | 198

Foreword

Two characters, theological interpretation of Scripture and missional hermeneutics, walk into a bar. . . . What happens next? We no longer need to wonder what direction this scenario might take. Instead, we can take and read this new book by Greg McKinzie. The results are profound and far reaching for practitioners of both discourses.

On the one hand, even though theological interpretation has prioritized the ecclesial location of scriptural engagement, it has struggled to identify what that means in practice. Surely, all agree, the act of reading of the Bible *as Christian Scripture* characterizes the gathered people of God as they come together to pray and worship. And many agree that, when we turn to Christian Scripture, our readings must be set in relation to the ecumenical creeds of the church. Indeed, one of the primary roles, if not the primary role, of the Nicene Creed, for example, is to teach us faithfully how to read Scripture. Prayer, worship, and confession—do these settings exhaust what is entailed in churchly readings of Scripture? We should add the importance of the history of interpretation of Scripture (or history of effects), not least among those historically and globally whose practices of reading theologically were and remain second nature. Even so, there is still more if we are to give priority to encountering Scripture in and with the church. For Greg McKinzie, participation in the church's mission—or, rather, in the ongoing *missio Dei*, in union with Christ and fashioned by the Spirit—is and must be indispensable to the theological formation of faithful readers of Scripture.

On the other hand, the discourse of missional hermeneutics has prioritized participation in God's mission but has needed to identify better what that participation entails, theologically. Moreover, at least among some missional hermeneuts, emphasis has tended to fall on reading the Bible for its understanding of mission and then applying that understanding to the life of the church. For these interpreters, the traffic is often conceived of or practiced as one way—from exegesis to ecclesia. Here again, Greg McKinzie raises hard questions. Most especially, he insists that participation in mission cannot simply be identified as the outcome of well-intended exegesis but is actually preparatory—essential, we should say—to faithful interpretation of Scripture. What is more, McKinzie makes his case through his sophisticated work in both trinitarian theology and philosophical hermeneutics, with that work firmly undergirding his approach to readerly formation and practice.

Unsurprisingly, then, what we have before us is a penetrating criticism of missional hermeneutics and theological interpretation of Scripture that shifts the conversation in both areas of inquiry—by pressing the one to be more missional and the other to be more theological, and, therefore, by narrowing the distance between these two. Undoubtedly, *The Hermeneutics of Participation* will stimulate fresh conversations and revamped practices for a sent church engaging its Scriptures.

Joel B. Green
Fuller Theological Seminary

Preface

I WAS FLATTERED WHEN my doctoral mentor, Joel Green, suggested that my dissertation did not read like a typical PhD program product. If you have read one or two of these gems formed by long years of academic pressure, you know what dissertationese sounds like. The most egregious examples aspire to sophistication through convoluted syntax, technical jargon, florid use of adverbs, and academic gamesmanship. Yet, they remain bloodless.

Though I trust Joel's judgment, I wonder how far I escaped such shortcomings. Having revised the original manuscript for publication as a monograph, I am aware just how "intricate," to quote my second reader, Dan Stiver, my argument remains—and how much I relish that intricacy because of what it can accomplish.

This is an unapologetically interdisciplinary work. I set about the task of identifying how diverse perspectives and methodologies might, together, offer answers to my questions that any one of them alone could not. Most of the academy looks askance at interdisciplinarity, with its many pitfalls. This fact led me to rigor regarding some of the conventions of the academic game that come to expression in dissertationese, namely, surveys and lengthy footnotes. These I have conscientiously retained for the sake of sustaining an interdisciplinary argument. I feel the need to show my work in the disciplines I have tried to weave together—to put all my cards on the table, as it were, so that critical readers can decide whether I have done justice to each thread.

I intend to offer the most compelling version of the argument I have constructed. I hope readers will find that, though technical and complex, the argument is sincere. I suspect this is, in part, what my dissertation committee perceived. The argument is not bloodless because it represents blood—and sweat and tears—for the sake of the church and, ultimately, the kingdom of God. Academics may be a game, but it is high stakes when the church's participation in God's mission is in question.

I am content with issuing the challenge to think more deeply and widely through the tremendous resources at our disposal when we come to the question of interpreting Scripture as participants in God's mission. Interpretation is complicated, to say nothing of the theological depths that words like *Scripture*, *God*, and *mission* betoken. How could we expect less than complexity, intricacy, and *work*? Indeed, scholarship is a part of the church's works seeking understanding. So I offer this book as a search for understanding in response to God's mission. May it serve God's purposes in the world!

Acknowledgments

No one deserves to be acknowledged more than my wife, Megan. I cannot imagine making this journey without her patient love and confidence. Through the years, my children, Ana, Maggie, and Cohen, have joined her as unrelenting supporters. Their love made this work possible.

The deepest of friendships have sustained my spirit. The good humor and encouragement of Kyle Smith, Bryan Tarpley, John Middleton, and Tim Ring have meant the world. Likewise, the fellowship and worship of the Hollywood Church of Christ and the Stones River Church of Christ have given me hope to carry on. The discipleship groups that formed the spiritual core of my last decade deserve special recognition, as do the ministry partnerships with Martin Rodriguez, Jon McPeters, and John King. And I can say confidently that my conception of the hermeneutics of participation would not be possible without my Peruvian sisters and brothers, in whom the grace of God was at work long before I met them.

The mentorship of Joel Green was a special privilege during my PhD work at Fuller Theological Seminary, where this argument took shape as a doctoral dissertation. His uncommon insight and gentle guidance made doctoral study a delight and strengthened this book profoundly. Dan Stiver, who led me into the depths of Paul Ricoeur's thought, has also made an indelible mark on my work. Additionally, study with Veli-Matti Kärkkäinen, Oliver Crisp, and Johnny Ramírez-Johnson has sharpened and refined my thought.

ACKNOWLEDGMENTS

The Society of Ricoeur Studies and the Society of Biblical Literature's Forum on Missional Hermeneutics have been vital as well. The warm collegiality of these organizations stands behind various dimensions of my argument. And the kindness and encouragement of John Franke and Michael Barram, who are both Forum on Missional Hermeneutics leaders and the editors of this series, are remarkable.

Finally, with all the church, I give thanks to God. None could put it better than the venerable words *Soli Deo Gloria*.

Abbreviations

ANF	*Ante-Nicene Fathers.* Edited by Philip Schaff et al. Peabody, MA: Hendrickson, 1994.
ASMS	American Society of Missiology Series
AUSS	Andrews University Seminary Studies
CBQ	*Catholic Biblical Quarterly*
CIT	Current Issues in Theology
CurTM	*Currents in Theology and Mission*
DFT	*Dictionary of Feminist Theologies.* Edited by Letty M. Russell and J. Shannon Clarkson. Louisville: Westminster John Knox, 1996.
Di	*Dialog*
DTIB	*Dictionary for Theological Interpretation of the Bible.* Edited by Kevin J. Vanhoozer. Grand Rapids: Baker Academic, 2005.
EDWM	*The Evangelical Dictionary of World Missions.* Edited by A. Scott Moreau et al. Grand Rapids: Baker, 2000.
EvQ	*Evangelical Quarterly*
FemTh	*Feminist Theology*
GOCS	The Gospel and Our Culture Series

ABBREVIATIONS

HTR	*Harvard Theological Review*
HvTSt	*HTS Teologiese Studies/Theological Studies*
IBMR	*International Bulletin of Missionary Research*
IJST	*International Journal of Systematic Theology*
Int	*Interpretation*
IRM	*International Review of Mission*
JAAR	*Journal of the American Academy of Religion*
JETS	*Journal of the Evangelical Theological Society*
JFSR	*Journal of Feminist Studies in Religion*
JPT	*Journal of Pentecostal Theology*
JR	*Journal of Religion*
JTI	*Journal of Theological Interpretation*
JTSA	*Journal of Theology for Southern Africa*
LTQ	*Lexington Theological Quarterly*
MDJ	*Missio Dei: A Journal of Missional Theology and Praxis*
Miss	*Missiology: An International Review*
MoTh	*Modern Theology*
NPNF2	*Nicene and Post-Nicene Fathers*. Edited by Philip Schaff and Henry Wace. 2nd series. Peabody, MA: Hendrickson, 1994.
NUSPEP	Northwestern University Studies in Phenomenology and Existential Philosophy
PCP	Perspectives in Continental Philosophy
ProEccl	*Pro Ecclesia*
PRS	*Perspectives in Religious Studies*
RelSoc	*Religion and Society*
SJT	*Scottish Journal of Theology*
ST	*Studia Theologica*
STI	Studies in Theological Interpretation

ABBREVIATIONS

SVTQ	*St. Vladimir's Theological Quarterly*
Them	*Themelios*
ThTo	*Theology Today*
TS	*Theological Studies*
TynBul	*Tyndale Bulletin*
VC	*Vigiliae Christianae*

CHAPTER 1

Introduction

Participation as Readerly Formation

"If a missional hermeneutic provides the fruit of an overall vision of the Bible's message (discerned and passed on) without the fruit of a robust set of habits of receiving the Scriptures and being formed by them in local missional responses, the project will have failed to achieve its full potential." —George Hunsberger[1]

SOME READERS ARE BETTER than others. In the discourse known as theological interpretation of Scripture, the notion of readerly formation entails this affirmation. Well-formed readers must be better than poorly formed readers or *theological formation* is an empty signifier. No doubt, the idea is contentious. It is challenging enough to substantiate in the relativistic context of postmodernism that some readings are better than others, more so the apparently *ad hominem* judgment that some readers are better than others. Still, some proponents of theological interpretation of Scripture contend the ecclesial practices that shape readers theologically stand to make them more perceptive, more faithful, more open in their engagement with the Bible. The corollary question, of course, is which practices offer such benefits. Moreover, the answer to this question calls for an account of *why* and *how* certain ecclesial practices shape readers. The

---

1. Hunsberger, "Mapping," 67.

present argument aims to show, in particular, why participation in God's mission should be counted among the church's hermeneutically formative practices.[2] In order to frame my argument, I begin by introducing two discourses that intersect in this study: missional hermeneutics and theological interpretation of Scripture, focusing especially on questions of readerly formation. I next specify my thesis and methodology. A summary of chapters concludes the introduction.

Theological Interpretation of Scripture and Missional Hermeneutics

Theological interpretation of Scripture and missional hermeneutics are discourses with significant affinities that appear to have developed in relative isolation from each other. Nonetheless, a convergence has begun in recent years. The present study unfolds at the nexus of the two discourses, testing the hypothesis that a vital new perspective on readerly formation emerges from the mutual encounter. I have argued elsewhere that missional hermeneutics is a radical reorientation of theological interpretation,[3] though the exposition of this position in relation to my present thesis is best delayed until chapter 7. At this stage, establishing the rudiments of each discourse will suffice to orient the specific line of argumentation that the ensuing chapters develop. The following definitions intend, therefore, to be condensed but representative articulations of complex, evolving ideas.

First, theological interpretation is a set of practices meant to cultivate (1) *perceptions* of the subject matter of Scripture as God's revelation, (2) *approaches* to the text of Scripture as canon, and (3) *dispositions* in readers of Scripture as the church.[4] As Richard Hays has succinctly stated, "Theo-

---

2. The question of *how* participation in God's mission shapes readers of Scripture must wait for a different argument. I have coauthored a study that begins to explore one possible understanding of formative effects: McKinzie et al., "Between," 133–56. Although this study makes use of concepts developed in the present argument (especially embodied narrativity), its method and concern are distinctive. I am engaged here not in empirical but theoretical hermeneutics.

3. McKinzie, "Missional," 157–79. Much of this argument is restated here and in ch. 7. See also Barram and Franke, *Liberating*, ch. 6.

4. These three components of my definition broadly follow Kevin Vanhoozer's summary of three approaches to theological interpretation, with their interests in (1) "divine authorship, in the God-world relationship 'behind' the text as it were"; (2) "the final form of the text," whether in narrative or canonical terms; and (3) the "function of the aims and interests of the community of readers for which the Bible is 'Scripture'" ("Introduction," 23).

logical exegesis is a complex *practice*, a way of approaching Scripture with eyes of faith and seeking to understand it within the community of faith."[5] The perceptions, approaches, and dispositions of theological interpretation can together be abbreviated as *faith*—faith in the God who speaks, through the canon, to the church. In the context of scholarly interpretive practices, however, this is specifically faith over against the "methodological atheism" typical of the modern academy.[6] Although we might refer to this alternative as *methodological faith*, it is important to note that theological interpretation is not a "method" as such, with sequential steps or techniques that determine meaning. In other words, cultivation of the perceptions, approaches, and dispositions that pertain to theological interpretation of Scripture may occur through a variety of practices whose criterion is *faith*fulness.

Second, missional hermeneutics, whose development is decades behind theological interpretation's, can likewise be understood as a set of practices. The discourse has been framed most influentially by George Hunsberger as four "streams" or "accents" among its advocates: "These accents have made proposals regarding the *framework* for a missional hermeneutic (the narrative of the *missio Dei*), the *aim* of a missional hermeneutic (ecclesial formation for witness), the *approach* of a missional hermeneutic (socially located questions), and the interpretive *matrix* of a missional hermeneutic (the gospel as the interpretive key)." Together, they contribute to the development of "a robust missional hermeneutic."[7] The introductory concern here is how these "streams" map onto what I have identified as the practices of theological interpretation.

The most important point to make definitionally is so obvious that it goes without saying in Hunsberger's review: what holds these streams together as a single robust missional hermeneutic is the doctrine of the *missio Dei*. David Bosch articulated what became the fundamental point of departure for missional theology: "The classical doctrine on the *missio*

---

5. Hays, "Reading," 11.

6. Rae, *History*, 38.

7. Hunsberger, "Mapping," 45–67, a revised and expanded version of Hunsberger, "Proposals," 309–21. Hunsberger's taxonomy has proven generative, though some key contributions might be parsed differently. See McKinzie, "Currents," where I note important distinctions between (a) the missional origins of Scripture and (b) the paradigmatic interpretive approaches of the New Testament authors as missional theologians, as well as the need to expand Michael Barram's notion of "social location" (Barram, "'Located' Questions") to consider both (c) missiological contextualization and (d) readerly formation. The final point (d) is the focus of this study.

Dei as God the Father sending the Son, and God the Father and the Son sending the Spirit was expanded to include yet another 'movement': Father, Son, and Holy Spirit sending the church into the world."[8] To restate the four streams of missional hermeneutics more clearly in these terms: the theological framework is the canonical narrative of God's mission, the aim is ecclesial formation for participation in God's mission, the approach to the text is the social location of participation in God's mission, and the interpretive matrix is the gospel of God's mission.

My working definition of missional hermeneutics, therefore, takes three of these streams to align respectively with the perceptions, approaches, and dispositions that theological interpretation is meant to cultivate, with the caveat that the *missio Dei* is a controlling theological assumption. Thus, missional hermeneutics is a set of practices meant to cultivate (1) a perception that the gospel of God's reconciling mission in Christ through the Spirit is the subject matter of Scripture, (2) an approach to the text of Scripture as the canonical narrative of God's mission, and (3) a disposition in readers of Scripture as the church called to participate in God's mission. The articulation of these interpretive aims in terms of the *missio Dei* is the basic challenge that missional hermeneutics issues to theological interpretation of Scripture. Several advocates of theological interpretation already speak in the Trinitarian and teleological terms that are essential to the doctrine of the *missio Dei*, and in this sense the basic challenge is to make explicit what may be already implicit in theological interpretation. The God who speaks in and through Scripture is the Father who sends the Son, who in turn with the Father sends the Spirit and the church in the power of the Spirit. The canonical narrative of God's redemptive purposes is the story of God's mission, into which the church is drawn. The formation of the church is purposive—the ecclesial community's transformation is *for* participation in God's mission.

Hunsberger notes that the missional hermeneutics discourse has been more attentive to concerns "behind and within the text" than to those "before the text."[9] He concludes, "If a missional hermeneutic provides the fruit

---

8. Bosch, *Transforming*, 390; see also the widely influential Trinitarian vision of mission in Newbigin, *Open Secret*.

9. The use of the "behind" and "before" metaphors represents another significant correlation to theological interpretation of Scripture. I expand on their significance in ch. 6. Notably, Barram and Franke's introductory volume in this series uses the *text itself*, *behind the text*, and *in front of the text* "lenses"—rather than Hunsberger's taxonomy—to locate the various streams of missional hermeneutics (*Liberating*, 68–69). Like my

of an overall vision of the Bible's message (discerned and passed on) without the fruit of a robust set of habits of receiving the Scriptures and being formed by them in local missional responses, the project will have failed to achieve its full potential."[10] In service to the fuller potential of missional hermeneutics, its third stream, which insists that the church's location as participants in God's mission is essential for interpretation, is the primary interest of the present study. More specifically, I am concerned with the question of readerly formation in view of missional hermeneutics' reorientation of theological interpretation. If participation in God's mission is the church's proper *locus theologicus*, what does it mean to say that some readers are better formed than others?

Readerly Formation

As the language of cultivating perceptions, approaches, and dispositions suggests, readerly formation is at the heart of theological interpretation of Scripture. Adapting Umberto Eco's "model reader," Joel Green represents this concern. Green's primary question is "what sorts of communities are open and able to hear the words of Scripture as God's word addressed to them."[11] The question behind the question, however, is What *makes* the sorts of readers who are able to hear? This puts a fine point on the distinction—and the relationship—between two separate hermeneutical concerns regarding readerly formation. On the one hand is the question of how Scripture forms readers. On the other hand is the question of what formation a reader needs in order to read Scripture well. It is hermeneutically no surprise that these two form a circle. A certain readerly disposition is necessary for Scripture to do its formative work; Scripture's formative work is necessary to cultivate that disposition. Green captures this reciprocity:

> As model readers generated by this text, we are guarded from too easily colonizing or objectifying the text, instead hearing its own voice from within its own various contextual horizons. At the same time, we remain open to God's challenge of developing those habits of life that make us receptive to God's vision, God's character, and

---

argument, theirs emphasizes the need for serious developments of the *in front of the text* lens and, like my argument, depends on liberation theology for crucial insights (see 169–75).

10. Hunsberger, "Mapping," 67.
11. Green, *Practicing*, 9.

God's project, animating these texts as Scripture and, then, textualized in and emanating from these pages. We come to Scripture with dispositions of risky openness to a reordering of the world, repentance for attitudes of defiance of the grace of God's self-revelation, hospitable to a conversion of our own imagination.[12]

Model readers are both generated by the text and approach the text with dispositions of openness. Taking James as a case study, the remainder of Green's discussion focuses on the way "James wants to shape a reader capable of hearing, of putting into play, his message."[13] But the other question remains: what disposes the reader to such shaping?

Missional hermeneutics assumes that not only the capability of putting the text into play but also *actually putting it into play* is at stake hermeneutically, not merely as a hermeneutical result but as that which disposes the reader to the text's formative work. In part, this is a matter of construing the narrative in explicitly missional terms. Green, like many advocates of theological interpretation, construes the narrative in implicitly missional terms, because narrative is inherently teleological, and Scripture's plot is that of God's purposes: "James sculpts his model readers by locating them, that is, us—on the plotline between creation and new creation."[14] Construing the narrative missionally is what Hunsberger's first two streams contribute. The purpose of the story is formation, as Green suggests, and it is the story that forms the church specifically for participation in God's mission. This is only one side of the coin, though. The stream in which Hunsberger locates Barram, "the missional locatedness of the readers," is the other side. What disposes readers to the story's formative work? Participation in the story—in God's mission. From this vantage, missional hermeneutics seeks to expand on Green's view of the relationship between theological interpretation and Christian formation: the purpose of the story is formation, this formation is for mission, participation in mission *is* readerly formation, and in this way, Scripture makes readers capable of hearing its message. The ideal reader is a participant in God's mission.

The practices that constitute theological interpretation are variable because the practice of theological interpretation as a whole hinges on the perceptions, approaches, and dispositions in play as readers engage

---

12. Green, *Practicing*, 20.

13. Green, *Practicing*, 42.

14. Green, *Practicing*, 36. Green has since offered an explicitly missional iteration of his earlier reading. See Green, "Reading," 194–212.

Scripture, not on the formulaic use of particular practices. Theological interpretation does, however, take for granted that certain established practices are known to cultivate the appropriate perceptions, approaches, and dispositions. Among these normal practices are the formative use of the Rule of Faith (particularly the liturgical confession of the ecumenical creeds), prayer and worship, canonical readings (both intertextual and narrative), attentiveness to Christian tradition (especially premodern exegesis), and reading as an ecclesial community with conscious convictions and interests. Together, these practices produce distinctive *theological commitments*, *narrative configurations*, and *hermeneutical virtues*. To establish the status of readerly formation in theological interpretation of Scripture, I represent each of these distinctives in turn, highlighting the ways missional hermeneutics challenges their limits.

Commitments and Readerly Formation

Stephen Fowl, a leading proponent of readerly formation for theological interpretation, argues: "Given the ends toward which Christians interpret their scripture, Christian interpretation of scripture needs to involve a complex interaction in which Christian convictions, practices, and concerns are brought to bear on scriptural interpretation in ways that both shape that interpretation and are shaped by it."[15] An essential hermeneutical circularity is evident, but Fowl places the accent on the way convictions, practices, and concerns shape interpretation. His thesis is limited, however, by the narrowness of the ends toward which he believes Christians interpret Scripture: "their primary aim . . . is to interpret scripture as part of their ongoing struggles to live and worship faithfully before the triune God in ways that bring them into ever deeper communion with God and with others."[16] Fowl's Trinitarian vision of communion has merit, but it unfortunately leaves theological interpretation with ecclesiocentric ends. This results in two shortcomings from a missional standpoint.

First, Fowl's vision of readerly formation moves in the right direction: "Christians need to be more intentional about forming their members to be certain types of readers, readers who, by virtue of their single-minded attention to God, are well versed in the practices of forgiveness, repentance,

---

15. Fowl, *Engaging*, 8.
16. Fowl, *Engaging*, 3.

and reconciliation."[17] Yet, forgiveness, repentance, and reconciliation are too limited as specifications of the convictions, practices, and concerns that shape interpretation. One might easily argue, of course, that reconciliation is a primary missional motif and that communion is one way of construing the goal of God's mission. To this extent, Fowl comes close to missional hermeneutics. But his discussion of theological interpretation seems to be keyed to the inner dynamics of a church communion that, like much of Western Christianity, imagines the struggle "to live and worship faithfully before the triune God" without reference to the mission of God. The admission that "there is a vast array of convictions and practices which should shape and be shaped by Christian interpretation of Scripture" leaves room for missional practices but does not dull the implication that intra-ecclesial practices of forgiveness, repentance, and reconciliation are the truly essential practices of readers well-formed for theological interpretation.[18] The fundamental problem is, perhaps, that the "relationships of self-giving love characteristic of the triune life of God"[19] in which Fowl roots the priority of forgiveness, repentance, and reconciliation are not relationships understood in terms of the *missio Dei*. The Triune life of God is marked by redemptive movement *beyond* the inner communion of those relationships.[20] Mission

17. Fowl, *Engaging*, 26–27.
18. Fowl, *Engaging*, 97.
19. Fowl, *Engaging*, 84.

20. This is one way of putting the matter, appropriate for an understanding of the Christian community rooted in a Trinitarian theology in which the accent falls on God's aseity. A prime example is Grenz, *Theology*, 76, who says that "as Christians our concern for humankind must begin 'at home' that is, with the needs of sisters and brothers within the community of Christ (1 John 4:11). But it must not stop there. Rather, we must see the entire world as the object of our care and concern, *just as the love of God spills beyond the boundaries of the trinitarian members to encompass all creation*" (emphasis added). Another approach to the issue is, in one way or another, to collapse the distinction between God's *opera ad intra* and *opera ad extra*, so that God's work *ad extra* (e.g., creation, preservation, or recreation) is not an overflow "beyond" the internal life of the Trinity but is "internal to his being." See Flett, "*Missio*," 10. From this it follows that, for a Trinitarian ecclesiology, the church's inner life as a community does not exist in distinction from its relationship to those outside the community. Hence, "it is only as a missionary community that human beings live in correspondence to God's own life of fellowship" (Flett, "*Missio*," 14). The doctrine of the *missio Dei* is not bound to either construal of the Trinity, and both construals indicate in different ways that God is missionary by nature. Whether one claims the church is not itself unless its love overflows the boundaries of the community or one claims that the church is not itself unless its work beyond itself is internal to the very existence of the community, it is fair to say the *missio Dei* reorients the church *beyond* itself. See ch. 2 of this study for further discussion.

is essential to the church's understanding of the Trinity and, in turn, the church's understanding of itself. Thus, Fowl's argument runs in the right direction but should be reoriented missionally. Theological interpretation needs to be more intentional about forming Christians *as readers* in the practices of mission rooted in the Triune life of the sending God.

Second, Fowl's claim that "reading the Spirit," which amounts to discerning the work of the Spirit in the lives of "others," is an aspect of theological interpretation that seems to move even closer to missional hermeneutics. As another dimension of readerly formation, reading the Spirit also requires certain "practical social structures, practices, and habits,"[21] yet the exegesis of Acts 10–15 by which Fowl identifies these fails to account for the fundamentally missional dimensions of the story. Although Fowl makes much of the hermeneutical role of hospitality (leading to friendship), which is a significant dimension of missional praxis, the "others" in whom hospitality allows one to read the Spirit are Christians.[22] The practices in view are still intra-ecclesial, meant to address interpretive differences between Christians on issues such as homosexuality in the church. Thus, Fowl makes the case that hospitality among Christians is vital for readerly formation, but this stops short of attributing the same formative role to missional practices. Again, the "trinitarian grounding"[23] of his discussion seems to bend toward an ecclesiocentric vision of the Spirit's work. For missional hermeneutics, however, a "plain sense" reading of the Acts narrative suggests the limits of Fowl's communion-centered concerns, for the "others" in view are those in whom the church finds the Spirit at work unexpectedly *beyond* the church (Cornelius), prompting fresh interpretation of Scripture regarding how the church should shape its life in order to participate in God's mission among the

---

21. Fowl, *Engaging*, 105.

22. One could assume that by "others" Fowl refers to those who are not the hermeneutically engaged church community, particularly when he mentions "welcoming strangers" (Fowl, *Engaging*, 119). He states clearly, however: "The only way to counter the privatizing tendencies of contemporary church life, which make it unlikely or impossible that Christians would be in a position to testify about the work of the Spirit in the lives of their sisters and brothers, is to enter into friendships with them" (Fowl, *Engaging*, 117). As Fowl applies his hermeneutic to the contemporary discussion of homosexuality in the church, it becomes apparent that his project as a whole is meant to address churches large enough, or at least privatized enough, that the members who are in theological conflict about homosexuality are effectively strangers to one another and in need of practices such as hospitality and reconciliation.

23. Fowl, *Engaging*, 98.

gentiles.[24] Furthermore, an account of the Trinity attuned to the *missio Dei* would push Fowl's notion of reading the Spirit beyond ecclesiocentrism. The Spirit that the church must learn to read is the Spirit sent by Father and Son, in whose sending the church is caught up as participants in God's reconciling work beyond and through the church. Murray Rae offers another confirmation that this hermeneutical consideration is already incipiently present in theological interpretation: "I recommend as a matter of considerable importance . . . that the identification of the church as the *primary locus* of theological interpretation be stated in such a way that it not preclude the work of God's Spirit taking place also outside the church. The Spirit blows where it wills!"[25] Fowl's thesis is essentially right: the convictions, practices, and concerns of the church shape interpretation. These commitments are hermeneutically formative. But missional hermeneutics challenges theological interpretation to reorient readerly formation in terms of the missional practices integral to the life of the church caught up in the mission of God.

Narrativity and Readerly Formation

Another facet of readerly formation in theological interpretation is narrativity, both the narrative nature of the text and the anthropological fact that human beings are fundamentally narrative creatures. The anthropological assertion requires considerable unpacking, which I undertake in chapter 4. For now, I limit the discussion to key expressions of a presumed narrativity in theological interpretation of Scripture. Green's claim regarding the formative function of placing the reader in Scripture's plotline has already signaled the assumptions that Scripture has a plotline and that the reader is capable of such narrative formation. These ideas reflect theological interpretation's strong affinities with narrative theology, from which wider reflections on narrativity have arisen.[26] The basic contention can be stated thusly: readers of Scripture are formed most decisively when their narrative

---

24. It is also worth noting that the practice of hospitality Peter needed to learn for the sake of discerning the work of the Spirit was that of *receiving* hospitality from the "other." Contemporary missiologists have been grappling with the inversion of the practice of hospitality for some time. See Gittins, "Beyond?," 164–82.

25. Rae, "Theological," 21.

26. See Green, "Narrative Theology," 531–33.

identities are "absorbed" by the biblical story, written into the biblical narrative, conscripted in the divine drama.[27]

Reference to *the* biblical narrative raises questions that biblical theologians have long debated.[28] Is there one biblical narrative or a multiplicity, and how might we decide? In this regard, the function of the Rule of Faith (*regula fidei*) in theological interpretation is vital. Stated briefly, the Rule of Faith (or Rule of Truth) is an articulation of the apostolic confession that, by the second century, had become a hermeneutical guide for proper biblical (i.e., Old Testament) interpretation among Christians.[29] How exactly the Rule functions hermeneutically is a matter of some debate, but many exponents of theological interpretation affirm a narrative function: one way or another, the Rule of Faith helps the church keep the biblical story straight as she interprets specific texts and, especially, contemplates their coherence with the rest of Scripture.[30] In other words, the canon's coherence

---

27. The metaphor of "absorption" originates with Lindbeck, *Nature*, 117–18, who extends the work of Hans Frei in narrative theology toward "the possibility of theologically reading Scripture once again in literary rather than nonliterary ways," namely, with a "postcritical focus on intratextual meaning" (123) derived from the "overarching story" (120) of the biblical text, which constitutes "the world of the Bible" (123) that absorbs the universe. Not all theological interpreters of Scripture take a narrative approach, nor do theological interpreters who make recourse to narrative theology espouse a single (say, postliberal) perspective. Still, the notion that the church relates hermeneutically to the biblical text in one way or another *as story* prevails. Among early soundings, see Wright, *New Testament*, 38–46; Watson, *Text*, 6, 10–11; Jenson, "Hermeneutics," 97–98. Green has been an enthusiastic proponent of narrativity in theological interpretation: see esp. Green, "Scripture," 5–20; Green, "Narrative and New Testament Interpretation," 153–66; Green, "Practicing," 387–97. The appropriation of Lindbeck's narrative theology in "postconservative" terms (also incorporating N. T. Wright's "dramatic" analogy) is particularly noteworthy in Vanhoozer, *Drama*.

28. Bauckham, "Reading," 38–53, represents the presumption of canonical narrativity among many theological interpreters. Although this is a point of contention among biblical theologians, theological interpretation largely assumes that "a narrative approach to biblical theology must be primary and foundational for all other methods" (Beldman and Swales, "Biblical," 164). As N. T. Wright puts it, "In principle the whole point of Christianity is that it offers a story which is the story of the whole world" (Wright, *New Testament*, 41–42).

29. See O'Keefe and Reno, *Sanctified*, 33–44, 119–28; Bokedal, "Rule," 233–55.

30. On the narrativity of the Rule of Faith, see Jenson, "Hermeneutics," 98; Blowers, "Regula," 199–228; O'Keefe and Reno, *Sanctified*, 119–20; Wall, "Reading," 90, 97, 101; Treier, *Introducing*, 34, 57, 59.

is narrative in nature, and the Rule of Faith helps the church emplot biblical interpretation according to that narrative.[31]

As I have mentioned, missional hermeneutics entails an approach to the text of Scripture as the *canonical narrative of God's mission*. Given that the determination of the plot of the biblical story is precisely what concerns a narrative understanding of the Rule, this claim raises further questions about the relationship between the Rule and mission. Historically and hermeneutically, the Rule of Faith is a missional phenomenon—a notion that

---

31. Detractors contend that the Rule of Faith does not serve a narrative function. The objection is often intertwined with concerns about the canonical unity of Scripture, especially the relationship of the Testaments. Among those who espouse Brevard Childs's "canonical criticism," canonical unity is internal to Scripture, so to take the Rule as a guide to narrative canonical coherence is to "claim the unity of the canon comes *from the outside*, through the lens of theological (or theocentric) cohesion" (Haydon, "Survey," 145–55). One worry that motivates the critique is that using the Rule in this way undermines the commitment to *sola Scriptura*, with the result that "canonical scripture is not normative (*norma normans non normata*)" without additional theological input (Finn, "Reflections," 228; see also Peckham, "Rationale," 89). The concern extends to a broader critique of theological interpreters' interest in ecclesially located reading, which purportedly "gives priority of the church over Scripture" (Rodrigues, "Rule," 264). In this regard, Fowl's comment is incisive: "Concerns that I take to be central to theological interpretation (i.e., doctrinal and ecclesiological concerns) are the very things biblical theology seeks to keep at arm's length, or further" (Fowl, *Theological*, 30–31). Among theological interpreters, Christopher Seitz has been the chief critic of the narrative understanding of the Rule. He states: "The canon of faith is not a pre-creedal (post-NT) digest that helps ground the authority of a two-testament canon, thus providing as it were the warrant for our recourse to Scripture as authoritative" (Seitz, *Character*, 199). He quotes John Behr with approval: "The point of the canon of truth is not so much to give fixed, and abstract, statements of Christian doctrine. Nor does it provide a narrative description of Christian belief, the literary hypothesis of Scripture [pace Blowers]" (Seitz, *Character*, 199n10; quoting Behr, *Formation*, 35–36). Instead, the "hypothesis" of Scripture identified by Irenaeus is "that Jesus Christ is one with the God who sent him and who is active in the Scriptures inherited, the Holy Spirit being the means of testifying to his active, if hidden, life in the 'Old Testament' and our apprehension of that" (Seitz, *Character*, 198). In other words, the Rule is christological but not narrative. In response to these objections, it is helpful to note that Green's careful delineation of the Rule's function, including the observation that "in early patristic exegesis the notion of 'economy' was paramount because, it was held, correct interpretation of Scripture must express its overall order or structure" (Green, *Practicing*, 79). The scriptural hypothesis represents a unity found not inside the biblical texts but "underneath them, in God's economy as this is understood in the narrative terms of the Rule of Faith" (Green, *Practicing*, 80n12). This affirmation highlights the fact that a nuanced understanding does not reduce the biblical narrative to the Rule yet affirms *the inherent narrativity of the divine economy*. It seems to me that detractors such as Seitz must demonstrate that the christological hypothesis of Scripture *could* be non-narrative.

some theological interpreters have begun to embrace. Robert Jenson, for one, describes the development of canon and creed by taking the "telephone game" as an analogy. In the game, a phrase whispered from person to person around a circle quickly becomes distorted. Jenson compares the game to the spread of the Christian message in the first centuries after Christ. "In the case of the church, the threat is made especially severe by the need repeatedly so to shape the message as to make it comprehensible for new sorts of hearers, by the need not merely to recite the gospel but to interpret it as its messengers enter new cultural or historical situations."[32] Mission, in other words, was the context of the emergence of both canon and creed, and it continues to be the context of their function in the life of the church:

> The problems that occasioned the emergence of the canon and the creedal tradition were far from the last of that sort that the church would encounter. The second-century appearance of the telephone-game problem was only the first of many. The mission—the mandate for one person to tell another person about the resurrection, who is to tell yet another, and so on—is constitutive of the church; indeed, the pursuit of the mission and the perdurance of the church come to the same thing. Therefore, the church is continually driven to cross geographical and temporal boundaries; for it, the harvest is always whiter on the other side of some cultural or historical fence. And beyond each fence new questions wait.[33]

For the purpose of reorienting theological interpretation missionally, the upshot of this account is that the hermeneutical relationship between canon and creed exists because of and for mission. "The canon without the creed will not serve to protect the church against perversion of the gospel, *and* neither will the creed without the canon."[34] This is not an assertion in abstraction from the mission that constitutes the church. On the one hand, the "plotted sequence of God's acts that Irenaeus called 'the economy'" (referring to the Rule of Faith) is what compelled the church from the beginning to "read the Old Testament as narrative of God's history with his people, the people that is now in mission as the church."[35] On the other hand, the canon compensates for "those essential aspects of the message

---

32. Jenson, *Canon*, 4.
33. Jenson, *Canon*, 63.
34. Jenson, *Canon*, 32.
35. Jenson, *Canon*, 23.

that the *regula fidei* did not—as our creeds still do not—directly support" precisely because "sophisticated theological reflection à la Paul or the evangelist John belongs to the mission itself."[36]

This is not an antiquarian observation about the Rule's, or even Scripture's, missional origins. Thanks to Bosch, missional theology takes for granted Martin Kähler's assertion that "mission is the mother of theology."[37] The point is, however, that mission is *still* the mother of theology. What Jenson's historical work reveals is that the function of the Rule of Faith in relation to Scripture, which is so integral to theological interpretation, is—continues to be—an essentially missional phenomenon. The Rule of Faith's proper hermeneutical function is to locate the message the church receives through Scripture in the narrative framework of God's *ongoing* mission, which is already constitutive of the church. The Rule of Faith, then, is not an interpretive key merely to the narrative of Scripture but to the *life* of the missional church that interprets Scripture as its story. Rae captures this idea well:

> There is, of course, a dialectical process at work here: the worship, the doctrine and the mission of the Church emerge and develop through engagement with Scripture, and then those same doctrines and practices successively constitute a hermeneutical guide to the reading of Scripture itself. . . .
>
> The story of the Church's life is long and complex of course, but it is possible to offer a brief description of this life and of its place in the divine economy. That brief description is known as the rule of faith. It is an account of God's action from creation to new creation and centered around Jesus Christ, in the course of which the community of faith is called into being as witness to and fruit of the action of God.[38]

J. Todd Billings helps drive home the point. In a section subtitled "Reading as Acting the Drama," he states:

> The church reads Scripture from within a narrative framework. . . . The rule of faith is a narrative emerging from Scripture that is also a lens through which to view Scripture. But this is not just a story about the past, or a fable of the imagination. This

---

36. Jenson, *Canon*, 41.
37. Bosch, *Transforming*, 16; see Kähler, *Schriften*, 190.
38. Rae, *History*, 146; Rae also discusses human participation in the action and purpose of the Triune God (53–54), deepening the connection to a missional vision of the church's life in the divine economy.

narrative is rooted in the action of God in history, culminating in the incarnation, life, death, and resurrection of Jesus Christ. Hence, we do not apply principles from a story to our lives so much as we enter into the ongoing drama being played out by God's work in the world around us. We are actors in the drama of creation, fall, and redemption in Christ, actors and not merely spectators of the triune God's work in the world.[39]

The Rule of Faith specifies the drama in which the church acts, and therefore, *as enacted drama*, the Rule serves hermeneutically to clarify the story of Scripture. This is the sense in which acting in the drama *is* reading. "Reading Scripture for the Christian involves nothing less than acting in our Christ-formed identity by the Spirit's power, in service to the Father."[40]

Missional hermeneutics reorients the role of the Rule of Faith in theological interpretation by bringing its missional origin and, more importantly, its missional function to the surface. Participation in God's mission was constitutive of the Rule's development and is constitutive of its ongoing hermeneutical function. The upshot of this construal is twofold. On the one hand is the narrativity of Scripture. The canon bears witness to the Triune *missio Dei* and, therefore, holds together narratively in keeping with the purposeful action of God in history expressed in the Rule of Faith. On the other hand is the narrativity of readers. Theological interpretation takes for granted the capacity of the church to be narratively formed—more, to enter into and participate in the narrative of God's ongoing mission. The correlation of these two hermeneutical axioms indicates the significance of narrativity for readerly formation in theological interpretation. The hermeneutical formation of the church is a function of the relationship between the narrative of God's mission, which extends through and beyond the biblical text, and the narrativity of readers.

Virtues and Readerly Formation

Like the other expressions of readerly formation, the role of virtue in theological interpretation represents a dialectic, this one comprised of "virtue through interpretation" (the ways that Scripture engenders virtue in readers) and "virtue in interpretation" (the virtue readers may bring to

---

39. Billings, *Word*, 200.
40. Billings, *Word*, 202–3.

interpretation).[41] Once more, the two are practically inseparable but heuristically distinguishable. Regarding the former, Richard Briggs's exploration of the "implied reader" results in interesting observations on Scripture's own contribution to readerly virtue.[42] More to the point here, however, is the question of which virtues beyond those supplied by Scripture should guide theological interpretation.

To begin, Fowl's discussion of ecclesial commitments extends to a consideration of virtues: "the good working of these practices will aid in the formation of virtuous readers who can exercise interpretive charity in the midst of interpretive disputes."[43] From one perspective, commitments and virtues might seem to compose a single idea in Fowl's work, but they are effectively two distinct sets of "practices." As we have seen, the "convictions, practices, and concerns" that I designated as commitments above prioritize "forgiveness, repentance, and reconciliation." These are, in short, *redemptive* practices—enactments of key elements of the biblical story of God's reconciling work that "result in relationships with both God and others that more closely resemble the relationships of self-giving love characteristic of the triune life of God."[44] By contrast, the "practices" in Fowl's discussion of virtues are "habits of perceiving and living in the world."[45] These are chiefly *liturgical* practices, such as "baptism and catechesis," "the liturgy of the church," "corporate Bible studies," and "common patterns of formation and prayer."[46] This vision of formation coheres with an established understanding of Scriptural interpretation as "ecclesial" reading. The practices of the community of faith instill the habits of perceiving and living that become indispensable for faithful reading.[47] Further, Fowl's ecclesial "habits" cohere

41. Fowl, "Virtue," 837.
42. Briggs, *Virtuous Reader*.
43. Fowl, *Engaging*, 75.
44. Fowl, *Engaging*, 84.
45. Fowl, *Engaging*, 74.

46. Fowl, *Engaging*, 200–201. I do not wish to maintain a firm distinction between redemptive and liturgical practices, as the two comprise one Christian way of life and mutually implicate each other. For this reason, I consider both sets to be "ecclesial" practices. It is noteworthy, nonetheless, that the habits of living and perceiving Fowl identifies are distinctively concerned with the formative effects of "the process of Christian formation more generally" (Fowl, *Engaging*, 200).

47. The Scripture Project's thesis 6 states, "Faithful interpretation of Scripture invites and presupposes participation in the community brought into being by God's redemptive action—the church" (Scripture Project, "Nine," 3). See also Jones, "Embodying," 143–60; Jones, "Formed," 34–52, for a leading representative of this claim.

with the communitarian ecclesiology in which contemporary virtue ethics is rooted.[48] The essential claim, then, is that these practices engender virtues, which are necessary for theological interpretation.

Two questions follow: which virtues are necessary, and which practices engender them? Missional hermeneutics reorients theological interpretation here as well. First, missional hermeneutics suggests that participation in God's mission is an indispensable ecclesial practice. This is a difficult claim to specify because missional practices are essentially contextual. Any attempt to state abstractly what participation in God's mission means must be accompanied by discernment of what God is actually up to in a particular place. Advocating missional practices without specifying what they are is too vague to be helpful, but specifying universal practices is its own variety of mortal generalization. The best we can do is work with categories of typical practices, which presents another reason this is a difficult contention. Categories of typical missional practices sound a lot like traditional Christian practices. For example, the watershed volume *Missional Church* states: "The ecclesial practices of missional communities are many and varied. Among them are baptism, the Lord's Supper, reconciliation, discernment, hospitality, the reading and interpretation of Scripture, the development and exercise of leadership, the loving care and support of one another, the proclamation of God's Word, the active evangelization of all peoples, the exploration and learning of the faith, as well as the responsible and responsive stewardship of all of God's abundant gifts."[49] Of the practices listed, only "evangelization" is traditionally qualified as mission work, and none of them is in any way novel.

By reframing these practices in terms of the *missio Dei*, however, they become something that they indisputably have not been in most Christendom churches: a means of forming congregations into missionary communities that engage their local contexts in order to discover and take part in the redemptive work of God.[50] Congregations that regularly engage in the same practices without being formed into such missionary

---

48. For a useful summary of the virtue ethics discourse that underlies virtue hermeneutics, see Briggs, *Virtuous Reader*, 23–34. See also Pardue, "Athens," 294–308; Treier, *Introducing*, ch. 3.

49. Guder, *Missional*, 159.

50. Conner, "For," 123–37, has recently related missional practices to the robust contemporary discussion of Christian practices, contending "what unites Christian practices is that they are Spirit-enabled means through which congregations participate in the life of God, which is missional" (Conner, "For," 127). But this is a *de jure*, not a *de facto*, claim.

communities (and they are legion) are not, I suggest, actually engaged in missional practices. To introduce a concept from Ludwig Wittgenstein that will bear significant weight in my argument, missional theology is a change of language game. The forms of life—the practices—of a language game constitute its most fundamental dimension, but the language of the language game is not therefore irrelevant. In fact, the practices of one game may mean something very different in another, depending on their respective rules. Consider, by analogy, the difference between throwing a ball in baseball and throwing a ball in dodgeball. Both games would list "throwing the ball" as an essential practice but not, thereby, mean the same thing. So it is with traditional Christian practices in the language game of missional theology. Many of them may appear to be the same but mean and effect quite different things in the life of a congregation.[51]

Second, missional hermeneutics expands the virtues on which theological interpretation depends. Kevin Vanhoozer identifies four key

---

51. For example, a survey of missional literature suggests that hospitality is "a preeminent missional practice" (Love, "Practices," 178–79); see Heuertz and Pohl, *Friendship*, which is an extension of Pohl's watershed work on hospitality, published before the proliferation of the missional movement: Pohl, *Making*; Roxburgh, *Missional*, 154–57; Hirsch and Ford, *Right*, ch. 8; Van Gelder and Zscheile, *Missional*, 132–33; Fitch and Holsclaw, *Prodigal*, 105–7; Heath and Duggins, *Missional*; Frost, *Surprise*, ch. 4. Hospitality framed by missional theology is neither merely fellowship within the community of faith nor simply a warm welcome for visitors to church gatherings and events. Both fellowship with one another and kindness to visitors are good, but in the language game of Christendom theology the former tends toward exclusion and the latter tends toward attractional models of evangelism. The missional practices of hospitality, by contrast, are those of a congregation actively engaged in seeking and embracing the stranger in its neighborhood or local context. Hospitality comprises contextual practices of loving the stranger, such as welcoming the marginalized into the "private" lives of the community, sharing resources, and, of course, eating together. Moreover, the missional practices of hospitality are not a church growth strategy. They are an expression of the life of a people graciously welcomed by God and sent to extend the same welcome in turn. Finally, to restate the point of practices in the present discussion, hospitality within a missional language game is *formative*. By engaging locally in contextual expressions of hospitality to the stranger, congregations cultivate a missional imagination. In this way, the church *becomes* a social location in which participation in God's mission is theologically constitutive, and in turn the community of faith reads Scripture anew. In other words, the practice of hospitality is not merely the result of the church's theology and biblical interpretation but is an example of participation in God's mission before and beyond the church by which the church learns to speak of God and read Scripture together. Missionally reframing ecclesial practices is necessary for determining the hermeneutical virtues of well-formed readers.

"interpretive virtues": honesty, openness, attention, and obedience.[52] Likewise, L. Gregory Jones names a number of exemplary readerly virtues: "receptivity, humility, truthfulness, courage, charity, and imagination."[53] Such lists are indeterminate, so how should theological interpretation specify which virtues are ultimately necessary for faithful interpretation, and, more to the point here, which virtues does participation in God's mission cultivate?

As Fowl mentions, following Augustine, love (or charity) is the Christian tradition's most outstanding candidate for interpretive virtue.[54] And faith is a term used in theological interpretation of Scripture to sum up the church's hermeneutical perspective—represented preeminently in the Rule of Faith already discussed.[55] One may naturally wonder, then, whether the third theological virtue of the Thomist tradition, hope, is not a vital missional addition. Along these lines, Ross McCullough argues:

> This is the rule of hope, then: that that interpretation is to be favored which discloses and enables us to participate in God's establishment of the new creation within the old, of eschatology within history.... This rule, like the rules of faith and love, is less a matter of following some algorithm and more a way of being, a capacity to discern and act—in a word, a virtue. And it will be a virtue that bears both on our reading of Scripture and our reading of history. Indeed, the virtue will be in how well we can read our story within the story of Scripture, to echo Hans Frei's famous concern—or, better, in how well we can write our story within the larger story of Scripture.[56]

Participation in God's mission calls for the virtue of hope as an eschatological capacity both to discern and to act. This is a necessary dimension of the practical wisdom (*phronēsis*) that Fowl advocates.[57]

From another angle, Ellen Davis observes that the biblical tradition roots wisdom in "a view of history stretching from the creation to the coming judgment."[58] Missional hermeneutics stipulates this is the narrative

---

52. Vanhoozer, *Is?*, 377.
53. Jones, "Formed," 32.
54. Fowl, *Engaging*, 87, 91–96.
55. See Johnson, "Reading," 110–16.
56. McCullough, "Hermeneutic," 270.
57. Fowl, *Engaging*, 188–96; Fowl, "Theological," 680–82.
58. Davis, "Preserving," 201.

of the Triune God's life with the world, necessarily recasting theological interpretation's formative practices. "How well we can write our story within the larger story of Scripture," therefore, becomes a matter of participation in God's mission. The question in not only how wise reading enables such participation but how participation in this ongoing narrative reconstitutes the habits of wise perceiving and living that readers bring to Scripture.

Argument

A hermeneutical circulation characterizes all three aspects of readerly formation—between the Scripture that engenders commitments and the commitments that direct interpretation; between the narrativity of Scripture and the narrativity of readers; and between the virtues that Scripture cultivates and the virtues with which the church reads. Missional hermeneutics reorients each of these dialectics toward the *missio Dei*: participation in God's mission is the commitment that Scripture should engender and with which the church should read; the narrative of God's mission is the narrative of Scripture in which readers' narrativity should participate; and the virtues that Scripture cultivates are for the participation in God's mission through which the church reads virtuously. The hermeneutical circle that consequently comes into view holds readerly formation in the tension between text and reader. The missional reorientation of theological interpretation affirms the notion of readerly formation but insists that *participation in God's mission* is its crux. While the nature of the text (the missional commitments it engenders, the missional narrative it presents, the missional virtues it cultivates) is one half of the issue, the question of "better readers" shifts the accent to the experiential dimensions of readerly formation. In view of the *missio Dei*, who are well-formed readers?

This question motivates my argument. On the one hand, theological interpretation of Scripture remains too missionally deficient to offer a convincing answer. On the other hand, missional hermeneutics remains too inattentive to the theological dynamics of readerly formation to address the question. The first need that my argument meets, then, is the integration of theological interpretation and missional hermeneutics. Because this integration places participation in God's mission at the crux of readerly formation, a second need appears: to specify theologically what participation in God's mission entails. Without a theological conceptualization of missional participation such as I develop here, it is difficult to identify well-formed readers in

INTRODUCTION

relation to the Triune God's work in the world. Finally, both of these needs—the integration of theological interpretation and missional hermeneutics and the theological definition of participation in God's mission—arise from a more basic need for the church to become better readers of Scripture. The question, *In view of the* missio Dei, *who are well-formed readers?*, confronts the church with the need for hermeneutical transformation. This need represents not a condemnation but a possibility, a hope rooted in the church's faith in the God of Scripture. I write in the belief that understanding the hermeneutics of participation might engender "better" readings—those born of the formative effects of missional participation.

This study is concerned, therefore, with a theological explanation of why it should be the case that participation in God's mission forms better readers. I limit the scope of this explanation to anthropological and hermeneutical explorations.[59] In short, I ask why the commitments, narrative configurations, and virtues that constitute well-formed readers should be conceived missionally. In other words, in view of a theological anthropology and hermeneutics, why is participation in God's mission especially important for readerly formation?

I claim that *the church is epistemically constituted as an interpretive community through participation in the ongoing* missio Dei *because that participation occasions a reconfiguration of human embodied narrativity in conformity with the life of the Triune God revealed in Scripture*. A great deal of the ambiguity about the status and role of missional practices in relation to readerly formation for theological interpretation reflects a more fundamental doubt about what participation in God's mission is in the first place. In other words, in order to affirm the formative hermeneutical role of missional practices, it is necessary to clarify what participation in

---

59. Bowald, *Rendering*, highlights the centrality of divine agency for theological hermeneutics by developing a threefold typology in which God, text, and readers are the foci. Bowald thereby accentuates a common criticism of approaches that focus on the text or readers, namely, that they are anthropocentric rather than theocentric. This is a welcome critique, but I suggest that *participation* theologically conceived is the category necessary to overcome the hermeneutical dichotomy his critique entails. Given the theological priority of the *missio Dei*, my argument assumes that God's agency is essential, not only in relation to such notions as divine speech "in, with, and under" (Bowald, *Rendering*, 36) the biblical text but in relation to God's active engagement with readers in history through missional participation (an idea toward which Bowald only gestures at the conclusion of his work; Bowald, *Rendering*, 242, 246). In other words, because my construal of participation is theologically determined, the anthropological and hermeneutical focus of the argument not only accounts for divine agency but adds to its conception a missing dimension of Bowald's typology.

God's mission means. The ensuing argument, therefore, hinges on a multi-dimensional theological definition of participation in God's mission. I will show that an understanding of participation in God's mission as *theōsis*, *embodied narrativity*, and *solidarity* explains why missional practices of participation are hermeneutically formative. This theological definition of participation in God's mission leads to a hermeneutics of participation that illuminates the epistemic reconstitution of the missional church's theological interpretation of Scripture.

Methodology and Chapter Summaries

Missional hermeneutics is an interdisciplinary discourse. It brings missiology to the intersection of biblical studies, systematic theology, and philosophical hermeneutics at which theological interpretation of Scripture emerges. Focused on concerns "in front of" the text, my argument emphasizes constructive theology rather than biblical studies, but it remains essentially interdisciplinary. I proceed in three movements: from a preliminary review of one aspect of missiology (i.e., theology of mission *cum* missional theology) to a theological proposal to hermeneutical considerations. Missiology is thus a point of departure for conceptualizing participation, but at the argument's heart is the interface of theological anthropology and hermeneutical theory.

Interdisciplinarity involves significant challenges, not the least of which is a sort of methodological schizophrenia, or at the least a tendency toward methodological inconsistency. The eclecticism that marks my argument might be perceived as such a failing, yet I offer it as an attempt to bring disparate voices into conversation despite the assumptions that seem to enclose them within their respective academic discourses. What does Christian mission have to do with Paul Ricoeur? How might the communitarian impulses of narrative theology cohere with the social praxis of liberation theology? Can the retrieval of ancient Eastern Trinitarianism really integrate with radically contextual biblical interpretation? Such are the tensions that this project attempts to maintain. From the highest methodological vantage, the attempt reflects a missional commitment to the encounter between others and the union of differences—a fundamental affirmation of discursive commensurability. At this level, I claim to be doing missional theology: not just theology that presumes the *missio Dei* is conceptually and practically axiomatic (though certainly that) but theology that is methodologically committed to the reconciliation of all things to God and, therefore, to each other in God. From a missional viewpoint, the Thomist notion of theology as the pursuit of understanding all things in relation to God (*omnia sub ratio Dei*) correctly affirms the *relatability* of all things without strongly enough affirming also the difficulties of alterity that necessitate the dialogical work of reconciliation. Thus, I hope to sidestep the accusation of imposing a systematic coherency on the disparate discourses I engage while still seeking to explore their generative relationships across real difference. The model I employ to this end is conversation: an encounter through which genuine mutuality gives rise to new understanding without eradicating substantial—sometimes extreme—difference.

There is no way to predetermine how the conversation unfolds. The fruit of conversation must arise from the untidiness and difficulty of the encounter. I do not, therefore, prescribe how the classical problem of relating theology and philosophy, of which the more recent problem of relating general and theological hermeneutics is a manifestation, should be resolved. I begin with the assumption that they are relatable and, when it seems necessary along the way, clarify the terms of the specific conversation in which they are engaged for the purposes of my argument.

Chapter 2 is an exercise in historical, comparative, synthetic missional theology. The aim of this chapter is to demonstrate the indeterminacy of the phrase "participation in God's mission" in missional theology and, therefore, in missional hermeneutics. The discussion proceeds in two sections. The first is an historical account of the theological developments that establish the language game of missional theology. The second develops a typology of "participation" language in missional theology. The conclusion of this chapter is that the meaning of participation in God's mission requires theological clarification if it is to explain the hermeneutical significance of participation in missional interpretation of Scripture. The following three chapters build toward a definition of participation in God's mission.

Chapter 3 explores a confessional, Trinitarian theology of participation in God's mission that relies on both the retrieval of ancient insights and contemporary constructive conclusions. I begin with the contemporary discussion of *theōsis*, taking the catalytic deployment of *theōsis* in the missional hermeneutics of New Testament scholar Michael Gorman as a point of departure. The argument then moves from the contemporary retrieval of *theōsis* doctrine to the significance of *theōsis* in recent theologies of atonement. The chapter concludes by relating my account of *theōsis* to the Trinitarian doctrine of *perichōrēsis*, thereby preparing for further reflection on the nature of the divine life in the world and human participation in it.

Chapter 4 adds a theological and philosophical exposition of human embodiment and narrativity in order to establish the significance of *embodied narrativity* for participation in God's mission. First, I account for the theological status of embodiment and narrativity respectively. Second, I develop their conceptual integration as embodied narrativity based on the philosophical work of Paul Ricoeur and the theological anthropology of Jürgen Moltmann. The chapter's conclusion brings my theological conception of embodied narrativity to bear on the idea of human participation in God's mission as *theōsis*.

Chapter 5 concludes the conceptual work on participation by bringing liberationist, missiological, and philosophical understandings of solidarity into conversation. I begin by exploring the theological significance of solidarity in Latin American liberation theology. I then broaden liberationist solidarity to a missional conceptualization. The final section brings together my claims regarding *theōsis*, embodied narrativity, and solidarity in a comprehensive definition of participation in God's mission.

Chapter 6 combines theological and philosophical hermeneutics in order to connect my definition of participation of God's mission to the concerns about biblical interpretation that occupy my thesis. I return to the work of Paul Ricoeur, focusing now on his hermeneutical phenomenology. This interest requires a methodological detour, along which I bring Ricoeur's own understanding of the relationship between philosophy and theology to bear on theological interpreters' reticence to rely on ostensibly atheistic hermeneutical resources. Having stipulated how general hermeneutics and theological interpretation relate in the subsequent argument, I develop a Ricoeurian model of the hermeneutical movement from embodied commitments to textual interpretation. Finally, I demonstrate how recontextualizing this model theologically in terms of my understanding of participation in God's mission illuminates the epistemic reconstitution of the church's theological interpretation of Scripture.

Chapter 7 concludes by specifying the implications of my argument for missional interpretation of Scripture. I first confirm that my understanding of participation in God's mission as theological interpretation's proper *locus theologicus* should reorient the notion of readerly formation toward the argument I have developed in the preceding chapters. Then, I relate the hermeneutics of participation to the commitments, narrativity, and virtues of readerly formation in theological interpretation discussed above. Finally, I end with the suggestion that, because the formation of missional readers is the process in which God opens the reading community's embodied eyes of faith, faith seeking understanding is works seeking understanding—readerly formation through participation in the mission of God.

CHAPTER 2

Participation in Missional Theology

"We cannot without ado claim that what we do is identical to the *missio Dei*; our missionary activities are only authentic insofar as they reflect participation in the mission of God." —David J. Bosch[1]

THIS CHAPTER SEEKS CLARITY about the problems with the conception of participation in God's mission that I must address before exploring why participation forms readers in unique ways. The contention that animates this chapter can be stated negatively: the diverse understandings of participation in God's mission that inhabit contemporary missional theology—and therefore inform missional hermeneutics—are theologically inadequate. Positively, the theological account of participation that I set forth in the next three chapters seeks to move farther down a trail blazed by missional theologians whose work is indispensable.

Although one might expect clarity about participation in mission simply to rely on a definition of mission, the question is not what *mission* means, or even what *missional* means, but what *participation* means when it is deployed within the language game of missional theology. Missional theology places the accent on the genitive—it matters *whose* mission is in question. The mission is *God's*. To characterize human participation by defining *mission*, therefore, shifts the accent in a way that conflates human mission and God's mission: stipulate what mission is, humans do that, and

---

1. Bosch, *Transforming*, 391.

there one has participation. But this undermines the force of placing the accent on the genitive. In what sense is it meaningful to say the mission is God's if it is ultimately—practically—what the church does? By using the language of participation in God's mission, the missional language game enforces a semantic rule that maintains a theological distinction between human *participation* and God's *mission*, a distinction that talk of *the church's mission* dissolves apart from the rule. Placing the accent on the genitive generates ambiguity regarding *how* the church's participation relates to God's mission. In other words, missional theology makes a theological distinction that requires further clarification.

In section 1, I trace the trajectories along which the concept of participation has developed and provide context for the emergence of missional theology as a distinct discourse. In section 2, I stake out the field of missional theology, on which the language of participation in God's mission is in play in missional hermeneutics. My aim is not to represent *missional* definitively but to delimit the arena in which the concept of participation needs the theological clarification that I will subsequently attempt. I then offer a typology of the major alternatives that have emerged under the influence of the early usage of participation terminology in the language game of missional theology. I conclude in section 3 by identifying the aporias that my account of participation in the following three chapters addresses.

The Historical Context of Participation Language

One might say that the problem facing contemporary understandings of participation is the success of David Bosch's argument in *Transforming Mission*. He lays claim to a presumptive consensus regarding *missio Dei* among Western theologies of mission following the 1952 meeting of the International Missionary Council at Willingen, Germany: "Mission is, primarily and ultimately, the work of the Triune God, Creator, Redeemer, and Sanctifier, for the sake of the world, a ministry in which the church is privileged to participate.... The recognition that the mission is God's mission represents a crucial breakthrough in respect of the preceding centuries. It is inconceivable that we could again revert to a narrow, ecclesiocentric view of mission."[2] This is a fair summary of *missio Dei* theology at the end of the twentieth century, but it raises numerous questions. What is participation in God's mission? How is the church's agency conceived in relation to

---

2. Bosch, *Transforming*, 392–93.

God's? Which Trinitarian theology informs the claim? Does God's mission proceed in the world regardless of the church's participation? What does the church's evangelistic commission have to do with this non-ecclesiocentric view of mission? The possible variety of answers to such questions indicates that the consensus is, in fact, minimal.

Yet, the givenness of this consensus became a key point of departure for the missional theology that emerged at the beginning of the twenty-first century. Darrell Guder, for example, sees the *missio Dei* theology issuing from Willingen as "a strong, global consensus that the church must be understood as essentially missionary." Though the missional church movement has done much to substantiate this claim in the last twenty-five years, the next section demonstrates that the consensus remains little more than a widely acknowledged "sense of theological priority"[3]—not a shared theological understanding of human participation in the Triune mission. The following discussion identifies key influences that inform the diversity of contemporary understanding.

The rhetoric of "participation in the mission of God" that characterizes missional theology finds its point of departure in the language of the statement on the missionary calling of the church that arose from Willingen: "We who have been chosen in Christ, reconciled to God through Him, made members of His Body, sharers in His Spirit, and heirs through hope of His Kingdom, are by these very facts committed to full participation in His redeeming mission. There is no participation in Christ without participation in His mission to the world. That by which the Church receives its existence is that by which it is also given its world-mission. 'As the Father hath sent me, even so send I you.'"[4] It is useful to begin with Willingen because the theology of the *missio Dei* that emerged from the conference establishes the Trinitarian parameters of participation language.[5] In order to understand the significance and the ambiguity of the statement, however, it is useful to consider four major influences on the development of participation language in the theology of mission leading up to the advent of missional theology: Karl Barth's emphasis on God's agency, Lesslie Newbigin's

---

3. Guder, "Multicultural," 22.
4. "Statement," 190.
5. See esp. Bosch, *Transforming*, 368–93; cf. Rosin, "Missio Dei"; Scherer, *Gospel*, chs. 3–4; Matthey, *IRM* 92.367 (2003), on the theme "*Missio Dei* Today," the whole of which is devoted to the fiftieth anniversary of the conference in Willingen; Kim, *Joining*, ch. 2; Wrogemann, *Intercultural*, chs. 5–6.

PARTICIPATION IN MISSIONAL THEOLOGY

Trinitarianism, J. C. Hoekendijk's focus on God's work in the world, and Donald McGavran's defense of the church's responsibility.

First, Barth's strong distinction between divine and human agency shaped the emergence of *missio Dei* theology. John Flett argues, to the contrary, that Barth's Trinitarian thought is not at work in Willingen's concern with the Triune *missio Dei*.[6] Trinitarianism aside, however, Barth's 1932 lecture "Die Theologie und die Mission in der Gegenwart," which is the first recorded instance of a theologian referring to the classical Trinitarian notion of *missio* in the context of modern mission theology, makes the point that *God is the subject of mission*. This idea comes through articulations of the *missio Dei* on all sides of the Willingen debate. The landscape of world mission was the same geopolitical upheaval that Barth had addressed earlier in the German context,[7] and by 1952 Barth had definitively shaped the theological discourse within which Willingen would construe mission in distinction from the faltering endeavors of the colonialist church.[8] The debates surrounding Willingen breathe this air and should be understood in terms of the problem that Barth's whole agenda (not just his 1932 essay) establishes: the emphasis on God's subjectivity in (infinite qualitative!) distinction from the church's. The phrase *missio Dei* became the token of a pivotal idea: the mission is God's, not the church's. In other words, the discussion as a whole is framed by the Barthian idea that God's Triune mission is distinct from the church's mission, reflecting the *diastasis* between God and humanity on which Barth's theology of witness depends.[9] Barth does not determine the Trinitarian conception of *missio Dei* following Willingen, for no single conception prevailed, but his influence shaped the basic question that participation language addresses: if the mission is God's, what is the church's role?

Second, Lesslie Newbigin's Trinitarian thought is especially influential on the development of participation language. As the author of the Willingen statement quoted above, Newbigin's wording marks the conjunction

---

6. See Flett, *Witness*, 120–30.

7. See Congdon, "Dialectical," 390–413, for a useful rendition of Barth's evolving concerns about mission in relation to German nationalism and the emergence of dialectical theology.

8. See esp. Chandran, "Christian," 95–100; Bingle, "World," 181–84, and throughout *Missions Under the Cross*, for the comments on the "revolutionary" context in which the church found itself at the time of Willingen.

9. Karl Hartenstein, in particular, mediated dialectical theology to Willingen. See Schwarz, "Legacy," 126.

of Trinitarian theology with participation language and provides the point of departure for the *missio Dei* theology. His subsequent work develops the claim that "there is no participation in Christ without participation in His mission to the world" through a Trinitarian ecclesiology: "The life of the Church is a real participation in the life of the triune God, wherein all life and all glory consist of self-giving, a *koinonia*."[10] Yet, although he stretched for a "fully and explicitly trinitarian doctrine of God," his writing never engaged the specifics of Trinitarian doctrine.[11] He consistently held the middle ground articulated at Willingen amid competing theologies, on the one hand articulating a doctrine that was profoundly ecclesiological while, on the other hand, contemplating the action of the Triune God "in the secular history of the world" beyond the church.[12] Consequently, Newbigin's Trinitarianism remained general, specifying neither how the church's witness is participation in the Triune life, nor in what sense the church's work in history amid the tides of culture relates to the Triune mission. This ambiguity has allowed missional theology to make room for diverse perspectives to reframe their missiologies in broadly Trinitarian terms. The cost of ambiguity, however, is that participation language is stretched thin, applied to notions of mission that make no Trinitarian claims.

Third, J. C. Hoekendijk, a Dutch missiologist, represents a key non-Trinitarian influence on participation language. In Hoekendijk's view, the church does not exist apart from "a communal and corporate *participation in Christ and his Messianic work* (apostolate) in the world."[13] Hoekendijk famously argued for the reordering of the missiological relationship between God, church, and world: "We must maintain the right order in our thinking and speaking about the church. That order is God—World—Church, not God—Church—World."[14] The reordering is about denying the church an essential mediating role: God does not act in the world through the church but rather *acts in the world*, and so the church happens—not as an end result or goal but in virtue of "participation in Christ's apostolic ministry."[15] Thus, Hoekendijk commends to the ecumenical church a

---

10. Newbigin, *Household*, 129. See Dodds, *Mission*, for an exposition of Newbigin's Trinitarian theology.

11. Newbigin, *Trinitarian*, 33.

12. Newbigin, *Trinitarian*, 21. See also Goheen, "'As the Father,'" 118.

13. Hoekendijk, *Church*, 44; emphasis added.

14. Hoekendijk, *Church*, 70–71.

15. Hoekendijk, "Church," 334.

view of itself as "nothing more than a mere instrument for God's apostolic action in the world, without 'an end in itself.'"[16] For him, participation is *mere* instrumentality, not indispensable instrumentality.[17] The church's participation in mission means being taken up in God's messianic dealings with the world, "drawn into Christ's office and . . . thus made into a missionary church," but Christ still functions in this office regardless of whether the church engages the world through it.[18] Hoekendijk's emphasis on God's acting in the world, which evinces no concern for Trinitarian theology, came to fruition in the ecumenical missiology of the 1960s. Though his view proved too extreme a reaction to ecclesiocentrism, the emphasis on God's relation to the world was crucial for the reformulation of the church's participation in the *missio Dei* as secondary to and derivative of God's primary, ongoing agency in relation to the world.[19]

Fourth, Donald McGavran represents the evangelical reaction to the emerging ecumenical understanding, further shaping participation language in non-Trinitarian terms. Preparatory material for the Fourth Assembly of the World Council of Churches in Uppsala, Sweden (1968), affirmed, "Participation in God's mission is . . . entering into partnership with God in history. . . . The central question then becomes to what extent is what we have inherited still serving the mission of God?" In response, McGavran wrote, "Quite on the contrary, for the Division of World Mission and Evangelism (DWME) and all Christian churches, the *central question* is: How many of the lost are we bringing back to the fold? How obedient are we to our Lord's command to disciple the nations? How faithful are we to the mission of God, the mission to which our Lord gave His life?"[20] A dichotomy between conciliar and evangelical understandings of mission looms in this exchange: "participation" in God's mission in history versus "obedience" to the church's evangelistic mandate. For evangelicals, the question was not whether mission is church-centered or world-centered but, assuming the church's commission and the goal of church multiplication, whether mission is essentially "evangelism" (verbal proclamation) or something broader. This shift is important for understanding contemporary participation language in evangelical

16. Hoekendijk, "Church," 336.
17. Cf. Barth, *Church*, 4/3.2, *Doctrine* §§72–73, 141.
18. Hoekendijk, *Church*, 101.
19. See Bosch, *Transforming*, 392–93.
20. McGavran, *Conciliar-Evangelical*, 237–38.

parlance, because so much theological attention is given to the nature of the church's evangelistic task that the concerns originally in question—the priority of the Triune mission, the work of God in the world beyond and apart from the work of the church, the existence of the church in virtue of participation in God's mission, and the limited agency of the church relative to God's mission—become marginal issues, at times completely lost from view.[21] In this context, appeals to *missio Dei* usually serve evangelical theology in defense of a holistic vision of mission: God's whole mission sets the parameters for the church's commission.

The Lausanne Movement's First International Congress on World Evangelization in 1974 was a watershed event, and it represents this trend. "The Lausanne Covenant," whose authoring committee was chaired by John Stott, is the culmination of an evangelical theology of mission articulated in contradistinction from that of the World Council of Churches under the influence of leaders like Hoekendijk. The "Covenant" takes a more moderate position than McGavran, representing Stott's well-known move toward a holistic understanding of mission—and in this sense moves beyond McGavran.[22] Stott effectively reframes the regnant Great Commission paradigm of evangelical mission with a Johannine theology (referring to John 17:18; 20:21), thereby establishing a Trinitarian evangelical understanding of mission, but this serves to promote a more holistic view of *what God sends the church to do*, in contradiction of the ecumenical vision of *the church's participation in what the Triune God does in the world*. It is not an accident of vocabulary, then, that participation language plays no role in the "Covenant." McGavran's challenges to Hoekendijk represent well the terms and driving concerns of the evangelical community at Lausanne.

Barth, Newbigin, Hoekendijk, and McGavran represent trends that problematize the presumptive consensus about the *missio Dei* in contemporary theology of mission. They also provide a backdrop for understanding the diverse uses of participation language that have emerged in the last fifty years, in which the relationship of divine and human agency, Trinitarian doctrine, the role of the church, and the scope of mission are

---

21. For example, while "The Lausanne Covenant" is confessionally Trinitarian (par. 14), its point of departure is the sending of the church "back into the world to be his servants and his witnesses, for the extension of his kingdom, the building up of Christ's body, and the glory of his name" (par. 1), and it maintains a fundamental distinction between evangelism and social action (par. 5) (Lausanne Movement, "Lausanne.").

22. See Stott and Wright, *Christian*, 22.

major variables. The next section takes stock of the variations in contemporary participation language.

Participation Language in Missional Theology

In this section, I review and critique the major alternative uses of *participation* in missional theological literature in order to devise a typology of participation. The typological exercise clarifies the problem of participation—the ambiguity of the language and the need for a more thoroughgoing theological explanation of human participation in God's mission. First, however, I stake out the field on which the missional language game is played.

The Missional Language Game

It has been over twenty-five years since the publication of *Missional Church*, which introduced the term *missional* into mainstream theological parlance in North America.[23] In the intervening decades, a recognizable discourse has emerged in connection with the term *missional* and taken on a life of its own. Its diversity, at the points where it gives way to incoherence, is the basic problem that confronts the theological specification of participation in God's mission.

Craig Van Gelder and Dwight Zscheile's *The Missional Church in Perspective* traces the emergence of *missional*, arguing that the word "displays an inherent elasticity that allows it to be understood in a variety of ways."[24] Their genealogy of *missional* presents a clear picture of its essential theological components: (1) a Trinitarian missiology, (2) a focus on the already/not yet reign of God, (3) a broadened understanding of mission as *missio Dei*, (4) an understanding of the church as missionary by nature, and (5) a transition from "theology of mission" to a hermeneutic of both Scripture and church history from the perspective of mission.[25] Indeed, the book attributes much of the diversity among supposedly missional churches to the underdevelopment or misappropriation of these key themes.

---

23. Guder, *Missional*.

24. Van Gelder and Zscheile, *Missional*, 3. See also Guder, *Called*, which consolidates key material that Guder had published to date.

25. Van Gelder and Zscheile, *Missional*, 25–35.

In scholarly discourse, however, the delineation of missional theology is not simply a matter of giving pride of place to the five theological components that Van Gelder and Zscheile identify. The fundamental complication is that missional theology exists in continuity with the twentieth-century missiological developments I have traced above.[26] Relatedly, Van Gelder and Zscheile contrast the convergence of missional theology toward *missio Dei* and the reign of God (represented by Newbigin) with the divergence precipitated by evangelical missiologists' entrenchment in "classical evangelical themes of the modern missions movement" (represented by Donald McGavran).[27] The contrast between conciliar *missio Dei* theology and evangelical theology of mission represents a major conceptual rift internal to the language game of missional theology and, therefore, of participation.

In that context, Van Gelder and Zscheile's claim that missional theology represents a "renewal of missiology" cuts two directions.[28] It might mean that *missio Dei* is a corrective to ecclesiocentric missiology in that it claims participating in God's mission is fundamentally distinct from participating in church missions, thereby producing the rift because evangelicals reject the distinction. Alternatively, it might mean that *missio Dei* is a corrective to ecclesiocentric missiology in that it claims the idea of participating in God's mission renews the church's understanding of what it means to participate in church missions, producing the rift because conciliar missiologists reject the persistent conflation of the two. Depending on whose missiology one reads, therefore, *participation* runs toward either synonymy or antonymy with what the church does.

Thus, the language game of missional theology is constituted by the conflict about what *missiones ecclesiae* have to do with *missio Dei*.[29] The

---

26. Guder, *Called*, ch. 1, usefully characterizes the transition from the convergence of "mission and theology" early in the twentieth century, through the emergence of "the theology of mission" midcentury, to the call for "missional theology" at the end of the century. This characterization represents the continuity between the historical overview of participation above and the discussion of missional theology in the remainder of the chapter.

27. Van Gelder and Zscheile, *Missional*, 33–36.

28. Van Gelder and Zscheile, *Missional*, 35.

29. This distinction has been a part of the contemporary discussion since Karl Hartenstein first introduced *missio Dei* terminology in his interpretation of the 1952 Willingen document "A Statement on the Missionary Calling of the Church." He says, "In a second section, the missionary obligation of the church is comprehensively established. The mission is not a matter of human activity or organization, 'its source is the Triune God Himself.' The sending of the Son for the reconciliation of the universe

distinction is a given for missional theology, but the nature of the relationship is not. I therefore pursue a theological explanation that addresses the essential tension of missional theology. On the one side, if participation is ultimately what the church would do regardless of reference to a Trinitarian understanding of God's ongoing mission in the world, what sense does it make to claim the mission is God's? On the other side, if mission is ultimately what the Triune God does in the world regardless of what the church does, what sense does it make to claim that the church indeed participates in God's mission? If we are to articulate what participation is according to the rules of this language game, we need a theological account of the way human and divine agency relate that can maintain the dialectic of *missiones ecclesiae* and *missio Dei*. Otherwise, claims about *missio Dei* become nothing more than a sort of theological therapy that convinces the church to compare its agenda critically with God's—which is important in view of the troubling history of church missions but insufficient to say why the reality of God's ongoing mission makes a difference for what the church does, much less how it interprets Scripture. En route to such a theological account, I take stock of the uses of participation language in missional theology.

Van Gelder and Zscheile's second volume, *Participating in God's Mission: A Theological Missiology for the Church in America*, represents the state of the issue in missional theology. Chapter 9, "Participating in the Triune God's Mission," is a rich overview of participation, yet it still leaves one wondering how participating in God's Triune mission might be conceived apart from "practices of discipleship and witness" or "practices of the gathered community" that can be—and often are—described and undertaken without any reference to Trinitarian theology.[30] Such practices are not necessarily distinct from participation in God's mission but, as yet, missional theology has not articulated how they are participation in the *missio Dei*—how they take part in the Triune life of God in such a way that they do not collapse back into mere *missiones ecclesiae*. The state of the issue, in other words, continues to be ambiguity.

To state more clearly what participation is, it is helpful to sort out alternative viewpoints, but to do so calls for a method of organization. My

---

through the power of the Spirit is the cause and purpose of mission. From the 'missio Dei' alone comes the 'missio ecclesiae.' Thus, the mission is placed in the widest possible framework of salvation history and God's plan of salvation" (Hartenstein, "Theologische," 62; my translation).

30. Van Gelder and Zscheile, *Participating*, 278, 283.

historical overview suggests some keynotes: the relationship between divine and human agency, the Trinitarian theologies that inform the various perspectives, and the nature of the church's instrumentality in God's relationship to the world.[31] Nonetheless, typologies are an imposition of order according to conceptually ideal types that highlight certain similarities among the constituents of a type and minimize differences between them. Unlike scientific taxonomies that arise from measurable data, a typology is ultimately a conceptual argument whose validity is relative to its usefulness for solving a problem beyond the classification itself. The validity of the following typology of participation is a function of its usefulness in identifying and critiquing the limits of contemporary understandings of participation—an exercise that serves a larger argument about what participation in God's mission means in this study's thesis. To that end, I have sought not to account for every conceivable understanding of participation or to catalogue every version of a given type but to trace the contours of the major alternatives in contemporary missiology in a way that identifies key distinctives and shortcomings. The problem I am addressing, however, goes beyond the identification of distinctives and shortcomings per se. The premise of the typology is the language game of missional theology that emerged from the history reviewed in the first section of the chapter. Therefore, their differences, contributions, and shortcomings ultimately have to do with the problem of articulating the relationship between God's mission and the church's missions. With an eye trained on the dimensions of this problem revealed by the historical development of the missional language game, the following typology represents the state of the question and serves to identify the aporias of participation.

---

31. I have been influenced by the hermeneutic of agency that Van Gelder and Zscheile use to map differences in missional theology in *Missional*, 70, according to which "the key issue, comprised of two closely related questions, is: to what extent are we simply dealing with human agency, and to what extent is God's agency operative and discernible within human choices? . . . The dividing line between branches [of the missional conversation] revolves around the extent to which one starts with the *mission of the church* and the extent to which one starts with the *mission of God*; when starting with the mission of God, it also has to do with how robust the trinitarian theology is." It seems necessary to me, however, to consider not just the extent to which God and humans are operative but *how* their agency relates, and not just how robust are the Trinitarian theologies that inform them but *which ones*.

A Typology of Participation[32]

Incarnational Witness

Guder is the chief representative of a limited view of human agency steeped in Barth's influence. This understanding of participation, which Flett's book also advances, is well-designated by Guder's own phrase, "incarnational witness."[33] Describing incarnational witness requires an account of Barth's foundational construal of witness in combination with Guder's more thoroughgoing vision of how the incarnation shapes the church's witness.

Barth's understanding of witness as participation in the work of God is doubly constrained. First, his insistence on the completeness of the event of reconciliation forecloses the possibility of any human contribution to the work of salvation. Second, his commitment to the infinite qualitative distinction between divinity and humanity limits participation to an epistemological function.[34] These constraints are interconnected. The strictly epistemological function of witness is predicated on the strictly cognitive character of faith in Barth's articulation of the doctrine of *sola gratia*: "As a human act, [personal faith] consists in a definite acknowledgement, recognition and confession. As this human act it has no creative but only a cognitive character. It does not alter anything. As a human act, it is simply the confirmation of a change which has already taken place, the change in the whole human situation which took place in the death of Jesus Christ and was revealed in His resurrection and attested by the Christian community."[35] In turn, therefore, the Christian's witness is purely passive participation: "In Christ's action for the world and the Christian as fully completed in His passion, [the Christian] can participate only passively in pure faith in Him, love for Him and hope in Him, without making even the slightest or most incidental contribution. Even the suggestion of Christian co-operation in this respect, let alone any attempt at it, could only be evil, because it would arbitrarily question and finally deny the ultimate foundation, support and consolation of the

---

32. Parts of this section are adapted from McKinzie, "Perspectives."

33. Guder, *Incarnation*, xii and *passim*.

34. I refer to infinite qualitative distinction without prejudice regarding the debate about the extent of Kierkegaard's influence on the later Barth. See, e.g., Oh, "Complementary," 497–512; Bender, "Søren," 296–318. Barth's understanding of the diastasis shapes the whole of the *Dogmatics*.

35. Barth, *Church*, 4/1, Doctrine §§61–63, 240.

whole world and therefore of the Christian."[36] Thus, the Christian community "can neither carry through God's work to its goal nor lead men to the point of accepting it. It transgresses the limits of its mission and task, is guilty of culpable arrogance and engages in a futile undertaking if it makes this the goal and end of its activity, assuming responsibility both for the going out of the Word of God and its coming to man. If this takes place at all, it does so in the power of the Holy Spirit over whom it has no power. Its task is simply to serve this happening, i.e., to assist both God and man."[37] The limit of its mission and task are set "by the fact that it is materially determined as a ministry of witness. . . . It is no less, no more and no other than the ministry of witness."[38]

Positively, witness entails *imparting and confirming information*.[39] As regards the revelation of God's love, however, "the concept of witness carries with it a restriction which we cannot ignore. When a man is a witness to another, he can only tell him about something, and answer for the truth and reality of what is told. He cannot produce the thing itself. . . . What can take place on this level, between man and man, as the one is witness to the other, can only be a reflection of what takes place on the vertical level, between God and both."[40] Reflection, repetition, imitation, and representation are important concepts for delimiting participation as witness. Barth is at pains to maintain the infinite qualitative distinction while affirming the reality of participation: "We may quietly admit that in relation to His action theirs will always be improper. But this action of theirs which imitates and reflects the love of God, the human response of love for God and the corresponding love for man as they are all actualised in Him, is as such a real action. Certainly the one will not be to the other—I prefer not to use Luther's expression—a 'second Christ.' But in the name and school of Christ he will represent what Christ is to them all."[41] As Barth struggles to say what it means for the Christian "to participate in what He does"—"the true and concrete participation of the Christian in the great context of the history of God with the world, and therefore of salvation history"—his overriding concern is that "we must not say anything which would deny

---

36. Barth, *Church*, 4/3.2, *Doctrine* §§70–71, 233.
37. Barth, *Church*, 4/3.2, *Doctrine* §§72–73, 148.
38. Barth, *Church*, 4/3.2, *Doctrine* §§72–73, 149.
39. See Barth, *Church*, 4/2, *Doctrine*, 200.
40. Barth, *Church*, 4/2, *Doctrine*, 203.
41. Barth, *Church*, 4/2, *Doctrine*, 211.

or even challenge the indestructible differentiation and irreversible order of their relationship. The participation of the Christian in that history, his function in that great nexus, can only be such as it is proper to him as a man who is not a God-man like Christ."[42] He shies from the word *cooperation* because of its association with synergism.[43] Nonetheless, "the Christian in whom Christ lives, and who lives in Christ, does participate as a subject, and indeed as an active subject, in the action of Christ and therefore in the history of salvation, doing things with Christ even if not himself effecting them."[44] The action in view is that of "the One who as a Prophet is not idle to-day in their time but is active as the living Speaker of the Word of God in the world." Thus, "being called by and to the Christ engaged in the exercise of His prophetic office, they have no option but to attach themselves to Him with their own action, to tread in His steps, to become with Him proclaimers of the reconciliation of the world accomplished in Him, heralds of His person and work."[45] This is the *ministerium Verbi divini*, which alone counts as "co-operation of the Christian in the work of Christ."[46] In summary, Barth limits human participation in the contemporary work of Christ in the world to witness, meaning the actions and words of the Christian community as reflections and representations of Christ's self-revelation—a sign that accompanies and confirms Christ's self-witness but in no way contributes to, manifests, or continues Christ's already complete work of reconciliation.

Guder's conception of witness is Barthian, though he interprets Barth in keeping with the argument that witness should be incarnational.[47] Thus, says Guder, "the church bears a marked resemblance to the incarnation of Jesus, who, being God, was equally real human flesh and life. It is no accident that the church is called the 'body of Christ.' It continues as an incarnate expression of the life of God."[48] This christological understanding of mission converges with *missio Dei* theology as Guder articulates the Trinitarian content of the revelation that the church's incarnational witness

---

42. Barth, *Church*, 4/3.2, Doctrine §§70–71, 226.

43. See Barth, *Church*, 4/3.2, Doctrine §§70–71, 227–28, 232; see also Barth, *Church*, 4/1, Doctrine, 109.

44. Barth, *Church*, 4/3.2, Doctrine §§70–71, 226.

45. Barth, *Church*, 4/3.2, Doctrine §§70–71, 234.

46. Barth, *Church*, 4/3.2, Doctrine §§70–71, 236.

47. See esp. Guder, *Incarnation*, 15–16.

48. Guder, *Missional*, 13–14.

discloses: "In every cultural expression of the gospel, as it is embodied in the life and witness of the emerging churches, the focus upon the person and work of Jesus Christ makes the Trinity explicit, disclosing, as it were, the eternal triunity of God in God's purposeful action to bring about new creation as well as the healing of the world."[49] Yet, witness to God's purposeful action remains extremely limited—even passive—in Guder's thought. In relation to the whole project of *Missional Church*, this seems to be not only because of his Barthian theology but also the rejection of the notion of "'building' or 'extending' the reign of God"—a critique that ends in an affirmation of Newbigin's passive *sign*, *foretaste*, and *instrument* language.[50] Guder's Barthian view of incarnational witness combines with Newbigin's embodied representation of the kingdom in a seamless account: "Christology defines mission, and Christologically defined mission that takes the earthly ministry of Jesus seriously will necessarily reshape the character and action of the church. As Lesslie Newbigin never tired of emphasizing, the church is not an end in itself, but a 'sign, foretaste and instrument of the kingdom.' The Jesus who is the Christ and the Lord embodies that kingdom. His message and how it is to be communicated are inextricably linked in the biblical witness."[51] The extremely limited agency that this entails in Guder's account is particularly clear in an essay on the mission of the church in which he suggests that "gospel witness works itself out" through "the formation of witnessing communities."[52] The formation of the church is the real work in view here: witness is a consequence of the church's existence as the church properly (incarnationally) formed, and the church's existence is missional because witness is its consequence. Guder's incarnational witness places the accent on *being formed* as a missional church, seemingly to the detriment of a positive account of what the church *does* as active participants in God's mission.

Participation as incarnational witness attends to major theological issues that overshadow any claim that the church participates in God's own Triune mission, namely, the relationship between the being of God and that of humanity and, by extension, the relationship of divinity and humanity

---

49. Guder, *Called*, 28.

50. Guder, *Missional*, 93, 101. This chapter, drafted by George R. Hunsberger, reflects his indebtedness to Newbigin, which Guder shares. See Hunsberger, "Newbigin"; Hunsberger, *Bearing*.

51. Guder, *Called*, 55; see also 22.

52. Guder, "Multicultural," 32.

in the incarnation of the Son. Ultimately, however, incarnational witness minimizes the agency of the church and limits it to the passive role of an instrument in the Triune mission of God. In Guder's view, the doctrine of the incarnation has implications for how the church witnesses, but not because the church relates to the Triune life.

Kingdom Collaboration

On the other end of the spectrum of human agency is the evangelical mainstream's understanding of participation, which the Lausanne Movement continues to articulate quintessentially:

> *Our participation in God's mission.* God calls his people to share his mission. The Church from all nations stands in continuity through the Messiah Jesus with God's people in the Old Testament. With them we have been called through Abraham and commissioned to be a blessing and a light to the nations. With them, we are to be shaped and taught through the law and the prophets to be a community of holiness, compassion and justice in a world of sin and suffering. We have been redeemed through the cross and resurrection of Jesus Christ, and empowered by the Holy Spirit to bear witness to what God has done in Christ. The Church exists to worship and glorify God for all eternity and to participate in the transforming mission of God within history. Our mission is wholly derived from God's mission, addresses the whole of God's creation, and is grounded at its centre in the redeeming victory of the cross. This is the people to whom we belong, whose faith we confess and whose mission we share.[53]

---

53. Lausanne Movement, "Commitment," part 1, sec. 10(A). A dualistic conception of mission remains strong among evangelicals, yet theological articulations like those of the Lausanne Movement have moved toward holistic mission, which embraces the more socially activist understanding of the kingdom of God traditionally associated with progressive conciliar and liberation theologies. Arguably, one weakness of my typology is that it does not include a liberationist understanding of participation. Stephen Bevans and Roger Schroeder, for example, argue persuasively that one of the three major types of theology understands "mission as participation in Jesus' mission in service of God's reign" in overtly liberationist terms (Bevans and Schroeder, *Constants*, 321). I would argue, however, that two factors merit consideration. One, liberation themes have infused and reshaped a number of understandings of participation. In this sense, a liberationist understanding of mission no longer stands apart but has become indispensable for multiple viewpoints. Two, the concerns of liberation and progressive ecumenical theology have ramified into political and postcolonial theologies. Recent decades have seen major publications in these areas, whereas liberationist discussions of mission per se have not

Both the watershed book *The Mission of God: Unlocking the Bible's Grand Narrative* and the Lausanne Movement's major document "The Cape Town Commitment" identify Christopher J. H. Wright as the chief representative of this perspective.[54] A second decisive voice is that of Ed Stetzer, the executive director of the Billy Graham Center for Evangelism at Wheaton College. Considering the two, the view of participation that I designate as *kingdom collaboration* becomes apparent. It is useful to begin with Stetzer and proceed to Wright's more expansive view.

Stetzer claims that "God's people are to participate in the divine mission to manifest and advance God's kingdom on earth through the means of sharing and showing the gospel of God's kingdom in Jesus Christ."[55] The crux of this understanding is its notion of the divine mission: manifestation and advancement of the kingdom. Thus, although Stetzer begins with the ecumenical *missio Dei* concept, God's mission is essentially an objective task, not a Trinitarian reality. Notwithstanding Stetzer's assertion that "sending is part of [God's] very nature," his emphasis is the idea that "God has a mission"—a "purpose," "agenda," and "plan."[56] This to-do is what the church undertakes when it participates in God's mission. The accent falls on the agency of the church. This is a corrective move: "While evangelicals have been helped by recognizing that, by and large, mission belongs to God, they have not forgotten that God calls the church to be the primary agent in his mission."[57] There is a pneumatology at work that softens this claim: "The church is born as a result of the Spirit's mission, and the Spirit empowers the church for its mission as it participates in God's mission."[58] Nonetheless, "God's mission is to advance his kingdom," and "Scripture bears witness that God advances his kingdom in this age through the lives of people."[59] In this regard, imitation of Christ, which Stetzer characterizes as "joining in Jesus's

---

enjoyed significant advocacy. In my view, therefore, the liberation option on its own is not a major contemporary understanding of participation, even though my argument in this study will take certain liberationist themes to be vital for a properly theological account of participation.

54. See Wright, *Mission*. Wright led the working group that prepared the "Commitment."

55. Stetzer, "Evangelical," 92.

56. Stetzer, "Evangelical," 97–99.

57. Stetzer, "Evangelical," 92.

58. Stetzer, "Evangelical," 105.

59. Stetzer, "Evangelical," 100, 103.

mission," is key.[60] By objectifying mission as God's agenda, Stetzer specifies what the church does as the primary agent of the kingdom. Unfortunately, he obscures God's Triune agency and reduces participation in God's mission to the dubious notion of advancing the kingdom.

Wright's view, though similar, is more expansive and holistic: "If we are to understand the mission of the church . . . we must understand the overarching biblical narrative within which the church participates as, on the one hand, the people of God in the present era between the first and second coming of Christ and, on the other hand, the people of God in spiritual and theological continuity with Old Testament Israel: in short, as those in Christ and thereby also in Abraham."[61] Wright deploys a narrative hermeneutical strategy that has become well known and widely accepted among evangelicals—the portrayal of the biblical stories as a drama that unfolds in discrete acts. By foregrounding the theme of mission in each act, he develops "a fully biblical understanding of the mission of God's people."[62] In the current act, the church is "to live within the Bible's own story and participate in its great unfolding drama. Mission is not merely a matter of obeying God's commands (such as, for example, the Great Commission—vitally important as that is), but of knowing the story we are in and living accordingly, bearing witness to the mighty acts of God (past and future)."[63] Whereas Stetzer places the burden of discerning the practical meaning of participation in God's mission on imitation of Jesus's life and ministry, Wright broadens the basis of this discernment considerably, in that "how we are to live, and what we are mandated to do as God's people in the world, are constantly rooted in the facts of who God is and what God has done"[64]—meaning, the whole story of God's being and doing revealed in the biblical narrative. This breadth results in "a truly holistic and integrated understanding of mission."[65] Wright's approach presents the problem that participation in God's mission is clearly participation in the drama, not participation in the Triune *missio*.[66] Therefore, Wright

---

60. Stetzer, "Evangelical," 106.
61. Wright, "Participatory," 65.
62. Wright, "Participatory," 73.
63. Wright, "Participatory," 77.
64. Wright, "Participatory," 65–66.
65. Wright, "Participatory," 81.
66. The relationship between participation in the mission of God and narrative identity will be a central issue in my constructive proposal. I am indebted to Wright's

sees participation in mission as essentially a function of the church's identity as God's people by virtue of their place in the narrative: "God has called into existence a people, in the midst of all the nations of the earth, to participate with God in his purposes for the world—'coworkers with God,' as Paul put it. This does not mean that we do everything God does. God is God, we are not. But it does mean that our understanding and practice of mission must reflect in some way, however imperfectly and provisionally, the comprehensiveness of God's biblically revealed actions, concerns, commands, promises, and intentions."[67] In this view, being coworkers with God proceeds on a distinction between what God does and what the church does rather than a notion of participation in that divine action. The phrase "reflect in some way" is key. Wright's vision of God's being and doing is robustly biblical, but the concept of the church's participation in God's mission is reductively imitative. A more Trinitarian approach is needed to push beyond this limitation.[68]

Participation as kingdom collaboration represents a strong sense of the church's agency as the people of God who share in God's work of "advancing the kingdom" in the world. Unlike the passivity of incarnational witness, in kingdom collaboration the church, as God's co-laborers, has a productive role in God's ongoing mission beyond making known what God has already done. Yet, the sense in which the mission is God's own Triune *missio* is attenuated by the paradigm of imitation.

---

narrative missional hermeneutic. The difficulty I find at this point is that his limited notion of narrative identity stands apart from a richer theological understanding of participation in God's mission.

67. Wright, "Participatory," 90.

68. "The Cape Town Commitment" attends to a Trinitarian framework in part 1, secs. 3–5, respectively titled "We Love the Father," "We Love the Son," and "We Love the Holy Spirit." The last of these begins: "We love the Holy Spirit within the unity of the Trinity, along with God the Father and God the Son. He is the missionary Spirit sent by the missionary Father and the missionary Son, breathing life and power into God's missionary Church. We love and pray for the presence of the Holy Spirit because without the witness of the Spirit to Christ, our own witness is futile. Without the convicting work of the Spirit, our preaching is in vain. Without the gifts, guidance and power of the Spirit, our mission is mere human effort. And without the fruit of the Spirit, our unattractive lives cannot reflect the beauty of the gospel." In such a statement, the *kingdom collaboration* view of participation takes a more theologically rounded stance in order to soften its clear emphasis on human agency. The distinction remains strong, however: the Spirit witnesses, and separately the church witnesses; the Spirit convicts, and separately the church preaches.

Contextual Dialogue

Among the most Trinitarian voices in missional theology are Roman Catholic theologians Stephen Bevans and Roger Schroeder. They have developed a view of mission called "prophetic dialogue," which attends to Roman Catholic, Eastern Orthodox, conciliar, and evangelical missiological developments with an unsurpassed inclusiveness, demonstrating the power of dialogue even as they argue for it.[69] From this view, mission is "a kind of continuum with dialogue on one side and prophecy on the other. Each context determines where the emphasis will be placed as the church engages in its missionary work."[70] On one end of the continuum is dialogue: "a basic attitude, indeed a kind of spirituality that underlies every aspect of mission"—"our basic stance is openness, an attitude of respect, listening, and docility (i.e., teachableness)."[71] On the other end is prophecy: "mission is ultimately about sharing the good news of God's reign with the peoples of the world." Yet, prophecy is a holistic endeavor, both nonverbal and verbal. On the one hand, it is "incarnated in the witness"[72] of Christians, so that "church communities are signs of the already present reign of God and give testimony to the merciful, life-giving, and true God revealed in Jesus." On the other hand, Christians also "*speak forth* a message of encouragement and hope" and "speak out in all sorts of ways against the evil in society."[73] This essential tension established, prophetic dialogue concretely includes six practices: "(1) witness and proclamation; (2) liturgy, prayer, and contemplation; (3) justice, peace, and the integrity of creation; (4) interfaith, secular (and ecumenical) dialogue; (5) inculturation; and (6) reconciliation."[74] By discussing these elements of mission as practices, prophetic dialogue puts agency front and center, which makes the construal of its Trinitarian foundations the critical issue: "the practice of prophetic dialogue is the full participation in God's trinitarian life and mission."[75] This turns out to be an essentially pneumatological claim. Bevans develops it in relation to the Spirit's general presence and work in creation and history

---

69. See Bevans and Schroeder, *Constants*, ch. 12; Bevans and Schroeder, *Prophetic*; Bevans, "Theology," 99–108; Bevans, "Prophetic," 3–20.

70. Bevans, "Prophetic," 9.

71. Bevans, "Prophetic," 6.

72. Bevans, "Prophetic," 7.

73. Bevans, "Prophetic," 8.

74. Bevans, "Prophetic," 10.

75. Bevans, "Prophetic," 13.

and special presence and work in the person and work of Jesus of Nazareth. The culmination of this line of reasoning is that the

> dialogical nature of God was revealed especially in Jesus's death and resurrection, where God's love for the world was poured out fully and then shared abundantly with Jesus's disciples as they are called to participate in God's very mission through the pouring forth of God's Spirit upon them (see the whole movement of Acts, and especially Acts 2). God's saving and redemptive purposes in creation and history, accomplished in a creative prophetic dialogue, had been worked out in the history of Israel and in the ministry, death, and resurrection of Jesus. Through the Spirit, the church became God's agent, God's partner even, in fulfilling God's saving purpose.[76]

The agency of the church—the church's action in mission—relates to God's presence and action in the world "through the Spirit." Furthermore, this relationship is predicated on the "nature of God" revealed in Jesus, which is Bevans's unique spin on social Trinitarianism: "God not only *practices* prophetic dialogue in God's saving presence and action in creation and history; God is in God's very self a communion of prophetic dialogue. In baptism, Christians are plunged into this communion and are called to share God's life of dialogue and prophecy within the created world and in human history."[77] Participation in God's mission through the Spirit is, then, realized sacramentally. In turn, the church itself becomes sacramental—in the words of the Vatican II document *Lumen Gentium*, "the church is 'like a sacrament or as a sign and instrument both of a very closely knit union with God and of the unity of the whole human race.'"[78]

Presbyterian theologian John Franke takes a view of participation that resonates deeply with that of Bevans and Schroeder. Franke is a colleague of Darrell Guder in the Gospel and Our Culture Network, yet I liken his understanding of participation more to prophetic dialogue for two reasons. First, Barthian witness does not loom so large in Franke's theology, and he seems not to align neatly with the extremely limited view of agency that Guder promotes. Second, his Trinitarian articulation of participation carries forward Lesslie Newbigin's focus on pluralism in a way that resonates deeply with the open, dialogical posture of Bevans

---

76. Bevans, "Prophetic," 14.
77. Bevans, "Prophetic," 14–15.
78. Bevans, "Prophetic," 15.

and Schroeder.[79] Hence, Franke's "contextual mission" perspective echoes Newbigin in seeking to explain what it means that the church "is sent into the world by the triune God for the purpose of bearing witness to the gospel as a sign, instrument, and foretaste of the kingdom of God."[80] Franke identifies and confronts our basic theological dilemma head on: the problem with the "consensus" on the *missio Dei* "is that, while it served to inseparably link the mission of the church with participation in the mission of God, it did not lead to specification with regard to the precise nature of the church's participation in that mission."[81] Furthermore, he develops the problem by reference to contextual complications:

> In keeping with the pattern of this sending, the mission of the church is intimately connected with the mission of God in the sending of Jesus and the Spirit. The church is called to be the image of God, the body of Christ, and the dwelling place of the Spirit in the world as it represents and extends the good news of God's love for the world as a sign, instrument, and foretaste of the kingdom of God. However, given the local and particular nature of the church in its various manifestations throughout history, culture, time, place, the expression of this mission is always contextual and situated in keeping with the commission to bear witness to the ends of earth.[82]

Thus, when Franke says the mission of God is, in short, "love and salvation," he is suggesting that "the salvific mission is rooted in the self-giving, self-sacrificing love of God expressed in the eternal Trinitarian fellowship and made known in the created order through the life, death, and resurrection of Jesus Christ."[83] To participate in love and salvation is to participate in the Triune fellowship—the *missio Dei*—further expressed in the world through the sending of the church. Franke therefore develops the metaphors of sign, instrument, and foretaste in terms of the image of God, the body of Christ, and the dwelling place of the Spirit, which is to say, as christological and pneumatological conceptualizations of participation in the Triune life. In regard to the image of God, Franke

---

79. For further methodological development of the relationship of pluralism to missional theology, see Franke, "Intercultural," ch. 4.
80. Franke, "Contextual," 118.
81. Franke, "Contextual," 108.
82. Franke, "Contextual," 112.
83. Franke, "Contextual," 114.

is attentive to the New Testament notion of being "in Christ," which he discusses in connection with "following the pattern of Jesus."[84] As the body of Christ, "the church is sent into the world and called to continue the mission of Jesus in the power of the Spirit,"[85] which is "to participate in the temporal, here-and-now activity of liberation."[86] And as for being the dwelling place of the Spirit, Franke highlights the eschatological peace that characterizes the community of the Spirit and its worship. Though all of these could be developed further biblically and theologically, Franke points to the potential of such development for clarifying in Trinitarian terms what participation in God's mission might be and how attempting to do so without reference to context is futile. The primary weakness of Franke's approach is precisely its ambiguity about what contextualization is. "All are called," concludes Franke, "to do their part in the mission of God in accordance with the particular social and historical circumstances in which they are situated and the gifting of the Spirit."[87] In this, Bevans and Schroeder's prophetic dialogue gives shape to Franke's contextual mission. Participation is, specifically, contextual *dialogue*.[88]

Participation as contextual dialogue places the accent on pluralistic encounters, making cultural contextualization and intercultural communication—and more fundamentally, the dialogical nature of interaction with the other—a central part of the church's understanding of God's Triune mission. These perspectives achieve a combination of Triune mission and human agency wherein the contextual, dialogical actions of the church are participation in the love and life of God. Still, doubt remains. Are the practices of contextual dialogue always participation in God's mission? Are all practices of, say, justice or liberation necessarily the work of the Triune God? In what sense, as the practices of the church, are they also God's own mission?

---

84. Franke, "Contextual," 119–21.
85. Franke, "Contextual," 121.
86. Franke, "Contextual," 123.
87. Franke, "Contextual," 133.
88. Furthermore, the tremendous missiological resources that have developed out of the imperative to contextualize mission work stand to offer help specifying just how *contextual* dialogue might proceed in the midst of cultural pluralism. See Moreau, *Contextualization*, for an overview.

Pneumatological Relationship

A fourth understanding of participation places the accent on the Holy Spirit. Once more, various angles on this type combine in a consistent emphasis—in this case on the *missio Spiritus Sancti*. Kirsteen Kim, whose body of work has consistently sought to critique and advance the purported consensus of Bosch's "emerging ecumenical missionary paradigm," is representative: "Although he propounds the theology of *missio Dei*, in which the church participates in the mission of God by the Spirit, Bosch binds the mission of the Spirit very closely to the missionary activity of the church. Thus, when he seeks to broaden mission to take account of the 'comprehensive' nature of salvation, he can do so only by increasing the scope of the church's missionary activity. In this way mission still appears to be in the mold of the Enlightenment project as a *work* to be achieved by organization and strategy, rather than as a participation in the Spirit."[89] Kim calls for "a mission theology whose starting point can be none other than a particular experience of the Spirit in the world, which interacts with other contextual theologies arising in different geographical locations, social conditions and religious milieus, where the Spirit is at work. The result of such an approach would be a theology that sees mission more as an attempt to live in the Holy Spirit than as a task to be accomplished."[90] Such a conception of participation in the Spirit relies heavily on the notion of discernment, for which Kim looks especially to Pentecostal theologian Amos Yong.[91]

Yong's charismatic missiology focuses on the Holy Spirit, but as a systematician his research began in religious studies, which gives his perspective on the presence and work of the Spirit in the world tremendous breadth. For Yong, discernment of the Spirit in a religiously plural world is predicated on a "universalistic reading of the Pentecost narrative" according to which the Spirit poured out on "all flesh" (Acts 2:17), which is "the theological basis for not only accepting but also valuing the plurality of cultures," including the religious dimensions of cultures.[92] This grounds the expectation of a deeply *relational* encounter between the Christian and the religious other in which the discernment of the Spirit poured out universally

---

89. Kim, *Holy*, 173–74.
90. Kim, *Holy*, 174.
91. See Kim, *Holy*, 160–69.
92. Yong, *Missiological*, 57.

on all flesh is at stake for the Christian.[93] This encounter is pneumatological not only in that the Christian missionary seeks to discern how the Spirit is at work in the religious other but also in that "even the discernment of spirits is a gift of the Holy Spirit rather than a creaturely capacity."[94] The dialogical exchange in which the Spirit is discerned and empowers discernment takes the shape of "a pneumatological theology of hospitality" in Yong's missiology.[95] A Trinitarian understanding of incarnation and Pentecost, he argues, manifests divine hospitality. In turn, "the hospitality of God is thus embodied in a hospitable church whose members are empowered by the Holy Spirit to stand in solidarity and serve with the sick, the poor, and the oppressed."[96] Such Christian praxis is itself "a theological posture characterized by a genuine epistemological humility, open to the surprising presence and activity of the Spirit."[97] In other words, the Spirit leads and empowers the practices of Christian hospitality, through which the Spirit enables "the possibility of authentic dialogue in the Christian encounter with those of other faiths"[98] that results in discernment of the Spirit's own work and witness to Jesus in a given context—which presumably leads the Christian deeper into mutual hospitality. Despite the sense in which this construal relies on the active praxis of Christian hospitality and dialogical discernment, it issues in "a generous Christian approach to interfaith relations that remains evangelical and missiological, while recognizing that Christians do *little more than participate* in the redemptive mission of the triune God."[99] The primary agency of the Spirit and the church's posture of humility and reliance profoundly limit the meaning of participation while at the same time specifying the significance of the church's indispensable praxis of transformative hospitality and dialogue.

---

93. Yong's relational, dialogical vision is deeply consonant with the contextual dialogue type, but pneumatology casts the notion of dialogue in a distinct light. In particular, Yong develops a "foundational pneumatology" on which his understanding of dialogical discernment of the Spirit depends. See Yong, *Beyond*, chs. 3, 6, and 7. This is merely indicative, however: apart from the specifics of Yong's proposal, I suggest the pneumatological relationship type understands participation in terms of the Holy Spirit to an extent that contrasts significantly with the contextual dialogue type.

94. Yong, *Missiological*, 73.

95. Yong, *Missiological*, ch. 4; see also Yong, *Hospitality*.

96. Yong, *Missiological*, 88–89.

97. Yong, *Missiological*, 95.

98. Yong, *Missiological*, 92.

99. Yong, *Missiological*, 221; emphasis added.

PARTICIPATION IN MISSIONAL THEOLOGY

Among North American missional theologians, Van Gelder is particularly attuned to the need for a more robust pneumatology in the articulation of *missio Dei* theology. He holds the agency of the church in tension with God's agency by virtue of construing participation in terms of two distinct questions: "What is God doing?—the issue of faith and discernment" and "What does God want to do?—the issue of wisdom and planning." Regarding what God is doing, Van Gelder says, "God is at work in the world beyond the church. Discerning this work of God is foundational for effective ministry. The church is called and sent to participate in God's mission in the world. The responsibility of the church is to discern where and how this mission is unfolding."[100] In view of the Acts narrative, he claims that the Spirit's leading takes the shape of unanticipated change and conflict accompanied by pain and disruption.[101] Contextual experiences call for discernment of the Spirit's work. Regarding what God wants to do, Van Gelder says, "Changes taking place in a ministry context present challenges that the church must seek to address. This requires careful planning. This work of the Spirit is related to the redemptive activity of God in the world. For a church to be a steward of the good news of the gospel, it must engage in focused missional planning in considering how to participate in what God wants to do in a particular context."[102] Discernment serves planning: what God is doing is an index of what God wants to do, and the church is responsible to respond intentionally and strategically. Both movements constitute participation. What the church does it would not do without the provocation and leadership of the Spirit, both because the church is attentive to the Spirit in discernment of God's contextual movement and because the Spirit is disruptive even when the church is inattentive, provoking change, reaction, and new strategic wisdom. Van Gelder and Zscheile's further discussion in *The Missional Church in Perspective* begins to stretch toward historically rich notions of participation by reference to the concept of *perichōrēsis*, the mutual indwelling that characterizes the relational union of the Triune life:

> Participation, grounded in a new appreciation for the relationality of God's Triune life, offers a much more helpful framework for conceiving of the relationship between God, world, and church. The theme of participation has received attention in several recent

---

100. Van Gelder, *Ministry*, 59.
101. Van Gelder, *Ministry*, 59–60.
102. Van Gelder, *Ministry*, 60.

Trinitarian works. Drawing on the biblical concepts of *koinonia*, communion, sharing, and fellowship, an understanding of participation describes the *perichoretic* (mutual indwelling) relationality of God's own Trinitarian life, as well as God's creative, incarnational, and Spirit-infused relationship with creation.[103]

I will discuss *perichōrēsis* further in the next chapter. Suffice it for the purposes of my typology to highlight the pneumatological accent of their argument. Like Yong's vision of relational discernment of the Spirit in all cultures and religious contexts, Van Gelder and Zscheile's description of participation in God's Spirit-infused relationship with creation entails a missiological commitment to relational openness to the world and imaginative discernment: "The missional church is a community led by the Spirit. It is a community that constantly looks for signs of the Spirit's leading in its own life and in the surrounding neighborhood. Its communal imagination must be pregnant with anticipation of the Spirit."[104] Borrowing Charles Taylor's conception of the social imaginary, they signal an important point already implicit in Yong's Pentecostalism: the ability to participate in God's ongoing work depends on an imagination that is not captive to modernist secularism, that can perceive "the Triune God's disruptive, graceful, provocative power and agency" in the first place.[105] Without this Spirit-shaped imagination, human agency and its missiological machination is all that remains. Perceiving and participating in God's redemptive relationship with all of creation, on the contrary, casts the question of agency in essentially different terms: "Ecclesial being—participating with a new identity in the body of Christ—is something that happens fundamentally *between*, between us and the Triune God, between us and others in the fellowship of faith, and between us and our neighbors in the world. This relationality and betweenness are the spaces within which mission occurs. Mission is not the transmission of a particular set of properties, ideas, goods, or concepts to people, but rather the entering into relational webs that transform us even as we engage in shaping others. The agency involved is God's, ours, and our neighbor's."[106] Like Yong's, this view culminates in a discussion of reciprocal hospitality.[107]

103. Van Gelder and Zscheile, *Missional*, 110.
104. Van Gelder and Zscheile, *Missional*, 118–19.
105. Van Gelder and Zscheile, *Missional*, 119.
106. Van Gelder and Zscheile, *Missional*, 121–22.
107. Van Gelder and Zscheile, *Missional*, 132–35.

Participation as pneumatological relationship moves beyond the limited view of the Spirit that has characterized missional theology, sometimes reducing it to binitarianism.[108] By highlighting the agency of the Spirit in the world beyond the church and by making the church's agency a function of its relationship to the Spirit, this perspective both amplifies the relational dimension of the contextual dialogue type and clarifies the subject matter of the dialogical exchange. The pneumatological relationship type insists that participation entails an involvement in the divine life beyond the paradigm of imitation. The Spirit enables mutual discernment in the church's relational encounters with the other. More, the Spirit is the agent whose actions are to be discerned and strategically joined. The primary weakness of this understanding of participation is that it needs a fuller account of the nature of the church's and the world's relationships to the Spirit, because it risks failing to articulate the difference between them. Additionally, the difficulty of determining "the norms and criteria with which we attempt to discern the presence and activity of the Spirit and of other spirits"[109] can become an insurmountable impediment to stipulating what counts as participation in what God is really doing in the world.

Sacramental Presence

Edward Rommen lays out a what he calls a "sacramental vision" understanding of mission from the Eastern Orthodox perspective. Appropriately named, sacrament—especially the Eucharist—is at the heart of this perspective, but it is a vision of sacrament rooted in an understanding of salvation as *theōsis*: "becoming increasingly and finally completely like God in his personhood and character."[110] "We understand the primary task of mission," says Rommen, "to be personally introducing Christ to those who do not yet know him so that they, through faith, can enter into communion with him and begin the journey to salvation."[111] In short, communion leads to salvation, so the mission of the church is to be the place where communion is made possible. Mission is profoundly church-centered from this perspective, in the sense that the sacraments are administered

---

108. See the critique of Bosch's limitation of the Spirit's role to initiating, guiding, and empowering mission in Kim, *Holy*, 28, 173.

109. Yong, *Missiological*, 73.

110. Rommen, "Sacramental," 71.

111. Rommen, "Sacramental," 69.

in the assembly of the church. Although church members are "dismissed into the world as witness of what they have seen," the invitation to "come and see" is the essential paradigm of mission.[112] The sacramental vision approach prioritizes relationship over information in evangelism: "Whatever else it might be, the mission of the church involves the facilitation of a personal encounter with the Lord of life, Jesus Christ."[113] This sacramental encounter, however, can only happen in the context of the church's authorized celebration of the Eucharist. There is a significant tension here: on the one hand, those to whom the presence of Christ is mediated through the Eucharist can "extend the liturgy into the non-ecclesial or pre-ecclesial world around them," but on the other hand, the real saving encounter with Jesus only takes place "in the eucharistic assembly."[114] The upshot of this construal is that church planting is extremely important, but only those with the apostolic authority to administer the Eucharist can plant legitimate churches. That is, "ecclesial authority or legitimacy"[115] is a matter of apostolic succession, marking Rommen's Eastern Orthodox perspective with a unique concern for "ecclesio-sacramental integrity." Yet, Rommen's contribution is the place he gives *theōsis*. Because *theōsis* is, for him, an understanding of the consequence of mission (i.e., salvation) rather than an understanding of mission itself, however, sacramental vision puts limits on the missional implications of *theōsis*. If the Eucharistic sacrament is not rightly administered, "the special manifestation of Christ is not present,"[116] without which *theōsis* is not sustained. The special presence—Christ himself available in the Eucharist—that nourishes *theōsis* is, in other words, precisely what is lacking outside the context of ecclesio-sacramental integrity. In contrast, the theology of *missio Dei* typically conceives of mission as attending to the saving presence of God in the world beyond the church assembly. Thus, the presence/absence binary in the sacramental vision approach indicates the key difference between *theōsis* as salvation and *theōsis* as mission. Rommen almost finds a mediating position in his discussion of the maturity (i.e., progress in *theōsis*) necessary "to direct attention to Christ's presence in the witness's own life."[117] This comes close

112. Rommen, "Sacramental," 77.
113. Rommen, "Sacramental," 78.
114. Rommen, "Sacramental," 81.
115. Rommen, "Sacramental," 87.
116. Rommen, "Sacramental," 84.
117. Rommen, "Sacramental," 86.

to a claim that Christ is present in the missional encounter with the other, but inviting-to-assembly is still the operative paradigm.

From a Protestant perspective, Peter Leithart similarly advocates a "sacramental mission" understanding. A major premise of his argument is that discussions of mission routinely ignore the importance of the sacraments. Humanity's problem as Leithart reads the biblical story is that, after Adam and Eve were exiled from the garden of Eden, "human beings no longer had access to the presence of God" so that although they continued to rule, "they no longer ruled as the companions of their Creator."[118] "That is the setting in which God set out on his mission to restore humanity, and his goal was to restore humanity to fellowship that would produce godly dominion."[119] Like Wright, Leithart takes the biblical story to construe "mission" as the goal of God. In this scheme, he casts Abrahamic "flesh-cutting [i.e., circumcision] and altar-building [i.e., sacrifice]" and the Mosaic "rhythm of life and liturgy" as sacramental—having to do with drawing near to the presence of God. Following the ministries of John the Baptist and Jesus, the sacraments of baptism and the Lord's Supper both proclaim and effect the restoration of humanity. Moreover, the baptized "who feast on the body and blood of Jesus are empowered by the Spirit as witnesses."[120] The conclusion toward which this construal drives is that "purification and meal, baptism and the Supper, have been centerpieces of the mission of God and the life of the people of God since the beginning. . . . God's mission is to restore the original harmony of liturgy and life, and . . . this intention comes to a focus in the Christian sacraments."[121] In addition to sharing Rommen's sacramental emphasis, Leithart provides another important pathway to an understanding of *theōsis* in relation to mission. Both sacraments entail "union with Christ" and "participation in Christ."[122] Leithart also pushes the discussion toward an overtly political theology. In his view, the reunion of humankind in Christ is at the heart of the church's mission: "she is sent to the world to disciple all people groups by baptizing them, teaching them the commandments of Jesus, and welcoming them to the table of the Lord. In this, the church is God's

---

118. Leithart, "Sacramental," 159.
119. Leithart, "Sacramental," 160.
120. Leithart, "Sacramental," 162–64.
121. Leithart, "Sacramental," 165.
122. Leithart, "Sacramental," 166–67.

instrument to fulfill his mission to reunite the human race."[123] But this unity is of overtly political significance; it constitutes a political body that "comes to visibility as the contrast society."[124]

This indicates the extent to which Leithart's view of participation envisions the church's "political" agency as passive. Foregrounding political agency in the context of God's mission also raises the questions surrounding both the church's historical relationship with colonial powers and God's revelation of the kingdom in the *saeculum* apart from the church. In considering the church's public presence, Leithart is not unique among the authors I have engaged. I highlight Leithart's construal in particular because the church's sacramental presence in the midst of the *saeculum* is indicative of his vision of participation. Here the vaguely neo-Anabaptist notion of the church as a "contrast society" is elevated to the level of a programmatic vision of participation.[125]

Participation as sacramental presence fundamentally reorients the conversation about the church's agency in relation to God's mission by recourse to rich theological conceptions of God's grace operative in and through the church in ways that do not easily fall into the trap of ecclesial activism. The implications of *theōsis* as union with Christ still need to be worked out, but the sacramental presence approach already signals its potential. At the same time, sacramental presence signals the difficulties that an appropriation of *theōsis* faces *prima facie*. The importance of the church's unique relationship with God can cast the church in the role of a dispenser of sacramental presence or even a reserve of sacramental presence apart from the world. The sense of the *missio Dei* in the world can ultimately fade from this view of participation, and with it the sense that the church is called to anything more than being sacramentally transformed and inviting others to do the same.

---

123. Leithart, "Sacramental," 168.

124. Leithart, "Sacramental," 174.

125. On the designation *neo-Anabaptist* in missional theology, see Fitch, "Other," 466–78. I acknowledge the irony of associating Fitch's position with Leithart's, given Leithart's resistance to the critique of Christendom typified by one of Fitch's decisive influences, John Howard Yoder (see Leithart, *Defending*). Nonetheless, Fitch has pioneered a position that, regarding the question of participation, hits the key notes of the sacramental presence type and contributes significantly to its development. See Fitch and Holsclaw, "Mission," 389–401.

Conclusion: The Aporias of Participation

I began with a brief review of early influences on participation language, establishing that questions regarding Trinitarian theology and the church's agency in relation to God's underlie the ambiguity of contemporary uses of *participation* in missional theology. Next, I proposed a typology of contemporary understandings of participation in God's mission that includes five alternative views: incarnational witness, kingdom collaboration, contextual dialogue, pneumatological relationship, and sacramental presence. Incarnational witness and kingdom collaboration both focus on Christology, emphasizing Christlikeness in consonant ways but ultimately taking polar positions on the nature of the church's agency in relation to God's. Contextual dialogue and pneumatological relationship both attend especially to the church's encounter with the other, but whereas contextual dialogue focuses on the loving, dialogical, situated nature of the church's relationship to the world, pneumatological relationship focuses on the Holy Spirit as the basis and meaningfulness of the encounter. Sacramental presence focuses on ecclesiology, highlighting the sense in which the church's union with Christ manifest in its sacramental practices is both the end of mission and its means.

Although differences in method and tradition are in play among the types, the point is not the banal observation that diverse theologies engender diverse understandings of participation. Rather, after taking into account the rich contributions of diverse perspectives and the nuance that comparison generates, the shared problem of articulating the relationship between God's mission and the church's missions remains unresolved among those playing the language game of missional theology. The argument that my typology serves is that once we have accounted for the distinctives of the major understandings of participation, no convincing response to its aporias has emerged. One might easily argue, in fact, that it is harder than ever to say, in a way that does full justice to missional theology's Trinitarian and ecclesial commitments, what the church's participation in God's mission actually is. At the same time, a number of concepts have proven profitable: incarnation (human-divine relationship, church as body of Christ), imitation (collaboration, in relation to *imago Dei*), Trinitarian relationships (love, dialogue, *perichōrēsis*), discernment of the Spirit, and *theōsis* (union with Christ, maturation). These will all find further purchase as I develop a definition of participation in God's mission.

The constructive upshot of the typological exercise, then, is greater clarity about both the aporias of participation and the resources available to address them. Any attempt to advance the conversation must, first, proceed from a thicker account of how human and divine agency relate. Second, given the grammar of missional theology, the relationship between human and divine agency must be conceived in fully Trinitarian terms. Third, this Trinitarian understanding of human agency in the *missio Dei* must give way to a concrete conception of ecclesial, human action in relation to God's action in the world. Accordingly, the proceeding three chapters will (1) begin by proposing an understanding of participation as *theōsis* that establishes the nature of human participation in the divine life in relation to the perichoretic union of Father, Son, and Spirit, (2) advance to a corollary theological anthropology that combines the concepts of human embodiment and narrativity in order to clarify the nature of perichoretic participation in the Triune life, and (3) arrive at an understanding of participation that appropriates and extends the notion of solidarity in liberation theology in order to specify concretely the nature of the church's missional action.

CHAPTER 3

Participation in God's Mission as *Theōsis*

"A triune doctrine of God encourages us to *discover* our roles as we participate in a God who is always in the movement of sending."
—Paul Fiddes[1]

To explain why participation in God's mission forms the church hermeneutically, it is necessary to address the aporias of participation that continue to mark missional theology. In this chapter, I begin to construct an account of how human and divine agency relate in mission by arguing that human participation in God's mission should be understood theologically in terms of human participation in the divine life. Missional theology has been largely inattentive to the relevance of the broader theological discussion of participation and its traditional cognates *union, divinization,* and *theōsis*. As I demonstrated in the previous chapter, even where *theōsis* or union play a more prominent role, as in the sacramental presence type of missional theology, they do not address the problem of participation but instead take union with Christ as the goal of mission or the result of sacramental grace, even tending toward an ecclesiocentrism that undercuts the logic of the church's participation in God's mission in the world. Accordingly, I attempt here to meet missional theology's need for a more

---

1. Fiddes, *Participating*, 51.

thoroughgoing engagement with the theology of *theōsis*. Conversely, a great deal of work has been done recently on *theōsis* and related ideas, but essentially none of it is concerned with God's mission. This is an oversight given the natural relationship between the traditional idea of participation in Christ through the Spirit common to exponents of *theōsis* and the idea of participation in the missions of the Triune God typical of missional theology. It is also a confirmation of missional theology's concern that too much of Christian theology leaves God's mission aside in favor of internal themes like those that have traditionally marked *theōsis* doctrine: spiritual progress, mystical communion, and beatific vision. Of course, none of these themes are antithetical to mission, but a tendency to construe such matters in basically non-missional terms prevails. This is clearest regarding the fundamental issue in the early patristic development of *theōsis*—atonement. In one of its earliest articulations, the idea of *theōsis* is that the Word of God "did . . . become what we are, that He might bring us to be even what He is Himself."[2] This soteriological claim has first to do with *our* benefit (from the church's perspective). I argue that, beyond the benefits enjoyed by those who experience salvation, our becoming one with the Savior through *theōsis* entails our participation in the ongoing divine work of atonement. Following Ross Hastings, I contend that the church's participation in God's mission is grounded in "the miracle of theosis, the union of Christ with his church."[3] Grounding a renewed articulation of the *missio Dei* in a Trinitarian theology that is open to the retrieval of patristic conceptions of union and *theōsis* provides a promising path toward a thick account of missional participation.

In section 1, I consider various dimensions of the contemporary discussion of *theōsis*, including the catalytic deployment of *theōsis* in the missional hermeneutics of New Testament scholar Michael Gorman, the flurry of retrieval work that has fueled a renaissance of engagement with *theōsis* doctrine, and the significance of *theōsis* in a variety of recent theologies of atonement. In section 2, I conclude by relating my account of *theōsis* to the Trinitarian doctrine of *perichōrēsis*, in preparation for further reflection on the nature of the divine life in the world and human participation in it.

---

2. Irenaeus, *Haer.* 5 preface; unless noted otherwise, the English text of *Haer.* is from *ANF*, vol. 1.

3. Hastings, *Missional*, 82.

PARTICIPATION IN GOD'S MISSION AS *THEŌSIS*

Toward a Missional Conception of *Theōsis*

First among the aporias of participation in missional theology that I identified in chapter 2 is the need for a thicker account of how human and divine agency relate. In this chapter, I demonstrate how a missional understanding of *theōsis* can answer this question. To move toward an understanding of participation in the *missio Dei* as *theōsis*, however, I must face two primary challenges: the diversity of understandings of *theōsis* on offer in the contemporary theological retrieval movement and the relationship of *theōsis* to a knot of soteriological issues, particularly among Protestants. Therefore, I first map my path through the retrieval movement. Then I locate myself theologically in relation to the debate about *theōsis* in relation to soteriology.

The purpose of these two procedures is to trace a missional understanding of *theōsis* that foregrounds a crucial point: the ongoing soteriological debate about *theōsis* is implicitly already a debate about the relationship of the church's participation in mission to the atonement. Therefore, working out the relationship between divine and human agency soteriologically in terms of *theōsis* begins to elucidate the chapter's main contention: *theōsis* is participation in the atonement, which is participation in God's mission. Before developing this claim in detail, I begin with a catalyst for my thesis, the work of New Testament scholar Michael Gorman.

Theōsis in Michael's Gorman's Missional Hermeneutics

Gorman's work is the first major argument that combines the language of participation in God's mission with a notion of *theōsis* retrieved from the Great Tradition. Moreover, he makes this argument to promote a missional theological interpretation of Scripture. Gorman focuses on interpreting Pauline and Johannine texts according to their own ideas of participation in mission.[4] My thesis breaks into the hermeneutical circle at a different moment, focusing instead on the interpretive community's participation in mission. Nonetheless, by representing the state of the question in missional hermeneutics, Gorman provides a propitious jumping-off point for this chapter.

---

4. Gorman, *Becoming*; Gorman, *Abide*; Gorman, *Participating*.

In two earlier works, Gorman develops a vibrant understanding of Pauline theology in terms of *theōsis*.[5] Then in his 2015 volume *Becoming the Gospel: Paul, Participation, and Mission*, he advances this understanding of Pauline *theōsis* through the theme of mission, arguing that "Spirit-enabled transformative participation in the life and character of God revealed in the crucified and resurrected Messiah Jesus—is the starting point of mission and is, in fact, its proper theological framework."[6] Two important consequences follow. First, Gorman says, "In 2 Corinthians 5:14–21 (and in shorter summaries of the gospel, such as Rom. 1:16–17), justification as inclusive of transformation, participation, and mission all find powerful expression. *To understand justification less robustly is simply to misunderstand Paul*."[7] Gorman's reading of Paul thickens the soteriological category of justification by including participation within it and then glossing participation with both transformation and mission. His reading of Paul ultimately issues in a missional revisioning of Pauline soteriology that overcomes not only the tiresome dichotomy of justification and sanctification but also the dichotomy of salvation and mission. The upshot is: "*To participate in Christ is both to benefit from God's mission of liberation and reconciliation and to bear witness to this divine mission—thus furthering it—by becoming a faithful embodiment of it.*"[8] Accordingly, a second consequence is that Gorman's theological exegesis of Paul in terms of *theōsis* helps close the gap between the typically instrumental view of Christian witness (e.g., "we are ambassadors for Christ"; 2 Cor 5:20) and the participatory view (e.g., "we might become the righteousness of God"; 2 Cor 5:21). As the book's title conveys, this gap is closed because the "becoming" that *theōsis* entails is "becoming the gospel," or in Paul's terms, "becoming the righteousness of God." The church "participates in the life of the God—Father, Son, and Spirit—who is the source and the content of that gospel. In other words, although Paul did not believe that all participants in Christ, all members of the *ekklēsia*, should become *euangelistai* (evangelists in the sense of traveling missionaries or public preachers), he firmly believed that they should all become the *euangelion* (the evangel, the gospel)."[9] In summary, all Christians are ambassadors for Christ, not

5. Gorman, *Cruciformity*; Gorman, *Inhabiting*.
6. Gorman, *Becoming*, 4.
7. Gorman, *Becoming*, 9.
8. Gorman, *Becoming*, 36.
9. Gorman, *Becoming*, 43.

because all are evangelists but because all participate in *theōsis*, which entails the church's embodiment of the gospel.

By reading Paul in terms of *theōsis*, Gorman offers a Pauline understanding of what *theōsis* is. In the final chapter of *Becoming the Gospel*, he summarizes his findings with a list of "missional virtues and practices" that constitute the church's embodiment of the gospel. Both the textual basis by which he stipulates the meaning of "participating now in the life and mission of the triune God"[10] and the consequent concreteness of his vision of participation are valuable. Yet, the chief difficulty of Gorman's proposal is the distance that remains between his list of "virtues and practices" and "the reality of communal, cruciform participation in the cross-shaped Trinity."[11] Gorman is careful to discuss the "reality" of participation with eschatological nuance, because the present reality is not the fullness of the future reality. Indeed, in Gorman's reading of Paul, the real conformation of human nature to the image of Christ by the power of the Spirit is the present ontological transformation that necessarily precedes and accompanies the embodiment of cruciform righteousness: "ethical conformity precedes and is the prerequisite for eschatological, ontological conformity, but the two are related, indeed inseparable: two dimensions of the same reality, the same narrative, participatory salvation."[12] Nonetheless, his emphasis on virtues and practices risks obscuring the ontological dimensions of participation that make sense of his ancient interlocutors' claims. Fortunately, his next volume, *Abide and Go: Missional Theosis in the Gospel of John*, confronts these issues more directly through Johannine categories.

In *Abide and Go*, Gorman takes the same methodological tack, reading the Gospel of John through the lenses of *theōsis* and missional hermeneutics. The result is much the same: an exegetical account of John's contribution to our understanding of *theōsis* as participation in God's mission. In Gorman's interpretation, the Gospel of John, particularly the "mission discourse" (chs. 13–17) and post-resurrection commissions (chs. 20–21), establishes not only "the reality of participation, of mutual indwelling, within God, particularly between the Father and the Son" but also the fact that human participation in this reality is by definition participation in the mission of God.[13] He contends: "Accordingly, for John, there is no spiri-

10. Gorman, *Becoming*, 5.
11. Gorman, *Becoming*, 8.
12. Gorman, *Becoming*, 282.
13. Gorman, *Abide*, 72.

tuality without mission, and no mission without spirituality; that is, *there is no participation in God without mission, and no mission without participation in God.*"[14] Though many of the particulars of Gorman's reading are illuminating, I will highlight just one idea that runs throughout the book, namely, that John's vision of participation is more than mere imitation. "In participating in God's holiness/goodness/love, we are participating in God's life," says Gorman.[15] As suggested by the phrase "reality of participation" in the quotation above, John's Gospel reveals that this divine life in which we participate, the life that just is Jesus, is "necessarily ontological."[16] Thus, "becoming children of God is a participatory reality—beginning to share in the sonship of the Father's Son."[17] It follows from this relational reality that participation in the Son's mission "requires more than obedience to, or imitation of, a person external to the disciple(s)."[18] Again, in the commissioning prayer of ch. 17, the unity in which mission is rooted is "more than *imitation* of the Father-Son unity; it is *participation* in that divine unity."[19] This ontological-relational reality is what Gorman means when he speaks of "missional theosis": "a mutual indwelling of the triune God and believers that entails the empowering and transforming work of God, by the Spirit, in and on believers individually and as a community. . . . To participate in the Son's union with the Father will be to participate in the Father's (missional) activity in and through the Son."[20] Gorman makes the expected caveats about the distinction between Creator and creation,[21] because his understanding correctly embraces a robust enough version of *theōsis* to require such caveats. "Participation in God's mission effects transformation"[22] is an ontological claim because participation is an ontological reality. In turn, the affirmation of "participation in the ongoing divine activity of salvation—the *missio Dei*—as the means of transformation" triggers the usual caveats about works righteousness.[23] Yet, Gorman does

14. Gorman, *Abide*, 74.
15. Gorman, *Abide*, 20.
16. Gorman, *Abide*, 50.
17. Gorman, *Abide*, 57.
18. Gorman, *Abide*, 89; see also 95.
19. Gorman, *Abide*, 115.
20. Gorman, *Abide*, 23.
21. See Gorman, *Abide*, 20, 23.
22. Gorman, *Abide*, 23.
23. Gorman, *Abide*, 23; see also 131.

not shy away from the implications of his reading: "For Jesus, there was an ontological unity with the Father that, in a sense, guaranteed his doing the Father's works. It was impossible for him not to do the works of God. His works were God's work (*erga*), his mission God's mission (*ergon*). Nonetheless, being fully human, Jesus needed to *willingly* do his Father's will. Like Jesus, disciples are in a relationship of mutual indwelling. Jesus has finished his work, as he will say again from the cross, and yet he continues his work in and through his disciples."[24] Gorman is clear that the church's work is derivative and dependent (as the doctrine of *missio Dei* already well establishes!), but through the Spirit who both instantiates the disciples' relationship of mutual indwelling with the Triune God and carries on the mission of God in the world, the church's agency and work are nonetheless real participation in the ongoing saving work of God, in a sense that surpasses mere imitative continuation of Jesus's ministry.[25]

Gorman's work is a watershed in missional hermeneutics, both for its conjunction of *missio Dei* and *theōsis* as an interpretive key and for its biblical exposition of their meaning. At least two difficulties persist, however. The first is, broadly, what the present study aims to address: exegesis of the biblical texts to determine what participation in God's mission means is only one segment of the hermeneutical circle. It is equally important to consider how participation in God's mission might shape that biblical exegesis in the first place.[26] The second difficulty is that the conception of *theōsis* Gorman brings to the text remains underdeveloped. His appeals to

---

24. Gorman, *Abide*, 131.

25. On the inadequacy of imitation for capturing Paul's idea of participation, see also Campbell, *Paul*, 381; Macaskill, *Living*, 35–37, 144–45.

26. I began this dialogue with Gorman in my article "Missional Hermeneutics as Theological Interpretation," 157–63, to which he responds in the first chapter of *Abide*. Though he expresses appreciation for my (and others') argument regarding the significance of participation in God's mission as a hermeneutically formative practice, his claim that missional hermeneutics is "inherently self-involving" (Gorman, *Abide*, 5; cf. 189) does not do any work in his own interpretation of John. His emphasis remains "heavily text-centered" (6), and the admission that there is "something of a hermeneutical circle" between mission discerned in Scripture and Scripture discerned through mission (5) is balanced against the observation that close readings of the biblical text "provide a basis for contemporary contextualized readings" (4n11). In other words, one side of the hermeneutical circle is the basis for the other, not vice versa. In this subtle affirmation of the *norma normans*, a recognizable and understandable position peeks out, but it is not a position that does justice to the implications of an inherently self-involving hermeneutical circle. I further address Gorman's dismissal of the liberationist dimension of my argument (5n16) in ch. 5.

Irenaeus and Athanasius are indicative but stand to offer much more, not least regarding the ontological questions involved in participation and the relation of the church's agency to God's. In the remainder of this chapter, I locate my argument in its contemporary theological context and then develop a theological understanding of missional *theōsis* that might further illuminate the meaning of participation.

Contemporary Retrievals of *Theōsis*

A spate of books on *theōsis* has appeared in recent years, marking a major retrieval movement that spans diverse Christian traditions.[27] Protestants have traditionally been averse to the implications of the doctrine that seem to run contrary to both the absolute distinction between Creator and creation and the Reformation's *sola gratia* and *sola fide* principles. Thus, although key figures throughout Roman Catholicism and Protestantism have held nuanced understandings of union with Christ, participation in the divine life, or even divinization, many Western theologians remain cautious about the language of *theōsis* so common among Eastern Orthodox theologians.[28] As I demonstrated in the previous chapter, the relationship between Creator and creation and the role of the church's works in relation to God's are at the heart of participation in God's mission. Therefore, if the doctrine of *theōsis* is to serve constructively in a theology of missional participation, it is important to trace the contours of these issues in the contemporary retrieval movement.

---

27. See Russell, *Doctrine*; Finlan and Kharlamov, *Theōsis*; Christensen and Wittung, *Partakers*; Kharlamov, *Theōsis*; Collins, *Partaking*. Participation, union, and *theōsis* are not absolutely synonymous terms, but they are, as Johnson, *Atonement*, 84n73, puts it, a "family of thought."

28. The phenomenon of Western theologians, including Protestants, rediscovering some version of *theōsis* in their traditions and embracing it constructively today has been documented. Gavrilyuk, "Retrieval," 656, goes so far as to say, "There are strong indications that we are living through a new wave of *ressourcement*." This has generated considerable debate about terminology, concepts, categories, and methods at use across such a wide spectrum of Christian thought. See Kärkkäinen, *One*; Olson, "Deification," 186–200; Habets, "Reforming," 146–67; Medley, "Participation," 205–46; and numerous articles in Christensen and Wittung, *Partakers*, esp. Hallonsten, "Theosis," 281–93. At this stage, rather than bogging down in methodological questions, I am addressing substantive issues that face a missional theology of participation.

Theōsis *and the Creator/Creation Relationship*

Through the christological idiom of the Niceno-Constantinopolitan Creed, Christian theology expresses the difference between Creator and creation, established by the biblical narrative, in ontological terms. The "one Lord Jesus Christ, the only-begotten Son of God, begotten of the Father before all worlds" is "begotten, not made, being of one substance with the Father," who is the "one God, the Father Almighty, Maker of heaven and earth," and through the begotten-not-made Son, "all things were made." The distinction between what is made and what is not made is not only one of createdness but also of essence (*ousia*): unlike the Son, what is made by the Father through the Son is *made* and is *not of one substance* (homoousion) *with the Father*. For this reason, the relationship between divinity and humanity in the incarnate Son establishes the grammar of divinization theology, as Athanasius demonstrates:

> Whence the truth shews us that the Word is not of things originate [τῶν γενητῶν], but rather Himself their Framer. For therefore did He assume the body originate and human [τὸ γενητὸν καὶ ἀνθρώπινον σῶμα], that having renewed it as its Framer, He might deify it in Himself [εν ἑαθτῷ θεοποιήσῃ], and thus might introduce us all into the kingdom of heaven after His likeness. For man had not been deified if joined to a creature [ἐθεοποιήθη κτίσματι συναφθείς], or unless the Son were very [ἀληθινὸς] God; nor had man been brought into the Father's presence, unless He had been His natural and true [φύσει καὶ ἀληθινὸς] Word who had put on the body. And as we had not been delivered from sin and the curse, it had been by nature human flesh [φύσει σὰρξ ἦν ἀνθρωπίνη] which the Word put on (for we should have had nothing common with what was foreign [ἀλλότριον]), so also the man had not been deified [ἐθεοποιήθη], unless the Word who became flesh had been by nature from the Father and true and proper to Him [φύσει ἐκ τοῦ Πατρὸς καὶ ἀληθινὸς καὶ ἴδιος αὐτοῦ]. For therefore the union [ἡ συναφή] was of this kind, that He might unite what is man by nature to Him who is in the nature of the Godhead [τῷ κατὰ φύσιν τῆς θεότητος συνάψῃ τὸν φύσει ἄνθρωπον], and his salvation and deification [ἡ θεοποίησις] might be sure.[29]

Accordingly, the biblical language of being "in Christ" becomes a question of ontological distinction and relationship.[30] Daniel Keating cor-

---

29. Athanasius, *C. Ar.* 2:70 (NPNF2 4:386); Greek text from Bright, *Orations*, 140.

30. The most representative to-and-fro on this point presently is that of Gorman and Grant Macaskill. See Macaskill, *Union*, 27–28, 75–76; Gorman, *Participating*, 212n15.

rectly asserts, therefore, that one "core element of deification is a concept of participation that enables us to maintain a clear distinction between Creator and creature while at the same time to make sense of the real relationship between them and the genuine conveyance of divine life and divine qualities fitting to the creature that the Scripture describes."[31] Furthermore, the doctrine of the hypostatic union stipulates the ontological distinction between Christ's two natures and, at the same time, their unity in one existence—an ontological union, Trinitarian caveats notwithstanding.

The notion of human union with Christ and participation in God is spoken rightly in this theological grammar. Yet, it raises persistent questions, especially regarding the provenance and implications of the ontological categories deployed in the creed. Indeed, much of the debate accompanying the retrieval of patristic conceptions of *theōsis* seems at root to be about the extent to which Greek metaphysics sets the terms of the discussion.[32] Nonetheless, Christian theology takes up Greek metaphysical categories to affirm the commensurability of divinity and humanity revealed in the person and work of Jesus Christ despite a given ontological divine-human dualism.

One of the most important problems raised by this intellectual history is the difference between the hypostatic union that pertains to Christ by nature and the union that humanity receives by grace, along with the underlying question of creation's participation in God apart from Christ. In other words, does the hypostatic union represent an ontological *novum* or an ontological actualization, whether by restoration, intensification, or development? This question, which addresses the relationships between God, church, and world, bears heavily on the issue of the church's participation in the Triune mission.

---

31. Keating, "Typologies," 282.

32. Norris, "Deification," 416, identifies the theological tradition in which the Eastern fathers developed *theōsis* and its cognates as "a contextualization project." By this, Norris highlights the idea that they made use of existing cognitive freight and terminology, appropriating, reframing, redefining, and redeploying them in Christian ways. More than merely resisting the influence of Greek philosophical notions that fail to comport with the biblical tradition, the Rule of Faith and, eventually, the ecumenical creeds, the development of *theōsis* in the patristic literature aims at a distinctly Christian theological vision of participation in the divine life. See also McGuckin, "Strategic," 95–114; Kharlamov, "Rhetorical," 115–31. A survey of the vocabulary related to *theōsis* indicates the complexity of this issue. See Russell, *Doctrine*, 333–44; Finlan and Kharlamov, "Introduction," 1–8.

PARTICIPATION IN GOD'S MISSION AS *THEŌSIS*

Radical Orthodoxy's retrieval of the Neoplatonic idea of *methexis* (the participation of imperfect, impermanent, individual things in their Platonic ideals) has occasioned the most thoroughgoing contemporary discussion of creation's participation in God.[33] Although participation is arguably the principal theme of Radical Orthodoxy as a whole, John Milbank's *Being Reconciled* is of particular interest because he relates *methexis* and the concern with participation as a general ontology and a "participatory worldview" to deification.[34] For Milbank, *methexis* is the metaphysical ground of the possibility of deification.[35] The question that Radical Orthodoxy rightly provokes is which ontology undergirds one's view of participation in God's mission, but various problems afflict Radical Orthodoxy's view. By addressing these, I deal with major issues regarding the Creator-creation relationship that concern *theōsis*.

Michael Horton suggests that Radical Orthodoxy's "account of participation is a form of univocity after all, with the Creator-creature difference being quantitative rather than qualitative."[36] Horton writes from a Reformed perspective but in this objection represents a broader Protestant viewpoint: "In the covenant theology of Scripture ... there are two distinct kinds of reality: divine and nondivine. This is the only ontological dualism

---

33. Neoplatonism is a philosophical school of thought that flourished from roughly AD 250–650, which combined the ideas of Plato with those of other notable philosophies of antiquity to produce a powerful synthesis that ultimately maintained the ontological distinction between a single divine cause and all subsequent effects. Participation (*methexis*) is the language Neoplatonism deploys to explain the relationship between cause and effect. See esp. Milbank, *Being*; Smith and Olthius, *Radical*.

34. Milbank, *Being*, 66, exposits Aquinas's view: deification "is extraordinarily in excess of the original goal—Creation—since it would be pointless for God to aim for deification, which is already himself." This gives rise to the verbal distinction between "participation" in Milbank's customary usage and "union": "*Now* it begins to be true, although it must also be retrospectively true ... that the Creation is sustained not only through participation in, but—in a mediated sense—through union with God" (71). Despite the verbal distinction, however, the two are conflated; union is incidental (not the goal) and is ultimately another expression of how creation is sustained.

35. This metaphysics is a casualty of the cataclysmic shifts around AD 1300 with which Radical Orthodoxy's genealogy of secularism is preoccupied: "the traditional centrality in theology of participation, deification, apophaticism, allegory and the vision of the Church as something engendered by the Eucharist all were abruptly challenged, in a fashion that proved epochally successful" (Milbank, *Being*, 111).

36. *Univocity* refers to the theological contention that the being of God and the being of creation can be expressed in the same terms: to "be" means the same thing in both senses. Horton, *Covenant*, 164.

that is finally decisive for Christian theology."[37] For Horton, the problem is ultimately that *methexis* is an ontological participation, which is an impossibility given the absolute ontological gap between God and creation that results from the doctrine of *creatio ex nihilo* (creation out of nothing, *not* creation out of God). For Horton, the proper account of participation is covenantal, not ontological; despite his attempt to move from "covenantal participation (*koinōnia*)" to "covenantal ontology," his understanding of participation is essentially nonontological.[38]

This is clearest in his critique of John Zizioulas's discussion of participation (*metochē*) and communion (*koinōnia*) in the Trinitarian theology of the Eastern fathers: he complains that Zizioulas identifies the problem that the fathers' theology addresses as "ontic rather than convenantal."[39] Hence, Radical Orthodoxy is wrong to claim that "created being participates ontologically in uncreated being as such."[40] What Horton means by "covenantal ontology" is spiritually profound intimacy: "The believer participates in the covenantal body of which [Christ] is the head. We can still affirm that we participate ontologically in the person as well as the benefits of Christ, but a covenantal ontology suggests that this is more like the relation of a commonwealth and its monarch or a husband and wife or parents and children in a family than a fusion of essences, personalities, or even wills. To be sure, this union is not merely legal or even relational, but spiritual, mystical, and real—since the Spirit accomplishes a more vital *koinōnia* than any natural community."[41] It seems to me that Horton is moving in the right direction by characterizing the relationship wrought by the Spirit as more than "merely relational," but it is not clear why Horton would consider this spiritual relationship to be ontological participation.[42]

37. Horton, *Covenant*, 164.
38. Horton, *Covenant*, 165, 202.
39. Horton, *Covenant*, 188.
40. Horton, *Covenant*, 205.
41. Horton, *Covenant*, 202.

42. The key to Horton's proposal, which brings together "speech-act theory, a Trinitarian perspective, a covenantal ontology, and the doctrine of analogy" (Horton, *Covenant*, 227) is the *declarative* nature of both creation and redemption: "Both our creation and our redemption are speech events, and the particular kind of discourse we are talking about is covenantal all the way down" (166; cf. 203). Thus, the legal declaration of justification establishes a "forensic ontology," "the forensic origin of our union with Christ" (139). Horton understands the forensic illocutionary force and the effective perlocutionary force of the declarative divine locution to be distinct but inseparable (143). Furthermore, this organic union is made effective *by the Spirit in contradistinction*

I will argue below for an understanding of participation as *relational ontology* precisely because the relationship and the transformation it entails are properly ontological, having to do with the nature and being of God and humanity. Horton is correct that the problem with Radical Orthodoxy is the Platonism of *methexis* but incorrect that "the church fathers were also infected by this virus."[43] True as that may be in some cases, it fails to account for how the ecumenical orthodoxy defined by the fathers conceives of participation in ontological terms over against Neoplatonic monism (the singularity of being derived from the One source of all being) *because* the dualism of the divine and the nondivine makes the relational claims of the New Testament nothing less than an ontological problem. Therefore, James K. A. Smith's more moderate Reformed critique of Radical Orthodoxy is correct: the use of Platonic metaphysics is not necessary, but participatory ontology is important.[44] More to the point, Neoplatonic ontology is a false path, and a patristic understanding of *theōsis* provides an alternative route to a Christian participatory ontology.

Much of the animus in Protestant critiques of participatory ontology relates to Karl Barth's sustained condemnation of the *analogia entis*, which he construed as any commonality of being that might constitute a point of contact between God and humanity apart from the revealed Word. It is now widely accepted, however, that Barth fundamentally misconceived the *analogia entis* in the Thomistic tradition, which somewhat reduces the irony of Radical Orthodoxy's retrieval of Aquinas's analogical ontology to overcome secularist univocity of being. That is, both Barth and Radical Orthodoxy desire to establish ontological dualism—Barth by denying "being" as a legitimate category of analogy and Radical Orthodoxy by taking "analogy" as a contradiction of the univocity of being. If Horton is right (as I suspect he is) that *methexis* ends in univocity anyway, then perhaps Radical Orthodoxy stumbles over the analogy of being just as Barth expects. Yet,

---

from ontological participation: "It is precisely in the covenant of grace that we come to participate in this kind of humanity that Christ mediates, not by mere imitation nor by ontological participation that would make the believer or the church an extension of the incarnation, but by sharing an inheritance that belongs to Christ by right and to us by gift. It is an inheritance not directly (by imitation or fusion), but by the Spirit through the means of grace" (203). The Spirit, then, "brings about the reality" (227) of nonontological union declared by God. It is not evident what that union is supposed to consist of apart from the declaration itself. "Forensic ontology" indeed.

43. Horton, *Covenant*, 206.
44. See Smith, "Will?," 61–72.

Barth fairs no better. Despite the work that his *analogia relationis* is meant to do in lieu of the *analogia entis*, some ontological basis for the divine-human relationship must exist, be it analogical or otherwise.[45]

In this regard, I agree with Alan J. Torrance's assessment that Zizioulas's work has "enormous ramifications for the analogy debate."[46] In particular, Zizioulas illuminates "the fact that 'being' may be given theological reinterpretation in dynamic, relational and personal terms."[47] It is such a relational ontology that allows us to navigate the Scylla of ontological monism and the Charybdis of ontological incommensurability toward a biblical vision of participation.

Zizioulas reads the fathers as navigating these straits: "It was necessary to find an ontology that avoided the monistic Greek philosophy as much as the 'gulf' between God and the world taught by the gnostic systems."[48] What emerged was the astonishing Trinitarian conclusion that "the being of God is a relational being." This is a relational ontology: "The Holy Trinity is a *primordial* ontological concept and not a notion which is added to the divine substance or rather which follows it. . . . The substance of God, 'God,' has no ontological content, no true being, apart from communion."[49] A detailed rendition of Zizioulas's retrieval work is unnecessary for my purposes here, nor am I content with every aspect of the Trinitarian theology that he deploys.[50] Rather, I affirm the basic insight that *"the identification of the 'hypostasis' with the 'person'"* gave "an ontological content to each person

---

45. Johnson, "Reappraisal," 3–25, explores Barth's realization that "his claims about participation in Christ and the analogy of faith . . . must presuppose an already existing analogy of being between God and humans" (20). Consequently, the *analogia relationis* developed through the doctrine of election avers "there is an analogy of being between God and humans, but this analogy is grounded in God's act of reconciliation rather than his act of creation" (22). The unresolved problem is that the human relationship to Christ still requires an ontological grounding. If reconciliation is the grounding for the analogy of being, then either some yet prior ontological basis makes reconciliation possible or reconciliation itself *is* the ontological basis. I will argue for something akin to the latter, but in either case Barth cannot avoid a fundamental, ontological point of contact between God and humanity.

46. See Torrance, *Persons*, 305.

47. Torrance, *Persons*, 186. Torrance does not make this statement in reference to Zizioulas, but it is clear that he thinks Zizioulas's work in particular signals such a possibility (see 256–57).

48. Zizioulas, *Being*, 16.

49. Zizioulas, *Being*, 17.

50. Torrance, *Persons*, 282–306, overviews critical issues.

of the Holy Trinity, without endangering its biblical principles: monotheism and the absolute ontological independence of God in relation to the world."[51] The key upshot of this development for the present study is that *theōsis*, "which means participation not in the nature or substance of God, but in His personal existence,"[52] is nonetheless an *ontological participation* that is not overcome by the ontological difference between Creator and creation. It remains to develop the connection between this Trinitarian relational ontology and *theōsis* in more detail, which I will undertake through a discussion of *perichōrēsis*, in conversation with Paul Fiddes below and Jürgen Moltmann in the next chapter. It suffices for now to affirm that not only is a Trinitarian relational ontology capable of answering concerns about the Creator-creation distinction that a retrieval of patristic *theōsis* teachings might raise, but also, in fact, participation and, by extension, *theōsis* are at the heart of the only theological understanding of the relationship between Creator and creation that emerged as tenable for patristic orthodoxy.

Finally, it is important to reiterate the stakes of this discussion: the relationships between God, church, and world as the church participates in the Triune mission. Like most theological discussions of participation, Radical Orthodoxy's discourse has remained disconnected from missional concerns.[53] This is not surprising given that *theōsis* is, for Radical Orthodoxy, just a redoubling of the grace of participation by which all creation exists. Such a perspective may expect its challenge to secularism to result in significant social transformation, but intensification of what already is lacks the alterity of truly radical transformation. I have also indicated the importance of avoiding an overreaction, which typically comes not in the form of Gnosticism, as in the patristic era, but of practical deism. Two iterations of practical deism are common: agnostic and ecclesiocentric.

For agnostic practical deism, God is epistemically unrelatable. The Christian expressions of such agnosticism comprise a spectrum running from postmetaphysical theology, which denies the possibility of predicating the nature of the relationship between God and world in ontological terms, to radical pluralism, which denies the possibility of shared criteria for assessing theological claims. Practically, then, God does not relate to the world, therefore the church relates to the world apart from God, on

51. Zizioulas, *Being*, 36, 37.

52. Zizioulas, *Being*, 50.

53. A notable exception is Peter J. Bellini's appropriation of Radical Orthodoxy in *Participation*.

the world's own terms.⁵⁴ Thus, although agnostic practical deism does not make ontological claims, it results in the same secularization that Radical Orthodoxy ascribes to modernity's presupposed univocity of being, because the issue is not that God's being relates to the world's being in a particular way but that we could neither know nor say in any case. The otherness of God overwhelms revelation and relationship. The prevalence of such perspectives even in the church makes them important for Christian missiology, but because they inherently preclude a notion of participation in God's mission, I forego further discussion here.

Ecclesiocentric practical deism, for which God is extra-ecclesially unrelatable, is the more relevant type. L. Roger Owens's study *The Shape of Participation* runs afoul of this tendency. Owens affirms Milbank's rejection of the univocity of being but critiques Radical Orthodoxy's "pre-christological account of participation."⁵⁵ For Owens, "the church's participation in God is Christ's practicing himself as the embodied practices of the church, in the Spirit, for the world,"⁵⁶ and this must be conceived in contradistinction from any notion of creation's participation in God. Says Owens, "If the church's practices are the church's participation in the life of God, then there must be some unique way—there must be some uniquely *Trinitarian way*—that the church's divine-human constitution, its embodied participation in God, differs from how the rest of creation and creation's rebellious powers relate to God's activity."⁵⁷ Owens therefore rightly stipulates that participation is both Trinitarian and embodied but rejects the idea that "the activity of God for the life of the world is happening somewhere other than in the practices of the church, so that through the church's practices the church must find where God is working, and join with God, cooperating, so to speak, in meeting human needs."⁵⁸ Quoting Lesslie Newbigin, he connects this idea directly with *missio Dei* theology, suggesting that such a view is now passé.⁵⁹

The complex problematic I established in the previous chapter makes dubious Owens's disregard of the idea that mission is participation in God's

---

54. Mission from this perspective consists of activities that are churchy versions of secular activities: marketing, social activism, and community development.

55. Owens, *Shape*, 139.

56. Owens, *Shape*, 16.

57. Owens, *Shape*, 56.

58. Owens, *Shape*, 59.

59. Owens, *Shape*, 59n42.

work in the world beyond the church. More fundamentally, however, one must wonder why the church's participation in God would be uniquely Trinitarian in contrast with the world's. Does God cease to be Triune in God's interaction with the world? No, the mistake Owens exemplifies is the restriction of all God's activity to the church; there is effectively no Triune relationship with the world apart from the church. His overdrawn distinction between church and creation pushes participation toward a disturbing over-identification of Christ and church and, in turn, a denial of the Triune mission in the world beyond the church. For, as Peter Kline describes, *missio Dei* theology needs the economic Trinity to determine materially the nature of the church's relationship with the world, lest "as—or rather, *if*— the church turns toward the world, the stability and reference point for this turning is not the ongoing history of Jesus Christ for the world in which God has his eternal being, but rather the church's own pre-established internal being, obtained by reference to God's own pre-established eternal being."[60] The understanding of *theōsis* toward which I am moving, then, takes participation as a continuous but differentiated model of mutual relationships between God, creation, and the church predicated on the creative and recreative *opera Trinitatis ad extra* revealed as *missio Dei*.[61]

Theōsis *and Works*

What we say about participation in mission is deeply connected to anthropological assumptions. In discussions of *theōsis*, the question of the relation of the church's works to God's is tangled with questions of "fallen" and finite human nature, "works righteousness," and the relationship between justification and sanctification. Veli-Matti Kärkkäinen's *One with God* is especially helpful for tracing the contours of these issues in various traditions.[62] Kärkkäinen's argument explores and challenges the dichoto-

---

60. Kline, "Participation," 40. Kline's article is an apt response to Owens because Owens leans heavily on the aspect of Robert Jenson's ecclesiology that Kline rightly critiques: "It is actually the church with its historically determined culture that becomes the goal of history, for him. It is, therefore, *the church* that comes to possess ubiquity as the condition for universality, and it possesses this before any engagement with the world" (59).

61. One suggestive proposal along these lines is Swart et al., "Toward," 75–87. The authors do not have *theōsis* in view per se, but they deftly outline a missional vision of "'participation' as a way of describing both the life of God and the interrelatedness of God, church, and world" (78).

62. Kärkkäinen, *One*; see also Kärkkäinen, *Spirit*, ch. 11.

mization of justification and sanctification, particularly in Protestant theologies.[63] The critical insight in this regard is that deification is about "divine-human synergy, the cooperation of the person with God"[64]—an idea that calls to mind participation in mission, although that is not the premise of his discussion. It is clear, nonetheless, that the underlying anthropology, especially regarding the doctrine of sin, is what ultimately causes the conflict between Eastern and Lutheran/Reformed understandings, an underlying anthropology that will inevitably delimit the significance of participation for the "works" of mission.[65]

As a point of departure, I affirm Kärkkäinen's statement: "The paranoid fear of 'works righteousness' of much of Protestantism has to be challenged and corrected by the 'synergistic' (Eastern Orthodox) and 'cooperational' (Roman Catholic) understanding of ('prevenient') grace—while at the same time (in agreement with the whole of Christian tradition) all forms of Pelagianism must be resisted."[66] The key to the remainder of the discussion of *theōsis* and works is that, for the missional theology articulated here, the relationship between justification and sanctification is not about the instrumentality of works for one's *own* salvation (works righteousness). Rather, assuming the instrumentality of faith alone for salvation, the instrumentality of works *in the economy of God's mission* is a separate issue. Articulated in the sharpest possible terms, the issue is the instrumentality of works in the generation of faith—that of others and, indeed, one's own. This does not put works in the position of causing or meriting faith but in a circular relationship in which, through the gift of faith, obedience becomes the instrument of God's continuous gifting.

The substantial, persistent concern regarding *theōsis* and human works in connection with participation in the mission of God is the uniqueness and sufficiency of Christ's already-accomplished work. Since the original discussion of the *missio Dei* among International Missionary

63. See also Marshall, "Justification," 125–39; Bloor, "New," 179–87.

64. Kärkkäinen, *One*, 31.

65. Gavrilyuk, "Retrieval," 652, observes that Western theologians frequently do not share the anthropological assumptions that make sense of Orthodox discussions of *theōsis*. Likewise, Hallonsten, "*Theosis*," 286, states: "Anthropology is the fundamental feature that marks the Eastern doctrine of deification and is thus the key to an accurate understanding of this doctrine. Further, this anthropology is connected to a view of the relation between God and creation that is significantly different from that of the Latin tradition."

66. Kärkkäinen, *Spirit*, 352.

PARTICIPATION IN GOD'S MISSION AS *THEŌSIS*

Council members sought to mark the difference between God's mission and the church's mission, significant baggage accompanies the discussion. At the same time, the very notion of participation in God's mission entails human (ecclesial) agency in God's not-yet-finished work. This fundamental tension remains unresolved. Thus, Reformed theologian J. Todd Billings argues for an understanding of "ministry as participation in Christ" over against the language of "incarnational ministry" common in mission theology, because "the incarnation of the Word in the person of Jesus Christ is a unique and unrepeatable event. As such, the incarnation is not an 'ongoing process' to be repeated or a 'model' to be copied in Christian ministry."[67] Instead of attempting to imitate the eternal Son becoming human, Billings wants ministers to conform to "*the pattern* of the God-human that Christians are to be conformed to by way of union with Christ—namely, the pattern of Christ's cruciform life."[68] Although the uniqueness and unrepeatability of Christ's crucifixion might logically compel Billings to put cruciformity under the same stricture as incarnation, he finds a preponderance of evidence in the New Testament for construing "union with Christ" in terms of cruciformity.[69] Nonetheless, relating the church's cruciformity so closely to Christ's cross requires a caveat: "While there is a necessary connection between Christians and the cross—particularly in the call to humble obedience and service, in self-denial (putting to death the old self)—there is also a profound difference between the two. Christians do not bear the cross on behalf of the sin of humanity—their cross reconciles no one to God. Only Christ's life and work is inherently redemptive."[70] In the end, then, Billings construes participation and union with Christ in terms of *the distinction* between the work of Christ and the works that Christians do as they are conformed to Christ's life. Unfortunately, his concern with "works" obscures the fact that participation, understood in terms of *theōsis*, does not make the church's works a problem but puts them in their proper relationship to the Triune God's work. Insisting on the distinction as Billings does erodes the meaning of union with Christ, limiting it to the status of justification and the

---

67. Billings, *Union*, 124.
68. Billings, *Union*, 142.
69. See esp. Billings, *Union*, 136–48.
70. Billings, *Union*, 149.

Spirit's work of sanctification, and this in turn makes participation nothing more than imitation of Jesus empowered by the Spirit.[71]

The understanding of participation in God's mission for which I am pressing requires a more robust vision of *theōsis*—one that sees the church's union with Christ as both its becoming the gospel (to use Gorman's phrase) and its collaboration in the Triune God's work in the world. For such an understanding, rather than threatening the primacy of God's grace that all orthodox theology assumes, the church's works just are its real union with the God who alone saves. This conclusion leads to the idea that missional *theōsis* can be correctly conceived of as the church's participation in the atonement.

Theōsis as Participation in the Atonement

Much of the energy generated by the retrieval work on *theōsis* has been directed toward atonement theology, particularly in relation to Irenaeus and Athanasius.[72] Certainly, the close connection (often synonymy) between atonement and reconciliation in typical theological discourse lends itself naturally to notions of union. Indeed, the oft-mentioned etymological parsing of "at-one-ment" provokes the basic question: what does it mean to be "at one" with God?

This section considers what the missional conception of *theōsis* may gain from atonement theologies that take notions of participation, union, and deification seriously. Conversely, conceptions of participation in God's mission that borrow the same patristic terms inform the doctrine of atonement in significant ways. The two connect at the level of ordinary theological language: the atonement is referred to regularly as the work of Christ and the mission of Christ, and missional theology commonly discusses the church's participation in or continuation of, precisely, the work and mission of Christ. These connections point toward a theological

---

71. Here is a Reformed account of union with Christ that justifies Roger Olson's doubt that Western participation language is comparable with Orthodox notions of deification (see Olson, "Deification," 193–97). Olson is wrong, however, to suggest that only the Palamite distinction between divine essence and energies properly defines deification.

72. See, e.g., Johnson, *Atonement*, 83–87; see also the role of union in Myers, "Patristic," 71–88.

substantiation of New Testament scholar Scot McKnight's claims that "a missional life is *participation in atonement*."[73]

Recent contributions to this idea include the works of Darrin Snyder Belousek and Hans Boersma. For Belousek, atonement theology determines mission's motive, means, and aim, helpfully epitomized as "cruciformity" (echoing Gorman). And this connection raises the vital question: is the cross just a "form" to be imitated or is the cross, the culmination of Jesus's very work and mission, determinative for mission in a more substantial sense? What does cruciformity mean for the claim that the church's mission is participation in Christ's ongoing work? Belousek's construal of atonement in terms of participation "in Christ" (including appeals to patristic understandings) in tandem with his idea of "carrying on" the work of reconciliation specifically as bodily participation in the suffering of Christ is provocative: "By suffering with and for the sake of others, the church and its members bear the sufferings of Christ and so continue identifying with and participating in the death and resurrection of Jesus."[74] The suffering of the church in a mode of cruciformity is, in some way, participation in Christ's own suffering. Once again, participation is distinct from imitation: "Suffering in the way of righteousness and faithfulness is both an imitation of and a participation in the suffering of Christ (1 Pet 2:21; 4:13)."[75] Unfortunately, Belousek balks at proposing a "theory of participation," which parallels the tendency in missional theology to discuss participation in mission without providing a "theory" there either.

Hans Boersma takes Col 1:24 as a biblical basis for the idea (with reference to Gorman's earlier work) that the church's cruciform suffering is participation in Christ's mission.[76] He points out the trouble this causes for traditional atonement theology and, in response, affirms that "neither the unique character nor the sufficiency of Christ's passion is at stake."[77] This is an important admission, given that the Protestant concern with works righteousness would cause many theologians to balk at the claim of human participation in the atonement. Even so, the startling implications of the idea that the church somehow participates in that unique, sufficient passion remain: "Believers share in the very suffering of Christ. . . . The

---

73. McKnight, *Community*, 141.
74. Belousek, *Atonement*, 320.
75. Belousek, *Atonement*, 447.
76. See also Leithart, *Delivered*, 172.
77. Boersma, *Violence*, 233.

work of atonement has its climactic and decisive moment in the crucifixion of Jesus Christ. He continues his work in the redemptive mission of the Church for the world."[78] With Boersma and Belousek, I share the perception that passages like 1 Pet 4:13 and Col 1:24 have something to teach us about the church's role as subjects, not in one's own atonement but in Christ's atoning work more broadly conceived. Indeed, the renaissance of *theōsis* theology calls interpreters anew to read these texts theologically in relation to participation.

Although this work cannot be undertaken in earnest here, it is worth noting that Col 1:24 is especially significant for the present discussion because it has long been considered a *crux interpretum* in regard to both the church's relationship to Christ (including in disputes about Pelagianism) and the soteriological sufficiency of Christ's work in relation to the church's (especially in Reformation disputes about merit).[79] Putting the matter in now familiar terms, C. M. Proudfoot succinctly states, "Paul knows suffering as a *participatio Christi* and not as an *imitatio Christi* only."[80] Proudfoot, writing in 1963, represents the old Christ-mysticism school of Pauline interpretation in the English literature.[81] Support for mystical readings was already waning by then, and apocalyptic and imitative understandings have dominated the field since.[82] Although some apocalyptic readings make room for a sense of the church's participation in the messianic woes, notions akin to *theōsis* do not characterize this line of interpretation. The contrast between imitation and participation remains the basic template for interpreting Col 1:24. The decreasing credibility of Pauline "mysticism" as a historical-critical claim has left some form of imitation as the only possibility, bolstered by the lingering suspicion of Pelagianism and works righteousness.[83] Accordingly, John Reumann quotes the conclusion of the Joint Lutheran-Roman Catholic Study Commission: "However the details

---

78. Boersma, *Violence*, 234.

79. For a useful, brief rehearsal of the passage's interpretation history, see Reumann, "Colossians 1:24," 454–61.

80. Proudfoot, "Imitation," 160.

81. On Christ-mysticism in relation to contemporary discussions of participation, see Campbell, *Paul*, ch. 2; Macaskill, *Union*, 17–24.

82. Bauckham, "Colossians 1:24," 168–70, concisely represents the apocalyptic view.

83. This is represented well by Jerry Sumney's rehearsal of options:

- Christ's sufferings may be supplemented from the treasury of merit earned by saints and martyrs.

of 1:24 are understood, there is no disparagement in the passage of the unique mediation by Christ through the cross. Nor does the 'filling up' contradict the reconciliation wrought by God through Christ 'in his body of flesh' and solely 'by his death,' a reconciliation of which the author regards himself a 'minister' (1:22–23)."[84] Assuming that this represents an orthodox consensus, then, the question is whether a theology of participation opens the way for something more than a merely imitative interpretation.

Paul Fiddes charts a way forward. Articulating the issue in terms of "past event and present salvation," he observes that the idea of the church's participation in Christ's suffering pushes participants' subjectivity back into the decisive event—Christ's own suffering: "In giving ourselves away to others, we find ourselves leaning upon a movement of self-giving and mission that is far deeper than our own, as we share in the 'sending' of the Son by the Father. In our suffering we find ourselves supported by a movement of suffering love which is more terrible than our own."[85] This account suggests what suffering in and with Christ means—indeed, what "completing what is lacking in Christ's afflictions" means—and, by extension, the sense in which missional *theōsis* is participation in the atonement. Fiddes will play a key role in extending the discussion of

- There is a distinction between suffering as a sacrifice for sin and suffering for edification.
- The passage illustrates the mystical union between Christ and Christians.
- These sufferings of Paul are part of the messianic woes that must be fulfilled before the *parousia*. (Sumney, "'I,'" 665; cf. Spivey, "Colossians 1:24," 44.)

Setting aside the apocalyptic vogue, Sumney argues for a yet more fully imitative interpretation, in which Paul's "vicarious sufferings" "are 'for you' because they demonstrate the extraordinary value of the gospel the readers had received and so provide a model for believers to imitate by holding fast to that teaching." Notably, he concludes: "This presentation of Paul must not cast doubt on the prior affirmations of the full sufficiency of Christ's work if the letter's argument is to be a success" (678). Anything more than imitation threatens the sufficiency of Christ's work. Likewise, Andrew Perriman, "Pattern," 62–79, argues for "an involvement in the sufferings and death of Christ that is objective rather than subjective, but which is essentially *imitative* and must be interpreted chiefly in the context of Paul's apostolic self-understanding. Any views that he may have had about the somatic or mystical participation of the believer in the reality of Christ have no significant bearing on the meaning of these passages; nor does the concept of a period of eschatological suffering play any part in his thought" (78).

84. Reumann, "Colossians 1:24," 461, quoting Anderson et al., *One Mediator*, Part Two, I.A.; Reumann concludes by affirming the notion of the church's participation in the quota of messianic tribulation, calling it "involvement in the struggle."

85. Fiddes, *Past*, 166.

theōsis into the concept of *perichōrēsis* in the next section. For now, his Trinitarian vision of the relationship between Christ's past atoning suffering and the present suffering of the church in mission points us toward a fuller understanding of *theōsis* as participation in the atonement and, therefore, participation in God's mission.

Summary

Before transitioning to the second major section of this chapter, I summarize the argument so far. Participation in God's mission should be understood as *theōsis*—specifically, *theōsis* as participation in the atonement. First, taking Gorman's work on Paul and John as a point of departure, I affirm the idea that (1) the real conformation of human nature to the image of Christ by the power of the Spirit is the present ontological transformation that necessarily precedes and accompanies the embodiment of cruciform righteousness and that (2) through the Spirit who both instantiates the disciples' relationship of mutual indwelling with the Triune God and carries on the mission of God in the world, the church's agency and work is real participation in the ongoing saving work of God, in a sense that surpasses mere imitative continuation of Jesus's ministry.

Second, pushing for a deeper understanding of what that ontological transformation and real participation entails, I confront two major issues in contemporary theological retrievals of *theōsis*: the Creator-creature distinction and works righteousness. Regarding the former, I conclude that Neoplatonic ontology (in which the *methexis* of creation in the divine Forms, rather than a Trinitarian relational ontology, explains participation) is a false path, and the retrieval of a patristic understanding of *theōsis* provides an alternative route to a Christian participatory ontology. Not only is a Trinitarian relational ontology capable of answering concerns about the Creator-creation distinction that a retrieval of patristic *theōsis* teachings might raise, but also, in fact, participation and, by extension, *theōsis* are at the heart of the only theological understanding of the relationship between Creator and creation that emerged as tenable for patristic orthodoxy. Additionally, I rule out two types of practical deism that unfortunately characterize the contemporary discourse, critiquing especially the ecclesiocentrism that makes God extra-ecclesially unrelatable. As concerns the Creator-creature distinction, the understanding of *theōsis* toward which I am moving takes participation as a continuous but differentiated model of mutual relationships between

God, creation, and the church predicated on the creative and recreative *opera Trinitatis ad extra* revealed as *missio Dei*.

Regarding works righteousness, I distinguish the notion of earning one's own salvation from the instrumentality of works in the economy of God's mission. By insisting that faith—including its integral works—contains no merit, I suggest that through the gift of faith, obedience becomes the instrument of God's continuous gifting. Accordingly, participation, understood in terms of *theōsis*, does not make the church's works a problem but puts them in their proper relationship to the Triune God's work. Therefore, the church's works do not threaten the primacy of God's grace that all orthodox theology assumes but rather just are the church's real union with the God who alone saves.

Third, I approach the notion of participation in the atonement itself, arguing that the suffering of the church in a mode of cruciformity is participation in Christ's own suffering. In view of theological readings of Col 1:24, I identify the church's role as subjects, not in one's own atonement but in Christ's atoning work more broadly conceived, as the core theological question for understanding participation in God's mission as participation in the atonement. Affirming once more the orthodox consensus regarding both the Creator-creature distinction and the primacy of God's grace over human works, I take the ontological transformation and real participation of *theōsis* to entail more than a mere imitation because, following Fiddes, the church's participation in Christ's suffering pushes participants' subjectivity back into the decisive event of Christ's own suffering.

The remainder of the chapter explores the relationship between *theōsis* and *perichōrēsis*, another patristic concept most at home in the Eastern tradition that has enjoyed appropriation in recent Western theology. My goal in section 2 is to further illuminate the idea of *theōsis* as missional participation through the Trinitarian doctrine of *perichōrēsis*. This provides a conceptual link between the idea of participation in Christ that is the heart of *theōsis* and the Triune work of God that is the *missio Dei*.

Theōsis and *Perichōrēsis*

Although theologians commonly discuss *perichōrēsis* without reference to *theōsis*, these concepts are mutually illuminating. Whereas *theōsis* explains the transformative nature of participation in the life of the Triune God and the proper end of that transformation, *perichōrēsis* explains more about what that participation entails. Far more than *theōsis*, *perichōrēsis* has become a vital doctrine among missional theologians who rely on a social Trinitarian understanding of mission. Grafting the two together in my account of participation, then, provides a way to elaborate the significance of *theōsis* in conversation with certain missional theologies. I begin with a review of the revival of *perichōrēsis* in contemporary theology, then turn to Fiddes for help extrapolating the significance of this teaching. I conclude by considering the ways the conjunction of *perichōrēsis* and *theōsis* enriches our understanding of participation in God's mission.

Perichōrēsis in Contemporary Theology

Retrieval of the ancient notion of *perichōrēsis* in the last forty years of systematic theology is steeped in a debate about the viability of social Trinitarianism. Grappling with distinct uses of *perichōrēsis* in this debate is the clearest way to shape a working definition for my argument.

Naturally, the context of this discussion is the renewal of Trinitarian thought led by Barth and Karl Rahner and, by extension, reflection on the relationship between the immanent and the economic Trinity. In particular, Rahner's Rule—"The economic Trinity is the immanent Trinity, and the immanent Trinity is the economic Trinity"—has spawned vigorous thought about the economy of salvation as an epistemological ground for Trinitarian theology, frequently in contrast with speculative thought in the tradition of classical Western theology following Augustine and Aquinas.[86] A major feature of these developments is the contrast between the focus on divine ontology typical of classical Trinitarianism and on divine relationality common to social Trinitarianism. As I have already discussed with reference to Zizioulas, a "relational ontology" has emerged, which I understand to play a mediating role. It is just here that *perichōrēsis* enters the discourse most generatively.[87]

---

86. Rahner, *Trinity*, 21; see Sanders, "Entangled," 175–82, for an outstanding review of major developments.

87. Zizioulas's *Being as Communion* was published in 1985. Equally important for social Trinitarianism is Jürgen Moltmann's appropriation of *perichōrēsis* in *Trinität und Reich Gottes* (1980), translated as *The Trinity and the Kingdom*, which I engage in the next chapter. My focus at this point is the mediation between classical and social Trinitarianism that Zizioulas's relational ontology uniquely offers, in contrast to Moltmann's markedly low view of classical Latin interests.

A notion developed in the Eastern tradition to explain, first, the relationship of Christ's two natures and, subsequently, the relationship of the persons of the Trinity, *perichōrēsis* is located squarely in the immanent Trinity.[88] The term and its verbal cognate *perichōreō* seek analogically to designate the unity of two natures in one person and of three persons in one being, without confusion in either case. While the earlier, christological use of *perichōreō* in Gregory of Nazianzus bears tangentially on the soteriological (and therefore economic) implications of human nature's union with divinity in Jesus, his emphasis lies on the concept of "interpenetration," the possibility of real unity-in-distinction.[89] Although Gregory also developed the idea of *theōsis* in terms closely related to *perichōreō*, the word does not play a role in his conceptualization of divinization.[90] It was, instead, Maximus Confessor who explicitly linked the language to God's relationship with believers as well as the rest of creation, apparently coining the noun *perichōrēsis* for this purpose.[91] For Maximus, the divinization of the human is an extension of the relationship of Christ's two natures; therefore, the analogy of *perichōrēsis* is useful precisely because it preserves the distinction between Creator and creation while denoting real union, hence an ontologically meaningful conception of *theōsis*. In one relevant passage, he writes:

> "The salvation of souls," properly speaking, "is the aim of faith." The aim of faith is the true revelation of the object of one's faith. *The true revelation of the object of one's faith is the ineffable relation of mutual love with that object according to the measure of each one's faith. The relation of mutual love with the object of faith is the final return of the faithful to their own beginning.* [Ἀληθὴς δὲ τοῦ πιστευθέντος ἐστὶν ἀποκάλυψις, ἡ κατὰ ἀναλογίαν τῆς ἐν ἐσάτῳ πίστεως ἄρρητος τοῦ πεπιστευμένου περιχώρησις. Περιχώρησις δὲ τοῦ πεπιστευμένου καθέσηκεν, ἡ πρὸς τὴν οἰκείαν ἀρχὴν κατὰ τὸ τέλος τῶν πεπιστευκότων ἐπάνοδος.] The final return of the faithful to their own beginning is the fulfillment of every desire. The fulfillment of desire is the ever-moving rest around the object

---

88. See Harrison, "Perichoresis," 53–65.

89. See, in *NPNF2*, Gregory of Nazianzus, *Epist.* 101; cf. *Or.* 18.42; *Or.* 22.4; see also Harrison, "Perichoresis," 53–65; Lawler, "*Perichoresis*," 49–66; Scalise, "Perichoresis," 58–76; cf. Stramara, "Gregory," 257–63.

90. See Scalise, "Perichoresis," 60–64; see also Russell, *Doctrine*, 213–25; Kharlamov, "Rhetorical," 123–27.

91. See Harrison, "Perichoresis," 56–59; Lawler, "*Perichoresis*," 50; Scalise, "Perichoresis," 65–73.

of desire by those who desire it. The ever-moving rest around the object of desire by those who desire it is the perpetual enjoyment of the object of desire unbroken by any interval. Perpetual enjoyment of the object of desire unbroken by any interval is participation in divine realities that transcend nature. *Participation in divine realities that transcend nature is the likeness of the participants to the participable.* [Μέθεξις δὲ τῶν ὑπὲρ φύσιν θείων ἐστὶν ἡ πρὸς τὸ μετεχόμενον τῶν μετεχόντων ὁμοίωσις.] The likeness of participants to the participable is the actualized identity of the participants with the participable, which they receive through the likeness. The actualized identity of participants with the participable received through the likeness is *the divinization of those made worthy of it* [ἡ θέωσις τῶν ἀξιουμένων θεώσεως].[92]

This soteriological use of *perichōrēsis*, in conjunction with *theōsis*, establishes the notion of human "participation in divine realities that transcend nature" in terms of the differentiated unity of Christ's two natures and, in turn, the differentiated unity of the Triune persons.[93] Further, as the translation of *perichōrēsis* above—*"relation of mutual love"*—indicates, Maximus specifies love as the essence of perichoretic union.[94] Accordingly, Verna Harrison concludes, "Perichoresis, which genuinely unites while preserving distinctness and enables mutuality and interchange of life itself among radically unequal levels of reality, thus stands at the heart of a Christian *ontology of love*."[95]

In this light, to say that the economic Trinity is the immanent Trinity and vice versa is not to say that the former displaces the latter epistemologically but to acknowledge that the way in which God reconciles created being with uncreated being is itself radically continuous with God's very way of being; indeed, the love expressed in the economy of salvation

---

92. Maximos Confessor, *St. Maximos*, 416–17; emphasis added. See Maximos Confessor, *Ad Thal.* 59; PG 90.608C–609B, for the Greek text.

93. The application of *perichōrēsis* to the Trinity begins with a contemporary of Maximus, Pseudo-Cyril (building once more on Gregory of Nazianzus), followed by John of Damascus a generation later. See Harrison, "Perichoresis," 59–63; Lawler, "*Perichoresis*," 50–52.

94. See Vishnevskaya, "Divinization," 134–36. Of Maximus, Zizioulas, *Being*, 98, states programmatically: "Maximus succeeded in nothing less than the miracle of reconciling a circle with a straight line. The way whereby he worked out a relationship between ontology and love, and developed an ontology of love out of the idea of *ekstasis*, may have immense value even in the theology and philosophy of our own days."

95. Harrison, "Perichoresis," 65; emphasis added.

through both incarnation and redemption is a revelation of the being of God, the object of faith in which creation, in Christ, may participate. This assertion inseparably joins the economy of salvation to the being of God, but being itself is now relational. The Trinity is "essentially" relational and, therefore, relatable *in se* to the being of creation.[96]

I have discussed three distinct uses of *perichōrēsis*: christological, Trinitarian, and soteriological. In summary, reflection on the relationship of Christ's two natures leads to a clarification of God's immanent way of being in Triune relation, which gives rise to recognition of an ontology of love that illuminates not only God's relationship to human nature in Christ but also God's relationship to humans in particular, along with the rest of creation. The premise that emerges from this line of thinking is that the Triune persons' way of relating to each other is ontologically continuous with God's way of relating to creation, and the name of this ontology is *perichōrēsis*. But in contemporary social Trinitarianism a fourth, anthropological, use of *perichōrēsis* has emerged.

In the anthropological use, the presumption is that the image of God in humankind corresponds, in some sense, to the Triune life. This notion is at least as old as Augustine's *vestigia Trinitatis*, but in view of *perichōrēsis*, the idea is that the divine image finds expression in the relationality—indeed, the relational ontology—of human being. *Imago Dei* therefore becomes *imago Trinitatis*, and social Trinitarianism becomes determinative of Christian anthropology in general and ecclesiology in particular.[97]

In turn, serious questions about the uses of *perichōrēsis* in recent theology have arisen, constituting what I consider the two major critiques of social Trinitarianism, which I label *ontological* and *apophatic*. The ontological critique insists fundamentally that, while the analogy of *perichōrēsis* in Trinitarian and christological doctrine may obtain given careful delimitation,[98] its application to God's relationship with creation breaks down, and its application to human relationship is untenable. This is essentially a continuation of the debate about the Creator-creature distinction discussed above, but it is useful to consider the specific objections to *perichōrēsis* in this regard. As I have indicated, Maximus innovatively applies *perichōrēsis* to *theōsis*

---

96. In response to Barth, then, one might say that the *analogia entis* is the *analogia relationis*, and the *analogia relationis* is the *analogia entis*.

97. Leading voices include Moltmann, *Trinity*; Boff, *Trinity*; LaCugna, *God*; Gunton, *One*; Volf, *Exclusion*; Volf, "'Trinity,'" 403–23; Grenz, *Social*.

98. See Crisp, "Problems," 119–40, for a thoroughgoing review of "coherent" versions of Trinitarian and christological *perichōrēsis*.

precisely because the union of Christ's two natures depends in orthodox confession on the union of humanity and divinity "without confusion."[99] Critics nonetheless claim that this distinction is frequently obscured in contemporary retrievals of *perichōrēsis*.

The upshot is a twofold ontological critique of social Trinitarianism. On the one hand, the ontological difference between divine and human nature precludes the application of *perichōrēsis* to God's relation to creation—the hypostatic union (somehow!) notwithstanding. For example, Randall Otto claims that one problem with *perichōrēsis* is "its appropriation to describe relationality apart from mutually shared being."[100] In other words, the analogy cannot properly extend beyond Trinitarian relations to divine-human relationship because a union of *being* among the divine persons is the essential idea: "Without the presupposition of their identity of essence perichoresis would be meaningless and could add nothing to the presupposition of the threeness of the persons."[101] This argument, however, ignores the idea that God's very being is relationality. Therefore, when Otto asserts that "perichoresis demands an ontological basis if the relations are to be *real* and not merely *logical*," he assumes that relations and ontology are two distinct categories.[102] The meaning of *perichōrēsis* is therefore limited by the supposed priority of being.[103] For Otto, it may explain the unity of three persons in one divine essence or the hypostatic union of two natures in one Christ, but the non-relational being of God in either case is the controlling assumption.

On the other hand, the anthropological use of *perichōrēsis* is further out of bounds. Because humans relate to one another through neither a unity of being like the Triune persons nor through hypostatic union like the natures of Christ, *perichōrēsis* may be a useful "analogy" or "metaphor" but nothing more.[104] In this vein, Kathryn Tanner writes, "Much of what is

99. See Wen, "Maximus," 6.

100. Otto, "Use," 366.

101. Otto, "Use," 370.

102. Otto, "Use," 376. This is, of course, simply a reassertion of the distinction between the immanent unity of essence and the economic diversity of persons, making *perichōrēsis* little more than a claim that the Three do indeed share one being by virtue of an "interpenetration" that leaves their distinction intact despite a primary "real" ontological unity.

103. This is precisely the priority that Moltmann, for one, struggles to overcome by retrieving *perichōrēsis*. See Moltmann, *Trinity*, 148–54.

104. Otto, "Use," 378–79.

said about the Trinity simply does not seem directly applicable to humans; human society could take on the very shape of the Trinity only if people were no longer human."[105] For Tanner, the gap between the Trinity and humanity appears unbridgeable.[106] The problem seems to be that, from her perspective, any bridging must happen from the human side, that is, in terms of imitation. To the contrary, *theōsis* is not imitation but participation, a divine-human synergy in which divine initiative is primary. Curiously, then, Tanner's own solution is to focus on participation instead of "modeling ourselves" on the Trinity: "The Trinity does not simply offer itself to us as an ideal or model for our imitation and leave it up to us to figure out how divine relations are applicable to humans. . . . The Trinity in the economy enters our world, closes the gap itself, to show how human relations are to be reformed in its image." The notion of the reformed image of God continues to provide the vital link for Tanner. Further, "Trinitarian relations need not be like human relations in order for humans to be taken up into them in this way—by being joined with Christ in the Spirit and thereby coming to share in Jesus' own relations with Father and Spirit."[107] Insofar as it is necessary to insist that social Trinitarianism should prefer *theōsis* to mere imitation, the critique is helpful, though I am unconvinced that most serious social Trinitarians do not already subscribe to a more robust vision of participation.[108] In any case, the vision of *theōsis* cast here agrees that the analogy of *perichōrēsis* means "Jesus' relations with Father

---

105. Tanner, "Trinity," 325.

106. Tanner, "Trinity," 326. So also Husbands, "Trinity," 120–41.

107. Tanner, "Trinity," 328. This is not a strong argument against the alternative since one might just as well say that Trinitarian relations need not be *unlike* human relations in order for human relations to be taken up into them in this way.

108. E.g., LaCugna, *God*, 228, writes: "Followers of Christ are made sharers in the very life of God, partakers of divinity as they are transformed and perfected by the Spirit of God. The 'motive' of God's self-communication is union with the creature through *theōsis*." The chief foil for Tanner's critique is Volf's article "'The Trinity Is Our Social Program.'" Volf, however, nuances his view with an acknowledgment of human finitude and fault, and other prominent social Trinitarians also recognize the serious limitations of human nature before the eschatological consummation of redemption. More to the point, the attempt to find a prominent social Trinitarian who prescribes a specific social or political program on the basis of *perichōrēsis* is bound to meet frustration. Perhaps the most likely candidate for such a politicized view is the liberationist Leonardo Boff. Yet, he writes: "It is not the theologian's task to devise social models that best approximate to the Trinity" (*Trinity*, 151)! His subsequent advocacy of "basic democracy" (152) remains exceedingly general and hardly means that his vision of *perichōrēsis* should be reduced to a political program in the sense Tanner seems to have in mind.

and Spirit are not the model for human relations; they are what our relations to the triune God are to be like—relations of worship and service to the Trinity's economic mission; relations that subordinate humans to God in a perfectly appropriate way."[109]

Karen Kilby is the chief proponent of the apophatic critique of social Trinitarianism.[110] Like Tanner, Kilby is suspicious of attempts to transition from the doctrine of the Trinity to notions of human relationality because of the difference between God and humanity. Taking aim especially at Miroslav Volf's perichoretic explication of human relations, Kilby states: "Everything that gives this discussion of identity, of the self/other relation, its richness, plausibility, and interest, is introduced precisely when considerations drawn from limitation, historicity, and fallenness quietly find their way into the discussion—precisely when Volf leaves behind anything that could possibly apply to or be derived from the Trinity."[111] Her proposal is that "the proper stance of Christian theology in face of the doctrine of the Trinity is non-comprehension, not knowing, not being in possession of a unifying grasp, idea, or model."[112] For Kilby, the problem is not just that modeling human relations on the Trinity is inappropriate but that it is impossible in the first place, because the doctrine of *perichōrēsis* says too much. We simply cannot know what the inner-Trinitarian relations are like and should not be so presumptuous as to apply them to humankind. Once more, however, the alternative is participation: "We are caught up in the

---

109. Tanner, "Trinity," 330.

110. See Kilby, "Trinity," 75–94.

111. Kilby, "Trinity," 81. As with Tanner, Volf is Kilby's primary target. Although she surveys Volf's argument thoroughly, noting how he makes allowance for the dissimilarity of Triune and human relations, she contends that such qualifications fail to limit Volf's argument as they should: "If he realizes the limitations of modeling creaturely, historical, and sinful human relations on eternal, perfect, divine relations; if he realizes the dangers of abstraction and theological emptiness that loom over general deductions about human relations deriving from the inner-trinitarian life; if he thinks that the primary weight must be given the *narrative* of the divine engagement with the world—why then does he not simply abandon the project of gaining political wisdom from the examination of inner-divine relations?" (81–82). The answer, as I have suggested, is that there is a critical difference between "gaining political wisdom" and suggesting that the Triune life is absolutely discontinuous with human life—much less that we could not say anything about divine relations in any case.

112. Kilby, "Trinity," 84. It is noteworthy, however, that Kilby is not actually suggesting an apophatic approach to the Trinity as such. Trinitarian theology is "backroom" (86) work that apparently remains quite cataphatic. She is actually advocating an apophatic approach to *the relevance* of the Trinity for human relations.

Trinity. The Christian life is a life of being brought into the Trinity—not a contemplation from a distance or a mimicry at a distance, but a genuine incorporation, a being taken up by the Spirit into the movement of the Son from and to the Father."[113] Kilby's apophatic Trinitarianism turns out to be "an incorporative, rather than a mimetic, trinitarian political orientation."[114] Christians trust, she explains, that "the Spirit may be at work aligning them with and incorporating them into Christ's own relation to the world."[115] Of course, alignment and incorporation are meaningless unless one can identify and articulate just what they entail in concrete situations. Given that this incorporation is in the life of the Triune God and therefore calls for a Trinitarian account of the Christian's relationship to God and the world, Kilby's apophaticism is ill equipped to say more.

Still, apophatic theology has in its favor the confession that words fail as we reflect on the Trinity, and I do not intend to delimit a missional understanding too tidily. As I explained in chapter 2, the difficulty of specifying what participation in God's mission means arises largely from the vagueness of its early Trinitarian moorings. At the same time, that vagueness served an ecumenical end, making room for the proliferation of missional theology in diverse corners of Christian thought. To advance the conversation about participation in the Trinitarian terms that are proper to the *missio Dei*, the remainder of the present argument appeals to Fiddes's novel construal of Trinitarian "persons." Adopting his view does not rule out the possibility of bringing other variations of Trinitarian thought to bear in the definition of participation that I am developing, much less does it overcome the failure of human words for the Triune God. But it offers a particularly compelling vision of *perichōrēsis*—one that coheres well with the understanding of *theōsis* I have developed.

Fiddes agrees that social Trinitarian accounts of *perichōrēsis* leave us with a considerable disanalogy between God and humans, arguing correctly that "we need more than a model of the triune God to copy. We need to become aware of the way that we are actually engaging in the triune life of God, sharing in the currents of the personal relationships of God."[116] The problem, he contends, is that accounts of *perichōrēsis* typically conceive of the "persons" of the Trinity as distinct subjects in relation. In turn, we are

113. Kilby, "Trinity," 84–85.
114. Kilby, "Trinity," 88.
115. Kilby, "Trinity," 91.
116. Fiddes, "Participating," 385.

left not with the possibility of real participation as subjects in the subjectivity of another but merely a model for imitation.

In response, Fiddes offers a genuine advancement of the relational ontology that Zizioulas identifies in the Greek fathers: "The notion of 'subsistent relations,' properly understood, . . . proposes that relations in God are as real and 'beingful' as anything which is created or uncreated, and that their ground of existence is themselves. If we use the term *hypostasis* as the early theologians did for a 'distinct reality' which has being, then the relations *are* hypostases. There are no persons 'at each end of the relation,' but the 'persons' are simply the relations."[117] This proposal represents a unique synthesis of Aquinas's "subsistent relations," which the Eastern tradition suspects of overemphasizing the one substance in which the relations subsist, and the "social doctrine" of those like Moltmann and Volf, whose rejection of "subsistent relations" tends toward "a kind of tritheism in which the threeness of God overbalances the oneness."[118] Thus, Fiddes contends, "there seems to be more potential for mutual indwelling (perichoresis) of created person and the triune God if the divine 'persons' are conceived as nothing other than relations."[119] This is a provocative idea that requires further explanation.

Rather than a *perichōrēsis* of persons-as-subjects, Fiddes argues for a "perichoresis of *movements*."[120] Extending Barth's notion of an "event of relationship," which Fiddes finds too static, he suggests "'movements of relationship,' or perhaps 'three movements of relationship subsisting in one event.'" The unity of event is important, as it signals his economic starting point, "the processions (actions) in God."[121] These are the Triune movements revealed in Scripture:

> The New Testament portrays prayer as being "to" the Father, "through" the Son and "in" the Spirit. This means that when we pray to God as Father, we find our address fitting into a movement like that of speech between a son and father, our response of "yes" ("Amen") leaning upon the child-like "yes" of humble obedience that is already there, glorifying the Father. At the same time, we find ourselves involved in a movement of self-giving like

117. Fiddes, *Participating*, 34.
118. Fiddes, *Participating*, 47.
119. Fiddes, *Participating*, 48.
120. Fiddes, *Participating*, 73.
121. Fiddes, *Participating*, 36.

that of a father sending forth a son, a movement which the early theologians called "eternal generation" and which we experience in the mission of God in history. To pray "in the event of Golgotha" [Moltmann] means that these movements of response and mission are undergirded by movements of suffering, like the painful longing of a forsaken son towards a father and of a desolate father towards a lost son. Simultaneously, these two directions of movement are interwoven by a third, as we find that they are continually being opened up to new depths of relationship and to new possibilities of the future by a movement that we can only call "Spirit"; for this third movement the Scriptures give us a whole series of impressionistic images—a wind blowing, breath stirring, oil trickling, wings beating, water flowing and fire burning—evoking an activity which disturbs, opens, deepens and provokes. The traditional formulation that the Spirit "proceeds from the Father through the Son" points to movement which renews all relations "from" and "to" the Other.[122]

The *perichōrēsis* of the Triune persons, then, refers to the interpenetration of these "three distinct movements of speech, emotion, and action which are like relationships 'from father to son,' 'from son to father,' and a movement of 'deepening relations.'"[123] Rather than presenting distinct subjects that humans might somehow perichoretically interpenetrate— apparently an impossibility—these movements constitute "the places opened out within the interweaving relationships of God." Participation in God, therefore, is far more radical than imitating a relational model; it is "sharing in this reality of relationship."[124]

Among the implications of this understanding is one of particular relevance to the present argument, namely, a revisioned perichoretic reading of the commission in John 20:21: "A triune doctrine of God encourages us to *discover* our roles as we participate in a God who is always in the movement of sending. The one who sends out the Son eternally from the womb of his being sends the Son into the world, and Christ after his resurrection from the dead says to his followers: 'as the Father has sent me, so I send you.'" This is not an unusual point of reference, considering it is a reiteration of the statement "As you have sent me into the world, so I have sent them into the world" (John 17:18), spoken just before the most

---

122. Fiddes, *Participating*, 39.
123. Fiddes, *Participating*, 38.
124. Fiddes, *Participating*, 50.

common text in discussions of *perichōrēsis*, John 17:20–23. Yet, Fiddes's notion of the *perichōrēsis* of movements illuminates the meaning of this sending relationship: "It is into these interweaving currents of mission that the disciples are drawn.... What is being portrayed here is no mere imitation of the ministry of Christ, not simply a modeling of human community on the relations in God. Participating in the movement of sending, disciples *represent* the actions of Jesus in their acts. There is an identification not of substance but of act and event."[125] With the identification of act and event, Fiddes provides a conceptual handle on the slippery surface of *perichōrēsis*. Yet, in view of missions history, a fearful question immediately arises: does *perichōrēsis* become in this scheme nothing more than a sophisticated justification for conflating the church's actions with God's mission? How can we speak of an identity of act when the actions of the church are fraught with sin? How, indeed, can we ever really speak of participation in God's mission when the church's missions are so commonly of her own design? So we come to the crux of the matter.

For Fiddes, the answer is to be found in the *perichōrēsis* of the Triune persons themselves, "three movements of relationship subsisting in one event." Here, unity of event does not preclude "a diversity of actions" by which the *hypostases* (movements of relationship) distinguish themselves.[126] By extension, diversity of actions delimits human participation in the event of God's missional action, differentiating the participating human from the participated divine. Fiddes notes, for example, "There will be some boundaries to the symmetry of relations, though not their reciprocity. That is, the movement of sending (mission) in which we find ourselves involved is always like that from a father to a son, not from a son to a father."[127] And again, "We become engaged in movements of love and pain which are like a handing over of the Kingdom, a returning it to its giver, and a raising from the dead, though we can never be as completely identified with them as was Jesus. In these active movements the *hypostases* distinguish themselves from each other."[128] I would add that *incomplete identification* with these movements further distinguishes the identity of the participant from the participated, even as the asymmetrical engagement of participation itself ensures the identity of event (mission).

125. Fiddes, *Participating*, 51.
126. Fiddes, *Participating*, 85.
127. Fiddes, *Participating*, 79.
128. Fiddes, *Participating*, 85.

Further, the diversity of actions in the case of human participants in God's mission is not only asymmetrical but also marked by sin. The church's participation in the perichoretic missions of the Trinity is always determined by a movement like that of a father to a son, but always a repentant prodigal son—a foolish and fallible son who shares in the father's work only because the father's embrace makes reciprocity possible.

Yet, having incorporated the reality of human fault in the differentiation that real participation in God entails, it remains to connect this understanding with *theōsis*. In what sense is *becoming*, to borrow Gorman's word, a dimension of missional participation? This question cuts to the heart of the contribution that my definition of participation offers because missional theology has paid significant attention to *perichōrēsis*, though largely without reference to *theōsis*.[129] As I have stated, however, *perichōrēsis* is an explanation of the transformative participation in the life of God that humans enjoy in the process of *theōsis*. Missional theology would, therefore, benefit from a conception of participation in God's mission in terms of the conjunction of these two ideas.

Conclusion: *Theōsis* and *Missio Dei*

Theōsis, the union of the church with God through an ontological transformation that necessarily precedes and accompanies the embodiment of cruciform righteousness, establishes the church's agency and work as real participation in the ongoing saving work of God, in a sense that surpasses mere imitative continuation of Jesus's ministry. By pushing the church's subjectivity back into the decisive event of Christ's own suffering, *theōsis* stipulates what the claim that the church participates in God's mission might signify: an ontological union by which the church's works in Christ, through the Spirit, become participation in the saving work of God. *Perichōrēsis* adds an idea of what such union entails. By designating the relational ontology through which unity in distinction may obtain even between the created and the uncreated, *perichōrēsis* further stipulates that human participation in the *missio Dei* involves an asymmetrical and incomplete yet truly reciprocal identification of human action with the divine movements of relationship subsisting in one event—the event

---

129. See Althouse, "Towards," 230–45; Van Gelder, *Ministry*, 88; Kline, "Participation," 38–61; Edgar, "Consummate," 112–25; Franke, "God," 105–19; Lang'at, "Trinity," 161–81; Van Dyk, "Church's," 225–36; Sexton, "Confessing," 171–89.

of mission. This concept surpasses the merely imitative and vaguely relational notions of *perichōrēsis* to which much of missional theology has appealed, offering instead a robustly Trinitarian vision of participation that maintains the distinction between the church's fallible missions and God's mission while indicating the sense in which the Triune movements of suffering, love, and reconciliation in the word include the church's work so as to instantiate a unity of action and event. Together, *theōsis* and *perichōrēsis* begin to address the aporias of participation.

I stated in the introduction that grounding a renewed articulation of the *missio Dei* in a Trinitarian theology of *theōsis* provides a promising path toward an account of missional participation, especially regarding a thicker account of how human and divine agency relate. Where, then, does a perichoretic account of participation as *theōsis* leave us? Chief among the questions that the foregoing argument raises is what the ontological transformation that *theōsis* entails might involve. If *theōsis* is "becoming a faithful embodiment"[130] of the gospel through participation in the perichoretic movements of the *missio Dei*, a theological account of embodiment is a necessary addition to the missional vision of participation. Further, the sense in which human embodiment may be transformed through participation in mission requires explanation. The pivotal issue is how embodied subjectivity participates, according to the notion of *theōsis* advanced here, in the triune movements through which God embraces the world. Fiddes offers a final clue: "To participate in God means that there is the ever-present opportunity to be aligned with a movement of communication beyond ourselves which is pure love, and which is also a movement of the will. We can lean upon a movement which is like a willing response of a son to a father, becoming *co-actors and co-narrators* with his 'Yes, Amen' to the Father's purpose."[131] The next chapter follows this insight, developing the concept of missional participation further through the idea of embodied narrativity.

---

130. Gorman, *Becoming*, 36.
131. Fiddes, *Participating*, 53; emphasis added.

CHAPTER 4

Participation as Embodied Narrativity

"By narrating a life of which I am not the author as to existence, I make myself its coauthor as to its meaning." —Paul Ricoeur[1]

THE CONCERN OF THE present chapter is to explain the relationship between the distinct claims that human life should be characterized in terms of embodiment on the one hand and narrativity on the other. Both claims are theologically significant, but the relationship between the two presents a conundrum. More to the point, the ambiguous relationship of embodiment and narrativity obscures their significance for understanding human participation in God's mission—and thus for understanding why participation in God's mission is particularly formative for interpreters of Scripture. My hypothesis in this chapter, therefore, is that the explanatory power of embodiment and narrativity for missional hermeneutics is far greater when the two are integrated into a single anthropological concept. I argue that human participation in God's mission as *theōsis* should be understood according to a theological account of human *embodied narrativity*. The argument proceeds in three sections. First, I account for the status of embodiment and narrativity respectively in contemporary theology and indicate why their conceptual integration is necessary. Second, I put an initial definition of embodied narrativity based on the philosophical work of Paul Ricoeur

1. Ricoeur, *Oneself*, 162.

in conversation with the theological anthropology of Jürgen Moltmann to stipulate a robustly theological account of embodied narrativity. The third section brings my theological conception of embodied narrativity to bear on the idea of human participation in God's mission as *theōsis*.

Theology Between Embodiment and Narrativity

Conceptually, both embodiment and narrativity have developed in literature beyond the bounds of theological discourse per se. To represent the anthropological concepts that theologians have engaged in recent decades, one would ideally attend to a broader set of interlocutors than theologians alone—especially philosophers, but also social scientists, linguists, and cognitive scientists. The burden of this section, however, is merely to establish the legitimacy of these developments from a theological perspective and to demonstrate their lack of integration. The modesty of this goal constrains my discussion and limits what follows to a broad overview of key ideas.

Embodiment in Recent Theology

In 1988, philosopher David Pellauer summarized the state of affairs: "Embodiment needs to be recognized more generally as a central component of philosophical and theological reflection, one that touches the full range of issues running from ontology to epistemology and back again (not to speak of ethics). Hence my conclusion must be that both philosophers and theologians need to get this project under way, not just because embodiment itself is a significant topic, but because it is central to their more general concerns for making sense of our lives."[2] Pellauer notes the general underdevelopment of the concept in philosophy following the groundbreaking work of Gabriel Marcel (1888–1973) and Maurice Merleau-Ponty (1908–61) and the even greater neglect in theology, though he identified theological works representing two streams of inquiry that would make much of embodiment in the ensuing thirty years: gender and sexuality.[3] A third stream, the theology of race, has emerged alongside these, heralding the importance of embodiment in postmodern, critical, and liberationist

---

2. Pellauer, "Embodiment," 177.

3. Pellauer attends more to the possibilities of feminist theology suggested by McFague, *Models*, though he also footnotes in passing the earlier work by Nelson, *Embodiment*.

theologies. A brief look at each reveals underlying dualisms that a theological account of embodied narrativity must address.

Within feminist theology, embodiment represents, first, a critique of epistemological universalism. As Susan Parsons states, "This emphasis on embodiment reveals a new epistemology in which knowledge is not deduced from abstract truths, but is formed in the midst of praxis and particularities."[4] Thus, "there are no places to stand outside our biology, there is no position to take up which is not intrinsically related to a web of personal and political power relations, and there is no truth that we can know which is disembodied."[5] The universalism under critique is not only a matter of disembodied abstraction but also of representation. The deconstructionist aspect of feminist theology endeavors to rewrite embodiment beyond the presumptive norms of patriarchy. "There is an urgent need," writes Elaine Graham, "for dominant, privileged groups to become critical about their own racial, sexual and gender identity, and begin to make it possible for everyone to think from the Body; or else bodily experience is restricted to a property of those speaking from a position of 'difference,' which in practice means the abnormal, problematic, victimized body. It is therefore essential that embodiment is affirmed as a common human trait, even though our experiences may be diverse and characterized by inequality of representation, access to resources and self-determination."[6] Feminist theology, along with other theologies of liberation, has been subject to criticism insofar as it recapitulates the privileging of experience in liberal theologies from Schleiermacher to Tillich.[7] Nonetheless, whatever role one grants experience methodologically, feminist theology elucidates experience's particularity as *embodied*. In this regard, Graham is surely right when she states: "A practical theology of the body/our bodies is therefore never merely the statement of principles; more the cultivation of the *habitus* of the body whereby the words of suffering and redemption may become flesh. If theological values have any substance, they will exist in primary form as bodily practices—clinical, liturgical, kerygmatic, prophetic—and only derivatively as doctrines and concepts."[8]

---

4. Parsons, "Feminist," 20.
5. Parsons, "Feminist," 23.
6. Graham, "Words," 115.
7. See Peacore, *Role*, chs. 1–3.
8. Graham, "Words," 120.

Patriarchal representation is not the only culprit for feminist theology, however. It also attributes the disembodiment of theology to a traditional, dualistic metaphysics, with its negative view of the flesh. Lisa Isherwood states: "Those of us who come from a Christian tradition have been taught in the bosom of mother church that flesh does not matter, that we can be misled and deceived by it and that as women we are the most fleshy, the most deceptive and the most misleading of all creations. This view has sprung from dualism which is deeply embedded in our tradition. . . . Dualism is a device lurking in the midst of an incarnational religion that has objectified us and made us aliens in our own skin."[9] Thus, the critique of dualism fits hand in glove with another of feminist theology's major contributions to the theology of embodiment—a retrieval of the christological doctrine of the incarnation. In Isherwood's words, the challenge of feminist liberation theology is "that we should take seriously the story we have told ourselves, which is that God left the heavens in order that the full reality of life in abundance may come to being. In order that we may embody justice seeking, mutual relation and radical risk taking."[10] Emphasis on the incarnation naturally leads to a difficulty for feminist theology regarding "the historical particularity of the maleness of Jesus," as Julia Baudzej puts it.[11] The dilemma arises because feminist theology, broadly speaking, refuses to screen out Jesus's embodiment; whoever Jesus is for all flesh, he is so as male flesh. Feminists, therefore, debate the significance of Jesus's sex. Baudzej, for example, highlights the distinction between Jesus's sex and the performance of maleness: "If it is taken in the context of embodiment then the emphasis shifts onto subjectivity—how this maleness is lived and acted out."[12] Regardless of one's strategy for resolving the question, the shared assumption is of enduring significance regarding the theology of embodiment: the incarnation entails a christological demand for an embodied vision of human subjectivity.

The theology of sexuality proceeds from the same ground, pushing farther into the murky dialectics of the biological and social constitution of human sexuality. Since James Nelson's 1978 volume *Embodiment: An Approach to Sexuality and Christian Theology*, the theological status

---

9. Isherwood, "Embodiment," 141.

10. Isherwood, "Embodiment," 144.

11. Baudzej, "Re-Telling," 88. In other words, as Rosemary Radford Ruether famously asked in *Sexism and God-Talk*, ch. 5, "Can a male savior save women?"

12. Baudzej, "Re-Telling," 88.

of human embodiment has been a centerpiece of the discussion. Nelson identifies two dualisms of traditional Christian theology—body-spirit ("spiritualistic") dualism and male-female ("sexist") dualism—as the major problematics to be addressed before proceeding to a constructive contemporary theology of sexuality.[13] The former is the arena of Nelson's major contribution.[14] Following Merleau-Ponty, Nelson argues: "If I do not realize the profound sense in which I *am* my body, if in a false spiritualization of my self-hood I deny my embodiedness, I will also tend to minimize the personal significance of activities which I carry on through my body."[15] The affirmation of a holistic self, which Nelson calls the "body-self," leads to a profoundly relevant question for the present study: what does it mean that "as body-selves we participate in the reality of God?"[16] The answer to this question must deal with the complexity of embodiment, however. As with feminist theology's view of gender, the debate about the nature of sexuality is ensconced in rigorous, unresolved philosophical disputes about the relationship between social construction and biology.[17] Nelson, for example, takes a moderate constructivist position, sensibly pointing out the reductionism that tends to replace dualism at the extremes: "Simply put, constructionism alone suggests spirit or mind without bodily reality, and essentialism alone suggests body without spirit."[18] These polemics demonstrate clearly: whether social or biological, the concreteness of human embodiment is the irreducible "matter" that theological discourse must address. Sexuality is a bodily phenomenon, and the question is what human bodies are and may become in relation to God.

Likewise, the theology of race, in conversation with critical race theory, attends to the embodied experience of socially constructed racial

13. Nelson, *Embodiment*, 45–46.

14. See also Nelson, *Body*.

15. Nelson, *Embodiment*, 20.

16. Nelson, *Embodiment*, 36. Moltmann-Wendel, *I Am*, represents the emergence in the mid-1990s of a theological view of the "self which is bound up in this multi-dimensional body and which experiences relationships and selfhood through it" (xv). See also Prokes, *Toward*, xi: "the search for adequate terminology to express the whole human person enfleshed in the world is ongoing, among philosophers as well as theologians."

17. These debates are typified by exchanges between philosophers Judith Butler and Susan Bordo in the 1990s, which have not reached any appreciable theoretical resolution. See the representative collection in Welton, *Body*, chs. 2–4, as well as the elaboration below.

18. Nelson, *Body*, 48. Louw, "Beyond," 111, similarly refers to sexuality in terms of "the 'ensoulment of the body' and the 'embodiment of the soul.'"

categories. In particular, problematizing the essentialization of the "black body" has become prominent in the discourse.[19] Anthony Pinn writes of "new black theological thought," which challenges the prior generation of black theology's tendency toward essentialism by attending to the complex particularity of embodiment:

> The new shape of black theological thought should involve a more complex and suspicious application of the trope of blackness as defining or foundational theological category. Rather than the privileged position normally afforded to this category, attention to the complex body as physical and discursive reality entails recognition of the rather flat nature of life meaning gleaned from the historical workings of blackness (over against whiteness). For the doing of black theology, blackness cannot stand alone but must be interrogated always in connection to other life modifiers.[20]

This emphasis on the particularity of embodied experiences creates a methodological dilemma because, despite its weaknesses, essentialization is in one respect the side effect of very useful—perhaps necessary and even inevitable—conceptual operations, namely, abstraction, generalization, and category formation. To speak of "the black body," for example, it is necessary to generalize. Accordingly, despite the fact that black persons' "uniquely individual experiences of their own body are constituted by a mélange of their complected or epidermalized experiences, class experiences, and gendered experiences among others," argues Harvey Young, "nevertheless, I submit that an acknowledgment of the multiple determinants that inform an individual's perspective on the world (and on herself) neither limits group identification nor prevents the theorization of the black body."[21]

Whether it is the fine-grain particularity of individual intersectionality or the broad-stroke particularity of shared black (over against white) experiences, both sides of this methodological dispute presume that the particularity of *embodied* experience is the *sine qua non*. Furthermore, I agree with M. Shawn Copeland that Christian theology is motivated by an imperative that justifies the methodological risks of attending to bodily particularity:

> Indeed, any formation of theological anthropology that takes body and body marks seriously risks absolutizing or fetishizing

---

19. See, e.g., Yancy, "Whiteness," 216; Yancy, *Black*.
20. Pinn, *Embodiment*, 50–51; see also Copeland, *Enfleshing*, esp. ch. 1.
21. Young, *Embodying*, 22.

what can be seen (race and sex), constructed (gender), represented (sexuality), expressed (culture), and regulated (social order). Moreover, such attention to concrete and specific, nonetheless accidental, characteristics also risks "fragmenting" the human being. But what makes such risk imperative is the location and condition of bodies in empire; what makes such risk obligatory is that the body of Jesus of Nazareth, the Word made flesh, was subjected in empire.[22]

Here as well, the incarnation draws theological anthropology inexorably toward the body.

This brief review of embodiment in theologies of gender, sexuality, and race suggests that concern with two major types of dualism mark the discourse: (1) body-soul (or body-spirit) dualism and (2) what I call material-social dualism. These comprise a kind of "double bind" for the body.[23] In order to do justice theologically to the concept of embodiment, I suggest it is necessary to address both dualisms in a way that leads to a comprehensively holistic understanding of humanity.

Body-Soul Dualism

In contrast with construals of the relationship between body and soul (and the other variations of dichotomous and trichotomous anthropologies) in which the body is a nonessential aspect of being human or, at least, of being the "image of God," a holistic vision of the human being increasingly characterizes theological anthropology.[24] This perspective has only

22. Copeland, *Enfleshing*, 56–57.

23. I take a cue here from the Nordic philosophers Mjaaland et al., "Introduction," 1, who refer to "a double bind" of the body in Christian thought: "On the one hand, it was perceived as a prison, binding the soul to transience, darkness, and confusion. On the other hand, it was itself controlled, bound and disciplined by reason and will, law and culture." Although this is a keen observation, they do not express the extent to which the latter, in which the Foucauldian category of "discipline" functions over against the material body, has become just as dualistically construed a bind as the former.

24. See Pannenberg, *Systematic*, 182. It is important not to overgeneralize the attribution of dualism to the tradition; Pannenberg nuances the portrayal of the early tradition: "Over against Platonism . . . the early fathers defended our psychosomatic unity as a basic principle of Christian anthropology. They did, of course, accept the view of the soul as an independent entity, which they corrected only to the extent of regarding both soul and body as partial principles of human reality, so that only the two together constitute the one human person. In spite of this emphasis on psychosomatic unity, however, the dualism of soul and body invaded Christian anthropology" (182). Augustine is a prime

become more pronounced following advances in neuroscience and cognitive studies, to the extent that some doubt traditional ontological notions of "soul" even represent the phenomena of consciousness that supervene on embodied existence.[25] New Testament scholar Joel Green is thus able to survey the broad acceptance of embodied anthropology in contemporary biblical studies in a way that leads to a conversation between neuroscience and New Testament interpretation.[26]

Among the variety of holistic models for theological anthropology currently in contention, the most compelling I have encountered is the Finnish systematician Veli-Matti Kärkkäinen's "multidimensional monism."[27] With this term, Kärkkäinen attempts to do justice both to the "more holistic and monistic" anthropology that marks contemporary biblical scholarship, theology, and philosophy and to the persistent fact that "for every nonreductionist, the distinction, yet not separation, between the physical and the mental is unavoidable in philosophical, theological, and scientific discussion."[28] This is not merely a concession to the heuristic limitations of anthropological language. Rather, as philosopher of religion Philip Clayton puts it, "a moment's reflection will reveal that an anthropology that would

---

example of this invasion. For him, man is made in the image of God "not according to the body, nor indiscriminately according to any part of the mind, but according to the rational mind, wherein the knowledge of God can exist" (*On the Trinity* 12.12). This rational mind is the soul, in distinction from the body: "We must find in the soul of man, i.e., the rational or intellectual soul, that image of the Creator" (*On the Trinity* 14.4). See also Taylor, *Sources*, 131. It is not necessary to lay every dualistic ill of Christian anthropology at Augustine's feet for the point to stand: powerful streams of the tradition have taken the soul, over against the body, to be the image of God and the essence of human nature.

25. See, e.g., the variety of perspectives in Green, *What?*; Green, *In Search*.

26. Green, *Body*, ch. 1. Certainly, advocates of dualistic anthropologies persist in the face of prevailing trends. It is noteworthy, nonetheless, that as prominent a representative of dualism as John Cooper, "Scripture," 30, demonstrates that even the dualistic tradition of formal Christian theology, when carefully articulated, takes the body to be, in one way or another, "essential" to human life. Whether this or any of the various monist construals of embodied anthropology on offer are satisfying in their particulars, the state of the discourse is fairly established with the claim that contemporary Christian theology largely assumes that human nature is essentially embodied.

27. Kärkkäinen, *Creation*, ch. 12.

28. Kärkkäinen, *Creation*, 339. The phrase "more holistic and monistic" calls for terminological clarity. Not every holistic anthropology is monistic: e.g., one need only hold that every aspect of human being is essential to its constitution as the image of God in order to qualify as holistic. Monism, by contrast, contends that human being is ultimately singular in essence—e.g., that the body and the soul are one. This basic differentiation is what makes Kärkkäinen's multidimensional monism a generative concept.

remain a listener to and learner from the sciences and other disciplines cannot rush headlong to the closure of a final conceptual scheme. Existentially as well as theoretically, ours must remain a multifaceted unity. If human being involves the quest to unify the diverse parts of our experience along multiple dimensions, then each axis must remain as a part of the overall project rather than being too quickly *aufgehoben* into a final, undifferentiated unity called 'the image of God.'"[29] Furthermore, I agree with Kärkkäinen that, for Christian theology, the multidimensionality of an inextricably embodied monism is a function of the human relationship to God: "Strictly speaking, ontological physicalism can only be penultimate for a theist. Hence, it seems to me that multidimensional monism . . . fits better the key belief in Christian faith . . . of the complex unity of the finite world as God's creation."[30] For a theology of embodied participation, this is a vital point. What humans are as embodied beings, they are in relation to God, as participants in God. Stated in terms of my argument thus far, participation in God's mission as *theōsis* is embodied participation. In turn, embodied participation in God's mission must be articulated in the christological grammar of the unity of Christ's two natures and the Trinitarian grammar of the incarnate Son's unity with the other persons of the Trinity.[31]

---

29. Clayton, "Emergence," 74. This entire volume is an exploration of "'multidimensional' approaches that could do justice to the 'complexity of human personhood'" (Welker, introduction to *Depth*, 1).

30. Kärkkäinen, *Creation*, 341.

31. Kathryn Tanner's discussion of the image of God in terms of participation provides an important clue in this regard. Marking the difference between two kinds of participation—which she calls "weak" and "strong," corresponding respectively to the broad ontological participation of creation and the limited "in Christ" participation of salvation—that my discussion of *theōsis* has already addressed, Tanner argues that Christ is the paradigm for the second, stronger type: "Despite the difference in nature that remains between humanity and the second person, the perfect hypostatic unity of the two of them in Christ makes him the perfect human image of the second person of the trinity in much the way the perfect unity of substance between first and second persons of the trinity makes the second the perfect image of the first. In both cases perfect unity makes for perfect imaging" (Tanner, *Christ*, 13). This is consonant with Oliver Crisp's proposal: "I bear the divine image in virtue of the fact that human nature is in principle created with the capacities and powers necessary and sufficient to be in hypostatic union with a divine person. This includes both my mind (and soul, if I have a soul), and body rightly configured" (Crisp, "Christological," 224–25; cf. Tanner, *Christ*, 50–51). The claim that I am building following Tanner and Crisp is that human participation in God—understood now as participation in the Triune mission—should be conceived of in light of the conjunctions of the very possibility of human union with Christ, the hypostatic union of Christ's two natures, and the intra-Trinitarian unity of persons. These linkages

As the primary argument of this chapter will demonstrate, human participation in the Triune mission as *theōsis* can be understood in terms of the perichoretic extension of the divine life in Christ, characterized according to the unity of the bodily and narratival dimensions of human life.

Material-Social Dualism

Turning to the problem of material-social dualism, social constructivists are represented supremely by Judith Butler, who identifies the powerful—and sometimes overwhelming—influence of the body's sociocultural context. Butler has brilliantly theorized how gender is a product of sociocultural "performativity," leading to the conclusion that the gendered body has "no ontological status apart from the various acts which constitute its reality."[32] The claim is strategically overstated: "To 'concede' the undeniability of 'sex' or its 'materiality' is always to concede some version of 'sex,' some formation of 'materiality.' Is the discourse in and through which that concession occurs—and yes, that concession invariably does occur—not itself formative of the very phenomenon that it concedes? To claim that discourse is formative is not to claim that it originates, causes, or exhaustively composes that which it concedes; rather, it is to claim that there is no reference to a pure body which is not at the same time a further formation of that body."[33] This is an insight into the hermeneutical constraints that the "facts" of biological discourse cannot circumvent, with which Christian theology still frequently needs to reckon. Carrying this point too far, however, leads to the replacement of embodiment with pure performativity—a reduction of the discourse about bodies to what Susan Bordo has called discourse foundationalism: "For the discourse foundationalist, insights into our embeddedness in discourse function as a 'bottom line,' a privileged framework which is used to deconstruct other frameworks of understanding to its own preferred elements."[34] This risks another kind of disembodiment. The trouble (so to speak) is that, taken at rhetorical face value, Butler's theory "leaves us with a disembodied body and a free-floating gender artifice in

---

substantiate *irreducibly embodied participation* as the modus of human engagement in the ongoing Triune *missio*.

32. Butler, "Gender," 41.
33. Butler, "Bodies," 77.
34. Bordo, "Bringing," 89.

a sea of cultural meaning production."[35] Bordo's moderate position seems most sensible. "For me," she says, "there is a big leap from acknowledging that the science of biology is mediated by historically located, conceptual frameworks . . . to reducing the concept of 'biology' to the status of 'fiction' or 'fantasy.' If biology is a 'fantasy,' so too is every other framework for understanding the body, social constructionism and performative studies included."[36] She urges attention instead to the "materiality of the body," which refers comprehensively to sociocultural and biological "finitude."[37] Following Bordo, I would move Butler's "concession" to the level of a given that establishes the material-social dialectic as irreducibly holistic.

Among the most insightful theological work along these lines is Ola Sigurdson's "theological somatology." His early soundings propose a phenomenological approach to the topic that highlights the difficulty lurking in the background of material-social dualism: the objectification of the body. The phenomenology of the body in the tradition of Merleau-Ponty is useful because it resonates with the emphasis on the particularity of bodily experience that we learn from theologies of gender, sexuality, and race.[38] A phenomenological methodology also resists the mistake of overcompensating for the objectification of the body by recourse to its total subjectification.[39] Giving due credit to Butler's insights, then, Sigurdson's approach yields a sensible conclusion: "The longer I have studied embodiment, the more I have been convinced that it is an abstraction to separate anatomy from history and discourse."[40] His study *Heavenly Bodies: Incarnation, the Gaze, and Embodiment in Christian Theology* is, from one angle, a far-reaching development of this holistic understanding. Sigurdson begins by establishing that a theological proclivity to speak about the incarnation

---

35. Bigwood, "Renaturalizing," 102.

36. Bordo, "Bringing," 89.

37. Bordo, "Bringing," 92, 90. By this, she refers to "our inescapable physical locatedness in time and space, in history and culture, both of which not only shape us (the social constructionist premise, which I share with other postmoderns) but also *limit* us (which some postmoderns appear to me to deny)" (90). Altogether, these are the "bodily, institutional, practical realities of our culture" (91).

38. Cf. Bigwood, "Renaturalizing," 99–114.

39. Foucault represents this move paradigmatically with his subversion of the Platonic axiom, "The body is the prison of the soul" (extrapolated from Plato, *Phaed.* 82e) by claiming, "The soul is the prison of the body" (*Discipline*, 30). Butler's reception of this point in terms of performativity is explicit in *Bodies*, ch. 1.

40. Sigurdson, "How," 30.

of Christ "on the basis of the idea of an autonomous modern subject" is ultimately a failure to grasp "the need for an understanding of the embodiment of the person in order to understand the incarnation."[41] The project is an exploration of "the anthropological implications of the doctrine of the incarnation for the human mode of being-in-the-world, or in other words, how Christ has been received in concrete human practices," which calls for an "anthropological supplement" that overcomes abstraction in favor of phenomenological particularity.[42]

This leads Sigurdson into an extended examination of the embodied human gaze as "a concrete reception of Christology in a significant practice"[43] and then of embodiment generally. The exercise hinges on Merleau-Ponty's insight that "the body is the vehicle of being in the world," and "our general means of having a world,"[44] according to which the difference between the "objective" and "phenomenal" body should be conceived. The body that has a world or is effectively one's being-in-the-world refers to the phenomenal (or "lived") body, which Merleau-Ponty defines as "the body insofar as it projects a certain 'milieu' around itself, insofar as its 'parts' know each other dynamically and its receptors are arranged in such a way as to make the perception of the object possible through their synergy" and more concisely as "the body such as we experience it," over against the body objectified by the scientific gaze.[45] The dualism this might suggest was apparent to Merleau-Ponty, and he furthered his thought through the conception of "flesh" as the "intertwining" of the objective and phenomenal bodies in a "chiasm."[46] Sigurdson takes this imagery on board: "One might say that the physical body and the phenomenal body have an interactive relationship, such that they both give the possibility for each other without the one being able to be reduced to the other."[47] In view of the socio-linguistic mediation of the phenomenal body, however, he extends the metaphor to the "constructed body," contending "it is critical to realize that the human body is invariably both nature and culture, and that these

---

41. Sigurdson, *Heavenly*, 141, 142.
42. Sigurdson, *Heavenly*, 147.
43. Sigurdson, *Heavenly*, 153.
44. Merleau-Ponty, *Phenomenology*, 98, 165.
45. Merleau-Ponty, *Phenomenology*, 262, 484.
46. See Merleau-Ponty, *Visible*, esp. 138–39, 160, 214–15, 259–60, 271.
47. Sigurdson, *Heavenly*, 330.

are indissolubly intertwined with each other."[48] In summary, Sigurdson says, "There are several aspects to the person's embodiment: her biological versus her phenomenal body, her individual and her social body."[49] This is a sort of double chiasm, one within the other, as individual experience and social mediation intertwine in the phenomenal body just as the phenomenal body and the objective body intertwine in the flesh. Much like multidimensional monism, Sigurdson's vision is of a complex, indissoluble holism that nonetheless yields to analysis of discernible parts.

From another angle, *Heavenly Bodies* advances a thesis anticipated in Sarah Coakley's essay "The Eschatological Body: Gender, Transformation, and God."[50] Coakley is specifically concerned with a theological reading of the *animus* that drives Butler's work and makes sense of its wide influence, but her theological lens is the "eschatological horizon" that orients gender subversion and transformation in the writings of Gregory of Nyssa. Her point is that the meaning of Gregory's subversion of gender categories derives from a *telos* and, ultimately, from "the horizon of a *divine* 'grand narrative.'"[51] Sigurdson likewise argues that "the Christian body is included in an existential drama of salvation, and in order to perceive the dynamic in the Christian understanding of the body, it is necessary to study this from a perspective that more clearly focuses on how the Christian body is a body that is transformed in the direction of an eschatological horizon."[52] This idea provides both a final addition to the conception of holistic embodiment and a transition to the subsequent discussion of narrativity. For as the body approaches the eschatological horizon, the resurrection looms, and the tensive question of what the body is and will become finally gives way to its last, most difficult iteration for a holistic, multidimensional conception: the continuity of bodily selves beyond death. Relying on the work of medievalist Caroline Walker Bynum, Sigurdson affirms that "the continuity of the changeable body lies in the narrative; it is the narrative that conditions the possibility of recognizing the body from one time to another."[53] I extend much the same insight below through Ricoeur's work.

48. Sigurdson, *Heavenly*, 332, 347.

49. Sigurdson, *Heavenly*, 570.

50. Coakley, *Powers*, ch. 9; Sigurdson engages this essay explicitly on pp. 413 and 573 of *Heavenly Bodies*.

51. Coakley, *Powers*, 157.

52. Sigurdson, *Heavenly*, 495–96.

53. Sigurdson, *Heavenly*, 574.

Unfortunately, Sigurdson recommends that "historical and theological research avoid too great an emphasis on continuity," instead placing an accent on the "unknown" character of the eschatological body.[54] He correlates this mysteriousness with the story's character: "The story is not done yet, and how the person's glorified body should be understood, as with Jesus's resurrection body, is still a mystery."[55] It seems to me that this correlation produces an undesirable reciprocal effect: because the body's narrative is what provides eschatological continuity, the mystification of the eschatological body in turn mystifies the significance that the eschatological *telos* may provide the body in history. Therefore, by allowing the mystery of the eschatological "heavenly body" to overwhelm the narrative that provides continuity, Sigurdson undercuts the potential significance that the narrative provides for conceiving the pre-resurrection body.

In a word, there is too much *not-yet* in Sigurdson's account and not enough *already*. From the perspective of a missional theology of participation as *theōsis*, the problem is that he does not recognize the "existential drama of salvation" as the story of the Triune *missio Dei*. This is particularly evident in that precisely when Sigurdson discusses humans being "made participatory" in the ecstatic overflow of Trinitarian love, no drama of redemption—much less of human participation in God's redemptive work through union with Christ—is in view; his account is non-narratival and non-missional. The failure to let the eschatological horizon fuse narratively with the ongoing story of human embodiment results in an erasure of the possibility that Sigurdson set out to explore: "the concrete reception of Christology in different significant practices."[56] Absent the eschatological possibilities provided by the particular narrative of the church's participation in the Triune mission through union with the resurrected Christ, present bodily reception of Christology becomes narratively and teleologically bereft, "a matter of the praxis of faith and the worship of the church, that is to say, of ritual practices like prayer, worship, Bible reading, and meditation"[57] that cannot not fully partake of the final holism of narrative

---

54. Sigurdson, *Heavenly*, 575, 588.

55. Sigurdson, *Heavenly*, 576.

56. Sigurdson, *Heavenly*, 148.

57. Sigurdson, *Heavenly*, 274. The argument that Sigurdson makes regarding the way such practices shape human embodiment for the reception of Christology resonates with the essential claim of Smith's *Imagining* (see ch. 1), both of which are consonant with certain notions of theological interpretation of Scripture. Yet, these practices will continue to struggle for full embodiment apart from the biblical narrative's inscription of participation in God's mission among the church's indispensable practices.

unity for which humans are destined. An account of human narrativity, to which I turn next, substantiates this critique.

To summarize, recent theological developments on embodiment indicate that body-soul dualism and material-social dualism each present deficiencies that a theological conception of embodied participation in God's mission must overcome. Taking the body seriously in view of the doctrine of *theōsis* requires a rejection of body-soul dualism in favor of a holistic anthropology such as Kärkkäinen's multidimensional monism. Theologies of gender, sexuality, and race consistently reveal that the dualism of the material body and the socially constructed body also demands a solution. But just as body-soul dualism can be erroneously resolved by reducing the human being to a body alone, material-social dualism can be erroneously resolved by reducing the body to a social construction alone. Here, too, a holism that accounts for the body's multiple dimensions can satisfy the requirements of a theology of missional participation. The resolution of both dualisms in a holistic theology of embodiment points toward an anthropology that accounts for human narrativity.

Narrative Theology Without Narrativity

The notion that "the formal quality of experience through time is inherently narrative" (which Stephen Crites articulated in 1971)[58] has, in one form or another, become a commonplace in a startling array of disciplines. Among cognitive scientists,[59] social scientists,[60] and philosophers,[61] the

---

58. Republished as Crites, "Narrative," 66.

59. E.g., Bruner, *Actual*; McNeil, "Homo," 331–60; Turner, *Literary*; Young and Saver, "Neurology," 72–84; Mar, "Neuropsychology," 1414–34; Boyd, *On*; Gottschall, *Storytelling*; Popova, "Narrativity," 1–14; Grishakova and Sorokin, "Notes," 542–61.

60. I refer particularly to the set of social scientific methods known as "narrative inquiry." Clandinin and Connelly, *Narrative*, 18, helpfully observe that some researchers have a "sense of a methodologist's opportunism. They seem to say that life and narrative are linked because the link seems to work." For these, narrative is essentially a useful, borrowed metaphor. Others "argue naturalistically along the line that 'this is the way the world is, and therefore this is how it should be thought about.' . . . Experience happens narratively" (19). See also, e.g., Polkinghorne, *Narrative*; Riessman, *Narrative*; Maynes, Pierce, and Laslett, *Telling*; Holstein and Gubrium, *Varieties*.

61. The primary point of departure is MacIntyre, *After*, ch. 15, in which he develops "the narrative concept of selfhood" (217). I will discuss Ricoeur at length below. A third standard point of reference is Taylor, *Sources*, 47–52, who is to a large extent riffing on MacIntyre and Ricoeur (along with Martin Heidegger's and Jerome Bruner's more

differences in method and particular claims cannot obscure the fact of a broad consensus that, in some sense, humans are *narrative by nature*.[62] I use the term *narrativity* in this study, in contrast with narrative, to denote a constitutive dimension of human nature.[63]

Attention to narrativity entered theological discourse through a back door. Narrative theology has significant roots in postliberal theological methods concerned principally with the nature of the biblical narrative(s) and the nature of doctrine, rather than with human nature as such.[64] Indeed, the claim that narrative interpretation is *not* about human nature is the so-called Yale school's bone of contention with the so-called Chicago school. For Hans Frei, narrativity is an essentially liberal notion: "There is a liberal sense of using the term, narrative theology, which generally says that to be human is above all to have a story. I am not sure that that's above all what it is to be human."[65] The comment is clearly, if passively, aimed at Ricoeur,[66] though it is more accurate to say, at "Chicago," which arguably means Ricoeur through the prism of David Tracy's work. At the risk of ambiguity, therefore, I will continue to refer to the two schools. The debate between Yale and Chicago has usually appeared to be a twofold disagreement about foundationalism, in which Frei and company vehemently deny either the need for a hermeneutical foundation in the form of a general hermeneutics or an epistemological foundation in the form of a theory of reference. Given that both have to do with an ostensibly shared "reality,"

---

rudimentary observations). Nevertheless, the monumental stature of *Sources* makes his assertion that the narrative conditions of identity are "inescapable structural requirements of human agency" (52) weighty indeed. Notably, Strawson, "Against," 428–52, has taken umbrage at such perspectives, suggesting they are not only wrong but potentially harmful. For an adequate rebuttal, see Rudd, "In," 60–75.

62. As Anne Foerst, *God*, 187, puts it, humans are *Homo narrans narrandus*.

63. For consonant discussions of embodiment and narrativity, see Bargár, "Christian," 93–104; Bargár, "Narrativity," 30–43. With the term *dimension*, I signal again the usefulness of Kärkkäinen's "multidimensional monism." Other terms, such as *aspect* and *facet*, similarly indicate a complex and differentiated but holistic conception of human nature.

64. Frei, *Eclipse*; Lindbeck, *Nature*. Notwithstanding Lindbeck's use of Ludwig Wittgenstein and Clifford Geertz to develop it, the cultural-linguistic model of doctrine carries with it significant anthropological entailments—something that many postliberals seem to ignore merely by virtue of the assertion that the nature of doctrine, not people, is in view.

65. Frei, "Response," 208.

66. See Frei, "'Literal,'" 117–52, for Frei's overt engagement with Ricoeur.

the two frequently merge confusingly in argumentation, so it is useful to separate them conceptually. On the one hand, Frei is ultimately concerned about hermeneutical foundationalism: "It is doubtful that any scheme for reading texts, and narrative texts in particular, and biblical narrative texts even more specifically, can serve globally and foundationally, so that the reading of biblical material would simply be a regional instance of the universal procedure."[67] One keen observer of the dispute, Gary Comstock, pointed out early on, however, that the charge of philosophical foundationalism does not obviously apply to the Chicago school.[68] It has become clear that the opposite is true of Ricoeur: though he does not endorse intratextuality in an *anti*foundationalist sense, as do many postliberals, Ricoeur explicitly insisted that, in Dan Stiver's words, "theology particularly should not be dominated by general hermeneutics, and sometimes the dominating influence would stream from theology."[69] Accordingly, Mark Wallace argues that Ricoeur and the Yale school are deeply compatible, and Boyd Blundell concludes that postliberals are actually the best candidates for appropriating Ricoeur's hermeneutics.[70] Furthermore, William Placher perceives that "perhaps Ricoeur's approach represents a theory sufficiently open and nuanced to overcome such objections [regarding general hermeneutics]."[71] Yet, Placher is ultimately concerned about the kind of reference that fills the void in lieu of a foundationalist theory of reference: "Ricoeur says that, since biblical narratives do not make historical claims and do not refer to the intention of their authors, their reference has to be to 'human experience,' to 'new possible modes of being-in-the-world' they open up for their readers."[72] For Placher, this is a critical theological shortcoming: "If—as Ricoeur sometimes proposes—the biblical narratives refer to our existence, then problems about how God acts or the historical reference of the Bible simply don't arise. Unfortunately, such a hermeneutic is finally inadequate to the meaning of the biblical texts. It fails to capture the sense in which the Bible offers us new possibilities for ourselves only on the basis of God's

---

67. Frei, "'Literal,'" 137.
68. Comstock, "Two," 688; see also Comstock, "Truth," 117–40.
69. Stiver, *Ricoeur*, 32. See esp. Ricoeur, "Philosophical," 14–33; Ricoeur, "Toward," 1–37.
70. Wallace, *Second*; Blundell, *Paul*.
71. Placher, "Paul," 42.
72. Placher, "Paul," 43.

prevenient action."[73] Wallace points out that this is not strictly true: "The problem is that Ricoeur appears to define the biblical world in three different ways: as human reality; as a new world or new covenant; and as God."[74] Regardless, the issue presently is not whether Ricoeur's understanding of textual reference was theological enough but what the debate reveals about the theological status of narrativity. Frei's tendency is to lump Ricoeur's understanding of textual reference under the heading "liberal" because the construction of "a general and inalienable human quality called 'narrative' or 'narrativity'"[75] is *a function of a general hermeneutic* that undermines the "literal reading," according to which "the direction in the flow of intratextual interpretation is that of absorbing the extratextual universe into the text, rather than the reverse (extratextual) direction."[76] But Placher's analysis reveals that the problem is actually theological, because the possibility of the intratextual universe absorbing the extratextual—in Ricoeurian terms, of the text opening up a new possible world—is *a function of an anthropology*. Stated generally, Frei's anthropological assumption is that human nature is such that the biblical narrative can absorb the reader's world. Placher clarifies that this possibility depends on God's prevenient grace, which is to say, not on a general human quality called *narrativity*.

I have taken this detour through a bygone debate because it is important to recognize that the unresolved "ambiguity of the phrase, 'to inhabit a narrative,' so central to narrative theology's interest in theological embodiment and performance"[77] is deeply connected to the insistence of certain narrative theologians that the literal reading *just does* function this way, as a matter of God's prevenient grace, which rules out that one should (or even could) say *how or why* a human being might be "absorbed by" or "inhabit" a narrative from an anthropological perspective. But this claim, too, represents a theological anthropology; it is a negative one in which divine prevenience precludes human capacity, despite the plausible claim that such capacity—namely, narrativity—might also be a gift of God. Such a claim is, in part, what my argument here is about, for which I find Ricoeur an exceedingly insightful (ad hoc!) conversation partner.

73. Placher, "Paul," 45.
74. Wallace, *Second*, 100.
75. Frei, "'Literal,'" 148.
76. Frei, "'Literal,'" 147.
77. Green, "Narrative," 532.

Notably, despite his rejection of narrativity, Hans Frei's Christology, focusing as it does on describing Jesus's unsubstitutable narrative identity, moves in an anthropological direction that reaches a denouement in the work of David Kelsey (who depends on Ricoeur), discussed below.[78] On another front, the ethics of Stanley Hauerwas has significant narrative dimensions, not least through its affinity with MacIntyre. Nonetheless, Hauerwas distanced himself from strong claims about narrative because, like other postliberals, he finds disturbing the notion that such claims are "trying to provide a theory about theology that is more determinative than first-order theological claims."[79] Given that even strong representatives of "narrative theology" are reticent about claiming too much, it is no surprise that despite the theoretical ubiquity of narrativity elsewhere, it remains a somewhat underdeveloped anthropological notion in contemporary theology. Where theological arguments regarding the narrative dimension of human nature do appear, they commonly stand in relation to an understanding of human embodiment. Four theologians—Robert Jenson, James McClendon, David Kelsey, and James K. A. Smith—are particularly noteworthy representatives of the conjunction of embodiment and narrativity in recent theology. I briefly consider each in order to sketch the conceptual limits of the discussion at present and prepare for a constructive argument that might more fully explain this aspect of participation in God's mission.

Embodiment and Narrativity in Recent Theology

Robert Jenson's Systematic Theology, vol. 2, The Works of God *(1999)*

The development of Jenson's thoughts on embodiment and relationality are straightforward. To begin, an irreducible characteristic of creatureliness is a material availability to others: "the body . . . is the person insofar as he or she is available to others."[80] He grounds this notion specifically in the creature's relation to God as the other: "If to be in the image of God is to be embodied before God, then to be specifically human is to be available to an

---

78. Frei, *Identity*. Ford, "What," 41–54, rightly says Kelsey's magnum opus *Eccentric Existence* "might be seen as the theological culmination of the Yale school."
79. Hauerwas, *Performing*, 136.
80. Jenson, *Works*, 60.

other."[81] Call this understanding *embodied relationality*. Next, Jenson argues phenomenologically that human self-transcendence is a function of this relationality, because "the structure of our mutuality is constitutive of my personhood."[82] Critically, however, since who I am is a function of "the story of my life," self-constituting mutuality is a narrative phenomenon: "Only in conversation do I occupy a position from which to interpret my life as a coherent whole, a position from which as a living subject I can anticipate the dead object I will be, and so from which I can grasp the identity of the I that does this with the life I remember."[83] That is to say, "the story of my life" is given to me through the mutuality of embodied relationality.

Further, the Triune God's personhood relating freely, opening communion to others, is what constitutes these others as personal. "Divine consciousness," Jenson states, "is focused because each of the persons God is has *dramatic location* in and by community with the others. And human consciousness is focused by its accommodation in this same mutuality.... Thus transcendental unity of apperception, wherever it occurs, is enabled by the triune life. And the unity of consciousness is therefore always a *narrative* unity. It has the integrity of a location within a story and is unitary because the story is coherent."[84] Though embodiment fades from view in the discussion of narrativity, it remains the working assumption: "the 'material' identity, the body, and this social identity are not really different things."[85] Ultimately, embodied relationality constitutes a narrative identity determined by its derivation from and coherence with the narrativity of the Triune life.

Although Jenson's account relates embodied narrativity to the Trinity in significant ways, he does so on a creational basis that ignores the distinctives of Christian participation. Indeed, humanity's "position within the Christological story" is a de facto reality regardless of one's awareness. This leaves numerous questions about what embodiment or narrativity might have to do with the church's participation in the divine life. At a minimum, however, Jenson establishes the conjunction of embodiment and the narrative self.

---

81. Jenson, *Works*, 64.
82. Jenson, *Works*, 74.
83. Jenson, *Works*, 75.
84. Jenson, *Works*, 98.
85. Jenson, *Works*, 104.

PARTICIPATION AS EMBODIED NARRATIVITY

James Wm. McClendon Jr.'s Ethics, *vol. 1 of* Systematic Theology *(rev. ed., 2002)*

Methodologically, McClendon's theology strikes narrative notes throughout. Though his discussion of human narrativity as such is limited, it sounds in concert with his discussion of embodiment. The third chapter of vol. 1, *Ethics*, begins with a discussion of "black religion as embodied ethics."[86] His defense of this idea concludes:

> Blacks learned in their understanding of the Jesus story to see that what they endured was not meaningless, but that by each son and daughter of them it could be said, "In my flesh *I complete what is lacking in Christ's afflictions* for the sake of his body, that is, the church, of which I became a minister" (Col. 1:24–25a). So encounter two necessary aspects of the black gospel: that it is irreducibly narrative in form, and that, as has been earlier implied (Chapter One), in it the baptist vision appears again—the story *now* echoes the story *then*, is the story then.[87]

The embodied, narrative ethics of the black church is paradigmatic for McClendon. "Concretely," he asks, "what focus will do justice to the Christian stories such as that of the black church—or to the whole Christian story, of which theirs is so poignant a part? The proposal here is that Christian ethics focus first on the *embodied selfhood* of the human species, seeking to understand our bodily nature both as the consequences of the natural history of *homo sapiens* (that is our link to the environment to its far limits) *and* as the locus of an interiority of shame, delight, guilt, and virtue with strong links to the narrative tradition of Christian faith."[88] In what sense, then, does he understand the conjunction of embodied selfhood and the "narrative tradition"?

The answer is found in the last chapter of *Ethics*, where McClendon explicates his view of narrativity:

> My suggestion is that what literary critics refer to understand the shorthand emblem of "character" is very close . . . to what ethics must address in its first strand, the witness of embodied selfhood (Chapter Three). Ethics' emphasis is a bit different from the critics', they emphasizing the *self* in its embodiment, we the *embodiment*

---

86. McClendon, *Ethics*, 86.
87. McClendon, *Ethics*, 90.
88. McClendon, *Ethics*, 94.

of such as self; but their "character" is nothing without (real or fictive) embodiment, and our "body" is nothing without the actual self thus made incarnate. It is the self in its continuity that is "embodied"; and it is the continuities of selfhood that both ethicists ... and literary critics understand as "character."[89]

Ethically, then, character is "the persistent qualities of my selfhood."[90] As with Jenson, the conjunction of embodiment and narrativity is essential. Moreover, the biblical narrative that Christians "enter" must be "real," and this is the narrative of the bodily resurrection of Christ.[91] While the meaning of embodied narrativity calls for the Trinitarian rationale that Jenson has signaled, McClendon adds a vital dimension with his discussion of character: the embodied self is determined by narrative continuity.

David H. Kelsey's Eccentric Existence: A Theological Anthropology *(2009)*

Kelsey's magnum opus *Eccentric Existence* engages the conjunction of embodiment and narrativity with a breadth of conceptualization surpassing the other authors considered so far. Like McClendon, his method is narrative, though more rigorously. Like Jenson, he portrays human identity in terms of narrative relationship to the Triune God, though more completely. To these, he adds Ricoeur's anthropology.

To hazard a summary, Kelsey's controlling idea is that Christian theological anthropology must be centered in the Triune God whom we know according to three irreducibly differentiated narratives of relationship with humankind: the Triune God relating to create, the Triune God relating to consummate eschatologically, and the Triune God relating to reconcile the estranged.[92] Accordingly, "no single monolithic story can be told about God's relating to us. God's mystery eludes that, which means that there can be no single monolithic theological story to tell about what and who we are and how we ought to be. If the ways in which God relates are irreducibly threefold, theocentric accounts of human persons will be irreducibly threefold. There is no single, simple Christian metanarrative."[93] This point

---

89. McClendon, *Ethics*, 329.
90. McClendon, *Ethics*, 351.
91. McClendon, *Witness*, 357.
92. For the material condensed here, see Kelsey, *Eccentric*, esp. ch. 1:3A.
93. Kelsey, *Eccentric*, 1:130–31.

of departure establishes the complexly relational, Trinitarian, and narrative basis of humanity's "eccentric existence."[94]

In connection with the Triune God relating to create, Kelsey explores "our having been born as living human bodies."[95] From this, he derives a variety of conclusions, but the important point for my purposes arises in his pivot from "living human bodies" to "personal living bodies."[96] Kelsey takes the phrase "personal body" from Ricoeur, more on which below. For now, suffice it to note the theological deployment of the term: "Personal bodies are called 'personal' because of a distinctive way in which God relates to them, not because of the ways in which they relate to God."[97] This is a body constituted as personal by Triune relationality alone. Kelsey insists, "The creatures to which God relates in this distinctive way are, *for that reason and no other*, 'personal bodies.' As a kind of shorthand expression, 'personal bodies' may then be called 'persons,' but being 'a person' is not a function of any particular human power or set of them."[98] This is a reiteration of the point that human existence is eccentric, centered relationally in the Triune narratives—in this case, the story of God relating to create. The givenness of the personal body in both its personhood and its embodiment is a function of narrative eccentricity.

Further, personal "identity" obtains in the same way: "Answers to 'Who?' questions that are deemed maximally adequate to precisely personal (or communal) identity are normally given in selected types of stories about the personal bodies or communities of personal bodies in question."[99] This is because stories both "describe a particular pattern of intentional actions done and undergone by the subject of the 'Who?' question" and "express the subject of a 'Who?' question, not at a particularly

---

94. Questions about the consequences of his intransigent separation of the three Trinitarian narratives need not delay us long. In my view, Pickstock, "One," 38, has the right of it in principle: "There is only one Christian story. In denying this, Kelsey denies the unity of the Trinity and the *communicatio idiomatum* in the God-Man." Yet, it remains to be seen whether—given that Kelsey does not deny the unity of the Trinity—his dismissal of the one story is as total as his rhetoric suggests. In any case, Pickstock's insight is correct: the unity of the Triune narrative is the unity of the Trinity. To this can be added Kelsey's insights about human narrativity even if his own conception of divine narrative unity comes up short. See also Lett, "Narrative," 618–39.

95. Kelsey, *Eccentric*, 1:250.

96. Kelsey, *Eccentric*, 1:286.

97. Kelsey, *Eccentric*, 1:291–92.

98. Kelsey, *Eccentric*, 1:292.

99. Kelsey, *Eccentric*, 1:334.

characteristic moment of interaction, but as she or it persists through change across time."[100] Once more, Kelsey emphasizes that "human persons' identities are given them by God and are not achievements constructed by their own effort, not even their efforts to respond appropriately to God."[101] One begins to wonder what might be the role of human agency beyond receiving the gift and, specifically, what Kelsey's answer means for participation in God's mission. If the relationship between embodiment and narrativity screens out participation—if the human's narrative relationship to God is one-directional—then my argument in this chapter encounters a conceptual barrier. In fact, however, despite his stark theocentricity, Kelsey does understand the role of human agency in terms that add to the conception of embodied narrativity: intention and interpretation. He explains: "A human creature's personal identity is the integrally dynamic singularity of his intentional actions and interactions with other human creatures in their shared proximate contexts and his way of interpreting the significance of what befalls him and of relating to it. . . . His identity lies in the sequence of these dynamic intentional interactions and events of interpretation that cumulatively are integral to one singular life."[102] This is one's "quotidian" identity formed in proximate contexts, over against one's "basic identity" formed in the ultimate context of the Triune narratives.[103] The critical issue, therefore, is the extent to which intention and interpretation play a role in the congruence of one's quotidian embodied narrative identity and one's ultimate embodied narrative identity.

How, then, does the quotidian relate to the ultimate? All three of the Triune narratives seem, for Kelsey, to relate especially to interpretation. Of particular interest is Kelsey's discussion of the third narrative: "The triune God relating to draw estranged living human personal bodies to reconciliation defines their basic identity. . . . The answer to the question about who they are is, 'As those who are structurally reconciled with God "in Christ," we are those who have their personal identities "in" Christ's identity, as the plot or narrative logic of God's relating to reconcile us by way of Incarnation becomes the plot or narrative logic of the dynamic of our own singular identities.'" But how does this basic narrative logic "become" the identity of

---

100. Kelsey, *Eccentric*, 1:334–35.
101. Kelsey, *Eccentric*, 1:339.
102. Kelsey, *Eccentric*, 1:379.
103. Kelsey, *Eccentric*, 1:381–82.

those "in Christ"? Certainly, it is "God's gift."[104] Yet, it is also a function of interpretation or "acknowledgment" that entails intention or "living": "The concrete quotidian identity is 'who' acknowledges its own basic identity by living in congruence with it. The human creature's quotidian identity is not replaced by its basic identity. Rather its quotidian identity is taken up into its basic identity and, across time, is shaped by it."[105] One's personal embodied identity may be found in Christ

> to the extent that the pattern of the movement of the sequence of acts, interactions, and so on, that constitute the lives in which they have those identities begin to be shaped by the narrative logic of the life in which Jesus has his personal identity. When that happens, the personal identities that participate in Jesus' identity are identities that coincide with rather than living at cross-grain to, at least one aspect of their basic identity—namely the aspect constituted by the triune God relating to them to reconcile them by way of incarnation to God when they are estranged from God.[106]

This imitative logic does not prevent Kelsey from asserting that being in Christ "has the ontological status of actuality, not ideality."[107] In regard to the Triune life, God relating to humans in this way has the effect of "drawing us into the pattern of [Christ's] relation to the Father, making the condition he is in by his relation to the Father our condition also."[108] I will return to the implications of this construal of narrative-relational interchange after developing my own understanding of embodied narrativity. For now, it is enough to establish the extent to which, for Kelsey, embodied narrativity is the paradigm of human participation in the Triune life.

James K. A. Smith's Imagining the Kingdom: How Worship Works *(2013)*

No contemporary work has addressed embodied narrativity more overtly than James K. A. Smith's series Cultural Liturgies, which develops what Smith calls a "liturgical anthropology." Its second volume, *Imagining the*

---

104. Kelsey, *Eccentric*, 1:384.

105. Kelsey, *Eccentric*, 1:385. Note that "taken up" echoes the standard narrative theological notion of being absorbed by the biblical narrative.

106. Kelsey, *Eccentric*, 1:390; see also Kelsey, *Eccentric*, 2:695–703.

107. Kelsey, *Eccentric*, 1:384.

108. Kelsey, *Eccentric*, 1:695.

Kingdom, gives special attention to "the nexus of body and story."[109] A part of his larger project "to situate theoretical reflection within the wider purview of our fundamental pretheoretical orientation to the world," he identifies the volume's focus as "further exploring the shape of a liturgical anthropology in order to articulate a Christian philosophy of action that (1) recognizes the nonconscious, pretheoretical 'drivers' of our action and behavior, centered in what I'll call the imagination; (2) accounts for the bodily formation of our habituated orientation to the world; and thus (3) appreciates the centrality of story as rooted in this 'bodily basis of meaning' and as a kind of pretheoretical compass that guides and generates human action."[110] Methodologically, Smith proceeds in a way similar to my own argument below, reflecting theologically in conversation with philosophical anthropology (Maurice Merleau-Ponty and Paul Ricoeur, among others). And, like my larger thesis, Smith takes the ultimate question to be one of formation, specifically for participation in the *missio Dei*.[111]

Smith echoes narrative theology in his frequent reference to "having absorbed, and been absorbed into" lived narratives.[112] Because of embodied narrativity, he argues that this absorption happens principally through liturgy:

> Liturgies are formative because—and just to the extent that—they tap into our imaginative core. As compressed narratives and tactile poems, the formative power of liturgies (whether secular or sacred) is bound up with their aesthetic force. Such liturgies are pedagogies of desire that shape our love because they picture the good life for us in ways that resonate with our imaginative nature.... We are conscripted into a Story through those practices that enact and perform and embody a Story about the good life.... We are incorporated into a social body when the stories of a people become the dominant landscape of our imaginative background—when those stories have worked their way into our "practical sense" in such a way that they now (automatically) govern how we perceive the world. In other words, this is how we "become native": because

---

109. Smith, *Imagining*, 108.
110. Smith, *Imagining*, 12–14.
111. Smith, *Imagining*, 156.
112. Smith, *Imagining*, 92. See key usages, e.g., on pp. 32, 53, 81, 96, 105, 109, 127, 134, 153, 165, 178, 181. *Absorb* is Smith's preferred term for the "aesthetic alchemy" through which "liturgies implant in us a vision for a world and way of life that attracts us" (137).

"nativity" is absorbed at the level of affect, on an aesthetic register. This is how worship works.[113]

In distinction from my argument, Smith understands liturgy or "worship" to be a formative process that leads linearly to participation in mission as a separate matter. His fundamental insight is that through embodied narrativity, "worship and the practices of Christian formation are first and foremost the way the Spirit invites us into union with the Triune God."[114] Yet, positioning mission as "the end or *telos* of Christian worship"—"worship *for* mission"—obscures the sense in which mission is itself participation in the Triune life of God and, therefore, is itself formative.[115] Nonetheless, Smith's account of embodied narrativity substantiates the anthropological insights that the present argument seeks to deploy. Considering participation in the life of God and its formative effects, embodiment and narrativity are, together, indispensable anthropological concerns.

This review of embodied narrativity in recent theology, though partial, represents the state of the discussion. On the one hand, the conjunction of embodiment and narrativity is, to a great extent, a given. On the other hand, the theological paradigms of their conjunction are by no means fully concordant. The hazy vision of embodied relationality, narrative identity, and participation in the Triune life that emerges from these overlapping accounts needs clarification. In the section that follows, I propose an understanding of embodied narrativity that, in relation to the conception of *theōsis* developed in the previous chapter, makes further sense of participation in God's mission. In a variety of ways, I follow the lead of the authors reviewed above, but my primary interlocutors are Paul Ricoeur and Jürgen Moltmann. A word more on methodology is due.

I take it that the existence of the dimensions of human nature here called embodiment and narrativity, each of which has been identified in diverse disciplinary fields, is established. The type of constructive anthropology I

---

113. Smith, *Imagining*, 137.

114. Smith, *Imagining*, 152.

115. Smith, *Imagining*, 153–54. This construal seems to be a symptom of Smith's understanding of mission not as participation in the Triune life but as "what it is for Christian to pursue their vocations to the glory of God and in ways that are oriented to the shalom of the kingdom." The aim of my critique is not to deny that "any missional, formative Christian institution that is bent on sending out *actors*—agents of reformation and renewal—will need to attend to the reformation of our *habitus*" (157), but to highlight the extent to which mission just is the formative, participatory practice that liturgy rehearses.

am engaged in here, like Smith's, assumes that when it comes to the human dimensions of participation, philosophy may offer genuine insights. The question, then, is whose account offers the best insight. Further, whose account combines the two in a way that might help us understand the human relation to the divine life? I engage Paul Ricoeur because he uniquely offers such insight—as numerous authors' use of his work already suggests. Ricoeur develops a robust philosophical anthropology that holds embodiment and narrativity together.[116] Moreover, his renowned work in textual hermeneutics allows me to extend these insights in the hermeneutical direction toward which my argument is bound. Finally, his understanding of embodied narrativity has an exceptional resonance with Moltmann's work on *perichōrēsis*. As I have shown, other theologians fruitfully relate embodied narrativity to participation in the divine life. But the synergy between Ricoeur and Moltmann proves useful for explaining participation in God's mission and, in turn, its hermeneutically formative effects.

Toward a Theology of Embodied Narrativity

Paul Ricoeur on Embodied Narrativity

To begin, I take a working conception of embodied narrativity from Paul Ricoeur's *Oneself as Another*. One of the greatest virtues of Ricoeur's exposition of narrative identity is that it serves to bridge the gap between two philosophical accounts of human identity, one in the tradition of René Descartes's subjective rationalism and the other in the tradition of John Locke and David Hume's objective empiricism. Onto these traditions, one can generally map the anthropological tendencies toward either radical body-soul dualism that prioritizes the soul (i.e., mind) or radical naturalism that reduces the person to the physical body.[117] Working in the Continental tradition of philosophy, Ricoeur spent much of his career interacting with

---

116. For recent but more limited explorations of the topic, see Menary, "Embodied," 63–84; Turner, "Individuality," 808–31; Mackenzie, "Embodied," 154–71.

117. Indeed, Ricoeur's work ultimately grapples with both of the dualisms critiqued above, construing their components in terms of a third, more essential dualism to be overcome: body-narrative. I've noted that Kärkkäinen and Sigurdson already gesture toward the ultimacy of narrative identity in relation to the story of God. Ricoeur's understanding of embodied narrativity establishes a philosophical basis for holding body, soul (mind), and social construction together in a holistic conception of the human self that integrally relates to God's story.

Descartes, unwilling to surrender the theme of selfhood to a physicalist reduction of the person. Yet, even Ricoeur's first major monograph, *Freedom and Nature: The Voluntary and the Involuntary* (1950), is at once a phenomenological description of "the Cogito" and a meditation on Gabriel Marcel's "rediscovery of incarnation."[118] Though the vast middle section of Ricoeur's work focused on the linguistic turn and hermeneutical theory, *Oneself as Another* (1990) is a return to the dialectic of selfhood and body, now with the insights of linguistics and narrative theory in hand. Thus, whereas for Descartes, "what tradition calls a soul is actually a *subject*, and this subject can be reduced to the simplest and barest act, the act of thinking,"[119] for Ricoeur, "the person cannot be held to be a pure consciousness to which would then be added, in a secondary role, a body, as is the case in all mind-body dualisms."[120] The problematic this position establishes, however, is precisely the self-body dialectic: "If it is true ... that the concept of person is a notion no less primitive than that of the body, this is to evoke not a second referent, distinct from body, such as the Cartesian soul, but ... a single referent possessing two series of predicates: physical predicates and mental predicates."[121] That is, this ascription of both sets of predicates to a single agent is rooted in the fact that "persons are bodies as well."[122]

Ricoeur, therefore, sets out to mediate between two poles of personal identity, which he characterizes as selfhood and sameness, or *ipse* and *idem*. On the pole of selfhood lie mental predicates, consciousness as a private entity, the subject of a body, the intentional motive of an agent, and ultimately the self-attestation of identity. On the pole of sameness lie physical predicates, the person as a public entity, the body as a fact in the world, the passivity and dispositions of an agent, and ultimately the reidentifiability of the human person. Selfhood-identity and sameness-identity overlap without complete coincidence. Selfhood also has an internal polarity: self-constancy and character. Whereas self-constancy is "faithfulness to oneself in keeping one's word,"[123] character comprises the "lasting dispositions by

118. Ricoeur, *Freedom*, 15. It is also noteworthy that Ricoeur saw this work as extending Merleau-Ponty's *Phenomenology*, with its stress on embodiment.

119. Ricoeur, *Freedom*, 8.

120. Ricoeur, *Oneself*, 34. See also the argument throughout *Freedom*, summarized by the formula "the voluntary is *by reason of* the involuntary while the involuntary is *for* the voluntary" in Kohák, translator's introduction to Paul Ricoeur, *Freedom*, xix.

121. Ricoeur, *Oneself*, 33.

122. Ricoeur, *Oneself*, 66.

123. Ricoeur, *Oneself*, 118; see also 123.

which a person is recognized," such as habits and "acquired identifications" (e.g., values).[124] Thus, character exists in the overlap of selfhood and sameness. Figure 1 represents this relationship:

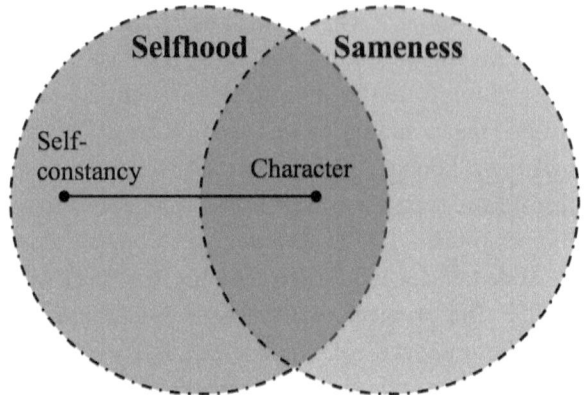

Figure 1: The Selfhood-Sameness Dialectic

Self-constancy (keeping one's word through time) and character (lasting dispositions acquired through time) are both "models of permanence in time," possessing thereby the quality of narrative. "Temporality," in other words, is the critical link to the notion of narrative identity.[125]

Ricoeur discusses the possibility and meaningfulness of accounting for the historical (i.e., temporal) nature of human life in this way as "intuitive apprehension," "preunderstanding," and "precomprehension."[126] Thus, following Wilhelm Dilthey's "spontaneous" apprehension that "the connectedness of life" is "equivalent to the concept of a life history," Ricoeur concludes: "It is this preunderstanding of the historical significance of connectedness that the narrative theory of personal identity attempts to articulate, at a higher level of conceptuality."[127] Similarly, literary narratology provides a "model of intelligibility" for human identity because "narrative is part of life before being exiled from life in writing."[128] The insights of narrative literary analysis serve anthropology because narrative

---

124. Ricoeur, *Oneself*, 121.

125. Ricoeur, *Oneself*, 124. The concept first emerged in *Time*, 3:244–49, wherein attention focused on narrative in historiography and literature.

126. Ricoeur, *Oneself*, 114, 141, 144, 145.

127. Ricoeur, *Oneself*, 141.

128. Ricoeur, *Oneself*, 162, 163.

literature is a derivative rendering of human life, which is always already an emplotted, historical "configuration."[129]

These observations about the relationship between narratology and narrative identity are important for my purposes because of their connection with embodiment. Ricoeur rejects the "puzzling cases" of science fiction in which brain-in-a-vat-type scenarios lend credence to a disembodied, neurological, reductive physicalism.[130] Accordingly, "literary fictions differ fundamentally from technological fictions in that they remain imaginative variations on an invariant, our corporeal condition experienced as the existential mediation between the self and the world. . . . What the puzzling cases render radically contingent is this corporeal and terrestrial condition which the hermeneutics of existence, underlying the notion of acting and suffering, takes to be insurmountable."[131] For Ricoeur, the body is an ontological given; therefore, what is inscribed in narrative fiction is none other than the emplotted, historical configuration of embodied human life. Narrativity is ineluctably incarnate.

Borrowing from narratology, then, Ricoeur grafts personal identity onto the concept of the character of a story:

> The decisive step in the direction of a narrative conception of personal identity is taken when one passes from the action to the character. A character is the one who performs the action in the narrative. The category of character is therefore a narrative category as well, and its role in the narrative involves the same narrative understanding as the plot itself. The question is then to determine what the narrative category of character contributes to the discussion of personal identity. The thesis supported here will be that the identity of the character is comprehensible through the transfer to the character of the operation of emplotment, first applied to the action recounted; characters, we will say, are themselves plots. . . .
>
> It is indeed in the story recounted with its qualities of unity, internal structure, and completeness which are conferred by emplotment, that the character preserves throughout the story an identity correlative to that of the story itself.[132]

The character's identity just is the temporal configuration of actions and intentions.

129. Ricoeur, *Oneself*, 141.
130. Ricoeur, *Oneself*, 129–39.
131. Ricoeur, *Oneself*, 150.
132. Ricoeur, *Oneself*, 143.

Finally, this narrativity has the shape of a "hierarchy of units of praxis" that includes (1) "practices," (2) "life plans," and (3) "the narrative unity of life," "narrative program," "life project," or "life story."[133] By examining the praxeological nature of narrativity, Ricoeur highlights two vital points. One, the historical actions configured in narration are embodied practices all the way down. Two, emplotment is teleological. Drawing together Ricoeur's insights, I suggest that narrative identity is *the ineluctably embodied history of the teleological self*. This, in short, is embodied narrativity. But this is a philosophical claim. To capture the theological vision of embodied narrativity that can help explain participation in God's mission, I turn to the theological anthropology of Moltmann.

Jürgen Moltmann: Perichoretic Participation in the History of God

Recourse to Moltmann reorients the discussion toward the inevitable topos of Christian theological anthropology: the *imago Dei*. His anthropology attends especially to the Trinity and Christology. By comparison, mission is a minor theme for Moltmann, though his anthropology does land in a missional posture of participation. What follows is an appropriation of key insights from Moltmann's expansive work, grafted onto Ricoeur's anthropology so as to substantiate embodied narrativity theologically in terms of perichoretic participation in the divine story. The result is a vision of embodied narrativity that extends the notion of *theōsis* as participation in the *missio Dei*.

Gestalt *as Emplotment*

The lynchpin that links Moltmann's anthropology to a Ricoeurian conception of embodied narrativity is the notion of the Gestalt, which Moltmann uses to describe the "perichoretic pattern of body and soul" in his discussion of embodiment.[134] He develops a threefold extension of Trinitarian *perichōrēsis* that includes (1) the relationship of God and world as perichoretic, (2) the human *imago Trinitatis* as communities of difference in perichoretic fellowship, and (3) the holistic relationship of body and soul as perichoretic. The last is in focus here, though it is important to note that

---

133. Ricoeur, *Oneself*, 153–63. He takes "narrative unity of life" from MacIntyre.
134. Moltmann, *God*, 258.

discussing these separately is a heuristic move, because they are ultimately an integrated human reality. Moltmann writes:

> We shall therefore view the relationship between soul and body, the conscious and the unconscious, the voluntary and the involuntary, or however this fundamental anthropological differentiation may be defined, as a *perichoretic* relationship of mutual interpenetration and differentiated unity; but we shall not introduce one-sided structures of domination into it. We are neither starting from the assumption of a primacy of the soul, nor assuming a primacy of the body. We are looking at the *Gestalt*—the configuration or total pattern—of the life lived. This supposes theologically that the presence of God in the Spirit is not localized solely in the consciousness or in the soul, or in the subjectivity of reason and will; but that its place is the whole human organism—that historical Gestalt which people, body and soul, develop in their environment.[135]

The Gestalt has two primary "fields": "'human being—environment' and 'body—soul.'"[136] That is to say, the "configuration" of body and soul is inextricably correlative to the environment, which has already been characterized in terms of both perichoretic human community and creation perichoretically related to the Spirit of God.[137] Hence, the configuration

---

135. Moltmann, *God*, 259.

136. Moltmann, *God*, 261.

137. Since Moltmann refers to the "soul," it is necessary to reiterate my affirmation of multidimensional monism. His argument describes the unity of body and soul, and multidimensional monism allows for the identification of distinguishable aspects of human nature without falling into dualism, so it seems feasible to use Moltmann in my argument without fear of an incompatible notion of embodiment creeping in. Admittedly, however, one wonders what, for Moltmann, the "soul" dimension ultimately is. In the attempt to map Moltmann onto my controlling, Ricoeurian notion of embodied narrativity, my interest is the unity of the bodily and narratival dimensions of human life in missional *perichōrēsis*. In this sense, I take it *soul* refers, for Moltmann, to the narrative self, ontologically inextricable from bodily sameness but distinguishable in the abstract. Finally, because the accent of Moltmann's theological anthropology falls on narrativity, embodiment seems to fade from view in the following discussion. Having affirmed the unity of embodiment and narrativity, however, for my argument this means the embodiment dimension in the abstract—not embodiment itself—is out of view. Indeed, the point is that because of the unity of embodiment and narrativity, there is no accounting for how a body participates perichoretically in God's mission except in terms of narrativity. The one just is the explanation of the other, because there is no such thing as disembodied narrativity.

of the life lived is a *historical* life lived *in community and in creation*—the "whole and particular bodily existence."[138]

The point of contact with Ricoeur is more than the strikingly Ricoeurian phrase "the voluntary and the involuntary," though the shared refusal to reduce selfhood to sameness or vice versa (as Ricoeur might put it) is significant. I see consonance between the "configuration" of Moltmann's Gestalt and the "configuration" of Ricoeur's emplotment. Both are attuned to the historicity of lived life as that which patterns the relationship of selfhood and sameness. The consonance is more evident when Moltmann clarifies that the way a continuously changing Gestalt becomes an identity is through promise: "In his promise, a person commits himself, acquires a particular Gestalt, and makes himself someone who can be appealed to. Through faithfulness the person acquires his identity in time. . . . The identity of the person in his life-history is denoted through his *name*. . . . The process whereby a person becomes a configuration or Gestalt is both inwardly and outwardly to be seen as a process of dependability and faithfulness."[139] Ricoeur likewise sees emplotment as the mediation between the self that promises and the public identity (identifiable by name) of the person on whom others depend. Moltmann's notion of combined dependability and faithfulness is represented by Ricoeur's term, *responsibility*, which "unites both meanings: 'counting on' and 'being accountable for.'"[140] Furthermore, as with Moltmann's Gestalt, Ricoeur indicates that when one's identity varies through changes in character (variations of sameness), it is the narrativity of human identity that maintains the unstable character's relationship with the self-constancy of the self who promises. One can still tell the story of that change as a narrative of the self. In Moltmann's terms, it is a historical configuration; in Ricoeur's, it is an emplotted life history.

Conformity to the Gestalt of Christ as Renarration

Moltmann's layering of *perichōrēsis*, therefore, allows us to see the perichoretic pattern of embodied narrativity in an environment that is creation already in perichoretic relationship with the Spirit:

---

138. Moltmann, *God*, 245.
139. Moltmann, *God*, 262.
140. Ricoeur, *Oneself*, 165.

PARTICIPATION AS EMBODIED NARRATIVITY

> The human being's soul—his feelings, ideas, intentions, and so forth—is a soul that is pervaded, quickened and formed by the creative Spirit: the human being is *spirit-soul*. The Gestalt of the human being, in which the body and soul have become united, is a Gestalt formed by the creative Spirit: the human being is *spirit-Gestalt*. But the Spirit whose efficacy forms body, soul and their living Gestalt is not merely the creative Spirit: he is at the same time the cosmic Spirit: for body, soul and their Gestalt can only exist in exchange with other living beings in nature and in human society.[141]

The inextricable pattern of soul and body is related inextricably as a whole to the creation (and the community) of which it is a part, to which the Spirit also relates perichoretically. This is already a basic vision of embodied narrativity as participation in God, but Moltmann carries it further. When the Spirit of creation becomes the redeeming and sanctifying Holy Spirit, "he lays hold of the whole human being, embracing his feelings and his body as well as his soul and his reason. He forms the whole Gestalt of the person anew by making believers 'con-form,' or 'like-in-Gestalt' to Christ."[142] A great deal is packed into the suggestion that the human being is capable, by the Spirit, of conforming to the Gestalt of Christ. The leading implication, of course, is that Jesus of Nazareth, truly God and truly human, has an embodied narrative identity like all humans. Moreover, participation in God from the perspective of embodied narrativity is somehow a matter of being renarrated by the Holy Spirit according to a narrative that is not one's own. This leads me to highlight the way Moltmann discusses the *imago Christi*.

The *imago Christi* is "an *imago Dei* mediated through Christ," as "the human being has been created 'in the direction of' the image of God which Christ is."[143] For this reason, the *imago Christi* is "the messianic calling of human beings," the eschatological culmination of a "historical process."[144] Moltmann summarizes his understanding in terms of *theōsis*:

> Participation in the divine nature and conformity to God, flowering into perfect resemblance, are the marks of the promised glorification of human beings. The God-likeness that belongs to creation in the beginning becomes God-sonship and daughterhood in the messianic fellowship with the Son, and out of the two springs the transfiguration of human beings in the glory of new

---

141. Moltmann, *God*, 263.
142. Moltmann, *God*, 264.
143. Moltmann, *God*, 218.
144. Moltmann, *God*, 225, 227.

creation. The image of God always corresponds precisely to the presence of God in the world, for it represents that presence. Consequently it is never fixed, once and for all, but is transformed, *in correspondence with the history of God's presence in the world.*[145]

The combination of two key ideas—calling in the direction of the *imago Christi* as a historical process and the *imago Christi* as the history of God's presence in the world—brings greater clarity to the notion of conformity to the Gestalt of Christ. Taking Gestalt narratively as the emplotment of a life history, the *imago Christi* is the life history of the Son of God incarnate—a historical configuration of embodied narrativity.[146] Conformity to the image of God is, correspondingly, a historical process of emplotment. Furthermore, "through the Son the divine Trinity throws itself open for human beings."[147] This process of emplotment according to the *imago Christi* is participation in the life of the Triune God. There is a certain slippage here, between *conformity* and *participation*, which requires more reflection. Nonetheless, Moltmann has thickened the concept of participation as embodied narrativity considerably by construing the Gestalt of Christ as historically and, therefore, narratively open human involvement.

Participation in the Open History of the Promising God

Returning to the discussion of the spirit-Gestalt, another coincidence appears. Moltmann describes the "anticipatory structure" of the person: "People always live in a certain direction." Like Ricoeur, he sees this teleological orientation as a mediation of two poles, which Moltmann calls "subjectivity and objectivity": "This subjectivity and objectivity are secondary forms of reflection in the totality of his lived life. This totality shows itself in his alignment towards *the project* of his life. As a totality, a whole, concentrated in himself and yet at the same time open, the human being lives in the project of his future." In relation to the Gestalt, therefore, "what people seek for, and their aim, is always reflected in the structure of their lives. The *history* of their lives takes its impress from what they *expect* of

---

145. Moltmann, *God*, 229; emphasis added.

146. "The history of Christ," "the history of the Spirit," and "the trinitarian history of God" are important themes in ch. 2 of Moltmann, *Church*, which I will discuss further below.

147. Moltmann, *God*, 243.

life."[148] This language resonates with Ricoeur's understanding of "narrativizing the aim of the true life."[149] The plot of embodied narrativity is always teleological—the configuration is governed by an aim, which is reflected in the hierarchy of praxis that comprises the "narrative program" and "life project" that a person is. In light of Moltmann's claim that humans live "in the direction of" the *imago Christi*, these coincidences of anthropological description become a fuller conception of embodied narrative participation in Christ. A twofold plot structure emerges. On the one hand, the vocation and process of conforming to the embodied narrativity of Jesus *is* the plot of a life renarrated by the Holy Spirit; participation itself is the *telos*. On the other hand, Jesus's own life project has an aim,[150] which a life conformed to the *imago Christi* comes to share.

The notion of sharing the aim of Jesus brings us close to participation in God's mission. In this sense, the throwing open of the Trinity through the Son casts participation in the historical terms of Jesus's embodied narrativity as a revelation of God's own life project. Indeed, Moltmann retrospectively characterizes the well-known eschatological bent of his theology as the "logic of promise."[151] The language is striking in comparison with his anthropological discussion of the role of promise in the acquisition of a Gestalt—and all the more so when he says, "The God who makes himself dependable through his covenant promises is fundamentally differentiated from the moods or caprice of other gods or forces of destiny. His essential nature is his faithfulness. His name is his identity, which is manifested in historical continuity."[152] The analogy with the dialectic of human faithfulness and dependability discussed above would seem to break down were it not for the incarnation of the Son, in whom the *telos* of "the trinitarian history of God"[153] comes to expression in the emplotment of human embodied narrativity.

Moltmann's theology makes evident that the "future of Christ" called the kingdom of God—the aim of Jesus's life project—is *God's future* made

---

148. Moltmann, *God*, 265.

149. Ricoeur, *Oneself*, 166.

150. Moltmann, *Church*, 29–37, refers to the "teleological interpretation of the history of Christ."

151. Moltmann, *Experiences*, 87–113.

152. Moltmann, *Experiences*, 97.

153. See Moltmann, *Church*, 52; Moltmann, *Trinity*, 90.

present by the promise of God.¹⁵⁴ "But God's promises must be understood historically not merely because they were uttered in history, and must ever and again be interpreted afresh in history, but also because they *throw open* a particular history. For the people who are concerned and who trust them, they throw open history in the possibilities of the promising God."¹⁵⁵ The particular history thrown open by the promises of God is the Triune life thrown open by the embodied narrativity of Jesus.¹⁵⁶ "As the one who will come, Christ is present now in his word and Spirit. In the present promise, the future is made present." Participation in Christ as sharing of the aim of Jesus's life project and as renarration according to the plot of Jesus's life story is a present participation in the future of God, made present by the "*pro-missio*" of the kingdom in the word and Spirit of Jesus.¹⁵⁷ Accordingly, missional participation is christologically, pneumatologically, and biblically delimited as "the eschatological becoming-one-with-God of human beings (*theosis*)" in which "participation in the divine nature and conformity to God, flowering into perfect resemblance, are the marks of the promised glorification of human beings."¹⁵⁸ By definition, this embodied-narrative becoming or flowering is a process of partial conformity, marked by both human failure and eschatological incompletion. It is no less, for that, a process in which both sharing the aim of Jesus's life project and renarration according to the plot of Jesus's life story are criteria by which the church must judge the authenticity of its embodied-narrative participation in God's mission.

Returning to Sigurdson's eschatological horizon of the body, whose narrative continuity was left shrouded in mystery by an overemphasis on the not-yet, I note that eschatological incompletion is part of the picture Moltmann helps us paint. But the accent falls—correctly, in my view—on the significance of present participation in the future of God for understanding embodied narrativity. Adding Ricoeur's incarnate narrativity to the picture reveals the extent to which the narrative continuity of the self beyond the eschatological horizon already manifest in present

154. Moltmann, *Experiences*, 98–102.

155. Moltmann, *Experiences*, 99.

156. For a fuller exposition of the throwing open of the Trinity as the throwing open of the history of God through the Son and the Spirit, see Moltmann, *Trinity*, 74–75, 88–90, 121–22.

157. Moltmann, *Experiences*, 102.

158. Moltmann, *God*, 229.

PARTICIPATION AS EMBODIED NARRATIVITY

participation in the story of God's future is necessarily an embodied continuity. This insight does not answer questions whose resolution awaits eschatological completion, such as the status of gender or sexuality beyond that horizon, but it does locate those bodily matters in the particular history thrown open in Jesus's embodied narrativity.

Embodied Narrativity and the Spiritual Hermeneutic of Scripture

The final turn in this exploration of Moltmann is a hermeneutic one, which is fitting given the textual medium of our encounter with the embodied narrativity of Jesus and the historicity of God's promise. The question remaining is how the narrative of Scripture functions in participation. In the context of the present discussion, it is necessary to ask about the role of Scripture in the Spirit's work of renarration or about the relation between the Spirit and the word of promise that comes through Scripture. In this relationship, I suspect, is the explanation of the slippage between conformity and participation. Whereas the embodied narrativity and aim of Jesus are inscribed in the narrative, rendering his Gestalt—and that of the history of promise thrown open in him—available for a conformity of mimetic participation, the Spirit remains the agent of the perichoretic relationship that finally constitutes the Gestalt of conformity to the image of Christ.

Thus, Moltmann acknowledges two sides of the narrative's function: on one side, it narrates the relationships of the Trinity in history; on the other, it functions "*in the trinitarian history of God*."[159] In other words, Scripture renders an emplotment of the Trinitarian history of God, but that rendering happens properly for a reader who is *in* the life history narrated. He states:

> From this we can conclude that a "spiritual interpretation of scripture" has to be *biographical* interpretation. Through the ways in which we express our lives we interpret the scriptural texts we live with. These utterances of life (as Dilthey called them) find expression through language and logic—through the praxis that furthers life—through our bodily configuration and the body language of mimic and gesture—through the experiences and remembrances which have shaped our lives—through our relationships in the communities we live in; and so forth. The book of the Bible is interpreted by our lived lives, for it is "the book of

---

159. Moltmann, *Experiences*, 144.

life," as it has been called from time immemorial. The sending of the Spirit (*missio Dei*) awakens life and multifarious movements of revival and healing. So *life* is the true interpreter.[160]

This passage demonstrates one of the clearest connections in his thought between the narrativity of the Trinity, an anthropology of embodied "configuration," and the *missio Dei*. A "spiritual" hermeneutic of Scripture, in which the dual function of the narrative is at work, holds these together. Yet, the nature of the human person at the nexus of the *read* narrative of the *missio Dei* and the *lived* interpretation of the *missio Dei* in the Spirit is critical. As embodied narrativity, that nature establishes the possibility of embodied participation in God's mission in precisely these narrative terms.

Moltmann's expansion of *perichōrēsis* contributes four key theological insights. One, he establishes a baseline emplotment of human beings in the bigger story of the Spirit of creation. Two, he characterizes the *imago Christi* as a renarration of human identity according to Jesus's embodied narrativity inscribed in Scripture. This renarration is both a process of conformity and adoption of a *telos*. Three, he indicates that *theōsis* in Christ is participation in the Triune history of God in the world. Four, coming full circle, he clarifies that bodily configuration, or embodied narrativity, is a matter of life lived hermeneutically in a dialectic of the inscripturated narrativity of the Triune life and the praxis that furthers life in the Spirit. Moltmann's understanding of the perichoretic configuration of the human person, therefore, extends a Ricoeurian conception of embodied narrativity theologically by explaining that the configuration of embodied narrativity—not disembodied human narrativity—is what participates in God's Triune history. In other words, given that participation in God's mission is *theōsis* understood perichoretically, Ricoeur adds that we might understand the human nature engaged in *theōsis* to comprise embodiment and narrativity inextricably, and Moltmann adds an understanding in which both dimensions are necessary to make sense of human participation in the Trinity historically, christologically, and hermeneutically.

Summary

I summarize the basic dimensions of embodied narrativity as follows. First, embodied narrativity is a holistic account of the human person in

---

160. Moltmann, *Experiences*, 146.

which selfhood and sameness designate the primary poles of *a single, multidimensional identity*. Selfhood refers to aspects of the person such as consciousness, agency, faithfulness, and subjectivity. Sameness refers to aspects of the person such as character, passivity, public accountability, and the body. Second, embodied narrativity entails *a dual narration of lived life*: "By narrating a life of which I am not the author as to existence, I make myself its coauthor as to its meaning."[161] A person's self-narration has an ontological limit: God is the author of the larger story; this story is the *missio Dei*. The Spirit's narration of a person has a hermeneutical limit: a person's self-narration may not conform to the Spirit's emplotment of his or her life according to the *imago Christi*. Third, embodied narrativity entails *teleological praxis*. On the one hand, the attempt to self-narrate without embodied, committed practices would result in the development of selfhood-identity without sameness-identity. Agency is meaningless without, for example, the public commitments and values that make one responsible. On the other hand, the attempt to engage in practices without narrative significance would result in the development of sameness-identity without selfhood-identity. Habits, public commitments, and values, for example, remain aimless without *meaningful* agency.

Conclusion: Embodied Narrativity and *Missio Dei*

My argument in this chapter is that a theological account of human embodied narrativity further explains human participation in God's mission. I argued in the preceding chapter that participation in God's mission is *theōsis*—perichoretic participation in the Triune life. How, then, does embodied narrativity clarify the meaning of perichoretic participation? Having accounted for the status of embodiment and narrativity respectively in contemporary theology and indicated why their conceptual integration is necessary, I turned to Moltmann's stipulation that Trinitarian doctrine is rooted in the scriptural history of God. Yet, although the narrative of Scripture may profoundly shape one's account of the Trinity, one's account of the Trinity may also determine the narrative of participation in the *missio Dei*. In other words, in the hermeneutical circle of the read narrative and the life lived in the Spirit, Trinitarian doctrine is (to borrow a postliberal term) the grammar by which the church coauthors its embodied narrativity—its participation in the *missio Dei*. Correlatively,

161. Ricoeur, *Oneself*, 162.

embodied narrativity is the ontological status through which humanity is *capax Dei*—capable of being taken up into the divine life thrown open for the world's redemption. The twofold dynamic of self-narration and Spirit-narration are, therefore, more than mere mimesis. Embodied narrativity describes a hermeneutic spirituality that constitutes the divine-human synergy of perichoretic participation in God's mission.

Furthermore, embodied narrativity is the ontological basis of the teleological praxis through which responsible, meaningful participation in the missional life of God takes place. Yet, missional ecclesiology's interest in practices can slip into a mode in which certain practices are presumed to be participation, without discernment of the church's embodied conformity to the Triune narrative unfolding in local contexts. We have seen the role of practices in the dialectic of embodied narrativity. In abstraction from the co-narration of God's story and the church's, however, they may fail to be participation, in Christ, in the perichoretic history of God's dealings with the world. Practices divorced from the narrative significance of the *missio Dei* fracture the narrative unity of the church's life. Furthermore, such participation can amount to doing certain activities that are simultaneously attributed to the Spirit, regardless of whether they are coherent with the story actually being narrated by the Spirit. Here the ontological limits of the church's self-narration come into view. One only has to think of the church's self-narratives in the midst of colonialist missions to see the possibility of practices emplotted with the wrong aim. But subtler forms of incoherent emplotment also exist in church practices that are not configured according to the story of God's mission. The doctrine of *theōsis* I have extended in terms of *perichōrēsis* finds in the theological anthropology of embodied narrativity a demand that the concrete practices of participation be more than a list of divine agenda items (even christologically mimetic ones) that, once completed, constitute participation in the Triune *missio Dei*. If we cannot abstractly identify the practices of participation, then what *can* we say about the perichoretic practices to which the hermeneutic spirituality of embodied narrativity calls us? Are we left with vague admonitions to "discernment" or encomiums about "love"? What more, theologically, might we say about embodied human co-narration in the story of God's mission?

By way of transition to the final piece of my theological account of participation, I return to Kelsey's *Eccentric Existence*, which provides the clue I investigate in the next chapter. Kelsey's Trinitarian, relational understanding of embodied narrativity relies on the term *solidarity* to represent the ways human personal bodies share in the Son's perichoretic relationship with the Father.[162] *Solidarity* designates the practices of those "in Christ," and—similar to my discussion of participation in redemption—"what distinguishes these practices is a recognizable set of patterns that reflects the distinctive plotline of narratives of the peculiar way in which God goes about relating to reconcile—that is, the way in which God goes about incarnation."[163] Kelsey recognizes this is a way of referring to *theōsis*, about which he adds, "To be appropriate to the peculiar way in which the triune God concretely goes about relating to reconcile estranged humankind, human love to God is precisely 'love to the Son sent with the Spirit by the Father,' love to God as one among humankind in solidarity with them in their estrangement and all its consequences."[164] *Solidarity* here serves as a theological designation of the concrete, perichoretic practices through which embodied narrativity as such shares in the reconciling labor of love that is participation in the *missio Dei*. To the development of this concept I turn next.

162. Kelsey, *Eccentric*, 2:641–42, 646, 694.
163. Kelsey, *Eccentric*, 2:698.
164. Kelsey, *Eccentric*, 2:708.

CHAPTER 5

Participation as Solidarity

> "The paradigmatic shift I am proposing calls for solidarity as the appropriate present-day expression of the gospel mandate that we love our neighbor. This commandment, which encapsulates the gospel message, is the goal of Christianity. I believe salvation depends on love of neighbor, and because love of neighbor can and should be expressed through solidarity, solidarity can and should be considered the sine qua non of salvation." —Ada María Isasi-Díaz[1]

I HAVE SO FAR developed the concept of participation in God's mission as *theōsis* according with a theology of human embodied narrativity. Despite the physicality that the fact of human embodiment fixes in the conceptualization of participation as *theōsis*, however, missional participation remains abstract. I argue in this chapter that a theological account of *solidarity* completes a missional understanding of participation by concretizing embodied participation in God's mission in history. Following the trajectory of perichoretic participation in the suffering of Christ (ch. 3) through embodied narrativity's entailment of concrete practices (ch. 4), I affirm that the church's suffering *with Christ* in the world is the essence of missional solidarity, through which Christian *marturia* comes to paradigmatic expression.

---

1. Isasi-Díaz, *Mujerista*, 88.

The chapter proceeds in three sections. First, I explore the theological significance of solidarity in liberation theology, especially that of Latin America. By representing solidarity as a practice, a virtue, and a theological method, liberation theology provides a wealth of insight into the essential nature of embodied missional participation. Yet the critical principle of the preferential option for the poor, without which liberation theology's understanding of solidarity would not have been possible, tends to put limits on participation that I will challenge. Second, therefore, I make recourse to broader perspectives on solidarity, especially in ethics, which open up the insights of liberationist solidarity for a fully missional conceptualization. The third section brings together the claims I have made regarding *theōsis*, embodied narrativity, and solidarity in a comprehensive definition of participation in God's mission. I conclude by returning to the question and thesis stated in chapter 1 and transitioning to the hermeneutical implications that chapter 6 will develop.

Solidarity in Liberation Theology

I noted in chapter 2 that liberation theology has shaped missiological conceptions of participation in God's mission.[2] Indeed, Latin American liberation theology in particular has a strongly missional resonance.[3] But this is not the case simply because many liberationists make reference to "mission." In this section I sound out two substantively missional dimensions of liberation theology: participation in God's work in the world and participation with Christ. Solidarity is the conceptual keynote that unifies these dimensions in clearly missional tones.

Foundational Conceptualizations of Solidarity

The language of solidarity in Latin American liberation theology is rooted in two idioms: Roman Catholic social thought and Marxian class theory. What emerges from the interaction of the two is a unique vision of solidarity as a practice, a virtue, and a theological method. This vision represents a critical development beyond the broader Roman Catholic and

---

2. See ch. 2, n. 53.

3. I agree with Dana Robert's assessment that Gutiérrez's *Theology* is "a seminal work of missional contextual theology"—*missional* being a retrospective appellation that much of Gutiérrez's and other liberationists' work deserves. See Robert, "Forty," 14.

Marxian understandings, and the theological essence of liberationist solidarity makes it irreducible to those earlier constituents. Furthermore, lest readers unfamiliar with the terminology be confused, I utilize the adjective *Marxian* to indicate a distinction from *Marxist*. The philosophical valance of Marx's reflections do not entail their subsequent deployment in the "Marxist" political program. Much of the Western Evangelical critique of liberation theology has overlooked this distinction.

In what follows I will briefly explain the nature of Roman Catholic social thought and Marxian class theory and their manifestations in the 1968 General Conference of the Latin American Episcopate in Medellín, Colombia, which served as a major point of departure of liberation theology. Then I will expound the three aspects of liberationist solidarity (practice, virtue, and method) as they ramify from their initial articulation in Gustavo Gutiérrez's groundbreaking volume *A Theology of Liberation*. In this way, I will identify the theological vision at the heart of liberationist solidarity in order to develop it further in section 2.

The Marxian Solidarity of Paulo Freire

As Rebecca Todd Peters observes in her survey of the term's development, solidarity emerged as a sociological concept through the work of Émile Durkheim and Max Weber and took a political turn through that of Karl Marx. Two interrelated Marxian "forms" of solidarity obtain: "the relationships and bonds between members of the working class due to their common struggle against oppression under capitalism" and the utopian vision of "true freedom and community that is only possible in a communist society."[4] *Solidarity* in Marxian usage designates both the means and the end of class struggle, defined in relational terms.

Paulo Freire played a vital role in mediating the Marxian sense of solidarity in the Latin American context through his celebrated book *Pedagogy of the Oppressed*, originally published in Portuguese in 1968. Freire developed the pedagogical notion of conscientization (*conscientização*)—"learning to perceive social, political, and economic contradiction, and to take action against the oppressive elements of reality"—in order to foster class consciousness.[5] The oppressed, he argues, frequently become oppressors, because "their vision of the new man or woman is individualistic;

4. Peters, *Solidarity*, 23.
5. Freire, *Pedagogy*, 35n1.

because of their identification with the oppressor, they have no consciousness of themselves as persons or as members of an oppressed class."[6] Conscientization is necessary, therefore, because "the pursuit of full humanity ... cannot be carried out in isolation or individualism, but only in fellowship and solidarity."[7] This is one half of the instrumental sense of Marxian solidarity, which identifies the utopian aim of solidarity, "humanization."[8] The other half of instrumental solidarity is the oppressor's relationship with the oppressed.[9] The oppressor, too, needs conscientization on the way to solidarity: "The oppressor is solidary with the oppressed only when he stops regarding the oppressed as an abstract category and sees them as persons who have been unjustly dealt with, deprived of their voice, cheated in the sale of their labor—when he stops making pious, sentimental, and individualistic gestures and risks an act of love. True solidarity is found only in the plenitude of this act of love, in its existentiality, in its praxis."[10] In praxis, Freire explains elsewhere, "action and reflection occur simultaneously."[11] Praxis therefore serves an epistemological function: the oppressed "whose task it is to struggle for their liberation together with those who show true solidarity, must acquire a critical awareness of oppression through the praxis of this struggle."[12] Conscientization leads to solidarity (in both instrumental senses) in the praxis of struggle for liberation; true solidarity as praxis engenders critical awareness—a truer consciousness of reality. In this way, praxis adds a depth dimension to both senses of Marxian solidarity, which effectively constitutes a third usage. In the epistemological depth of solidarity as an *instrument*, the "act of love" serves the end of humanization as both a concrete practice of liberation and the cultivation of critical consciousness. In the epistemological depth of solidarity as an *end*, critical consciousness becomes the

---

6. Freire, *Pedagogy*, 46.

7. Freire, *Pedagogy*, 85; likewise, 174.

8. Freire, *Pedagogy*, 49, 85.

9. The "oppressor" in Freire's usage is also the dupe of false consciousness. Of course, consciously malicious oppressors exist, but of greater concern in the practice of conscientization are the "beneficiaries of a situation of oppression" who "do not perceive their monopoly on *having more* as a privilege which dehumanizes others and themselves" (Freire, *Pedagogy*, 58–59).

10. Freire, *Pedagogy*, 49–50.

11. Freire, *Cultural*, 7.

12. Freire, *Pedagogy*, 51.

full transformation of both the oppressed consciousness and the oppressor consciousness as an aspect of humanization's achievement.[13]

The Marxian sense of solidarity that Freire mediates, then, has three dimensions: practice, epistemology, and *telos*. This is a significant interpretive accomplishment, because Peters's simpler, twofold construal of Marxian solidarity is justified—the epistemological significance of solidarity does not sit on the surface of Marx's thought. Richard Bernstein gives the epistemological significance of praxis for Marx a much-needed treatment in *Praxis and Action* (1971), published three years after *Pedagogy of the Oppressed*. "Marx was only incidentally interested in metaphysical and epistemological issues," notes Bernstein, "and after early writings they receded into the background for him. We find, at best, hints and suggestions, not a well-developed theory."[14] Bernstein elucidates these hints and suggestions masterfully, explaining that "it is *praxis* that turns out to be the key for understanding the full range of man's developing cognitive activities."[15] That is to say, critical consciousness is a function of praxis—the "'practical-critical' activity" of Marx's first thesis on Feuerbach.[16] So, Bernstein explains, "if it is true that man's present reality and world is an objectively alienated one, then the abstract possibility of a 'humanized world' only becomes a real possibility through a radical transformation of this objectified alienated condition—by revolutionary *praxis*."[17] To this we can add that a humanized world becomes a possibility because, through the epistemological function of praxis, it is *perceived to be a possibility*. What Freire brilliantly adds to this understanding of Marx is that solidarity—as it foments class consciousness, effects liberation, and transforms consciousness—*is* the praxis and its goal. This is the threefold sense of solidarity that Freire unleashes in the Latin American context of the late 1960s.

---

13. Freire, *Pedagogy*, 54, identifies two "distinct stages" of the pedagogy of the oppressed. "In the first, the oppressed unveil the world of oppression and through the [*sic*] praxis commit themselves to its transformation. In the second stage, in which the reality of oppression has already been transformed, this pedagogy ceases to belong to the oppressed and becomes a pedagogy of all people in the process of permanent liberation."

14. Bernstein, *Praxis*, 75.

15. Bernstein, *Praxis*, 73. He notes that "Georg Lukács first underscored this aspect of Marx's thought." Freire, *Pedagogy*, 52–53, 174, attends to Lukács.

16. Reproduced in Bernstein, *Praxis*, 11.

17. Bernstein, *Praxis*, 75.

PARTICIPATION AS SOLIDARITY

Roots in Roman Catholic Solidarity Ethics

At the same time, the conceptualization of solidarity in Roman Catholic social thought was undergoing profound development.[18] Two documents in particular reflect the emerging understanding of solidarity in this context. First, the Vatican II document *Gaudium et spes* (1965) takes initial steps beyond the earlier notions of solidarity as human interdependence and political cooperation.[19] Quoting the 1891 encyclical of Pope Leo XIII, *Rerum novarum*, *Gaudium et spes* says that solidary is "social unity" rooted in the work of Christ that creates "a new brotherly community composed of all those who receive Him in faith and in love."[20] Meghan Clark observes: "Theologically, solidarity [was] beginning to be used in a broader sense. It [was] more than simply the statement that as human beings we are all part of the one human family. It [was] a call for that community to live and act in particular ways."[21] Second, the encyclical of Pope Paul VI titled *Populorum progressio* identifies "*mutual solidarity*—the aid that the richer nations must give to developing nations"—as one of the church's "major duties" in the work of international development.[22] This sense of solidarity as a duty (alongside justice and charity) is a call back to earlier notions of obligations rooted in "the reality of human solidarity."[23] But Paul VI also strains to get free of the distortions that plague the observation of interrelatedness from the perspective of the "developed" nations:

> An ever more effective *world solidarity* should allow all peoples to become the artisans of their destiny. Up to now relations between nations have too often been governed by force; indeed, that is the hallmark of past history. May the day come when international relationships will be characterized by respect and friendship, when mutual cooperation will be the hallmark of collaborative efforts, and when concerted effort for the betterment of all nations will be regarded as a duty by every nation. The developing nations now emerging are asking that they be allowed to take part in the

---

18. In this subsection I rely on Clark, *Vision*, ch. 1. See also Bilgrien, *Solidarity*; Beyer, "Meaning," 7–25.
19. These are reviewed in Clark, *Vision*, 9–19.
20. Paul VI, *Gaudium et spes*, §32; emphasis added.
21. Clark, *Vision*, 20.
22. Paul VI, *Populorum progressio*, §§43–44; emphasis added.
23. Paul VI, *Populorum progressio*, §17.

construction of a better world, a world which would provide better protection for every man's rights and duties.[24]

The initial theological grounding and ethical framing of *Gaudium et spes* and *Populorum progressio* put solidarity on a new footing in Roman Catholic thought. It is now oriented christologically and eschatologically in addition to being refined deontologically as a fully mutual obligation that assumes and serves the agency of "developing" nations.

Solidarity at Medellín (1968)

The Marxian and Roman Catholic understandings of solidarity converged at the Medellín conference, which had a catalytic effect for Latin American liberation theology. James Kirylo and Drick Boyd observe that "based on a Freirean model of 'liberating education,' the concept of 'participation' was illuminated as a result of the conference."[25] That is, at Medellín, *participation* becomes a conceptual key for explicating and operationalizing the solidarity of *Populorum progressio* that emphasizes the agency of the poor.[26] *Solidarity* and *participation* appear throughout the "Conclusiones" of Medellín. Two primary senses of solidarity as participation emerge: collaborative participation in the liberating mission of Christ and loving participation in the suffering of the poor.

The first sense of solidarity as participation emphasizes the agency of Latin Americans in their own social change. As in the broader European usage of the term and the earlier Roman Catholic understanding, solidarity is participation in political cooperation and organization for the purpose of social "development."[27] "Socialization, understood as a sociocultural process of personalization and growing solidarity, induces us to think that all the sectors of society, but in this case, principally the socioeconomic sector, ought to overcome antagonisms through justice and fraternity, in order to become *agents of national and continental development*. Without this unity,

---

24. Paul VI, *Populorum progressio*, §65; emphasis added.

25. Kirylo and Boyd, *Paulo*, 89 (and ch. 8, "A Freirean Imprint on Liberation Theology," more broadly); see also McLaren and Jandrić, "Paulo," 246–64.

26. Notably, Paul VI gave the opening address at Medellín, interweaving mission, solidarity, liberation, and participation in suggestive ways. See Consejo Episcopal Latinoamericano, "Discurso," 76–77, 80.

27. Consejo Episcopal Latinoamericano, "Medellín," 90. English quotations of Spanish works in this chapter are my translation.

PARTICIPATION AS SOLIDARITY

Latin America will not manage *to liberate itself from the neocolonialism* to which it is subjected, nor consequently to actualize itself in freedom, with its own cultural, sociopolitical, and economic characteristics."[28] This "unity of action" is a practical exigency in the face of neocolonial socioeconomic oppression. Already, however, the seeds of the subsequent doctrinal reflections are present in the reference to *la fraternidad* (fraternity). Expounding a Christian vision of peace, the bishops root the possibility of solidarity in Christ: "Peace is, finally, a fruit of love, an expression of a real fraternity among humans: a fraternity provided by Christ, Prince of Peace, upon reconciling all humans with the Father. *Human solidarity cannot be truly realized except in Christ* who gives the Peace that the world cannot give. Love is the soul of justice. The Christian who works for social justice should always cultivate peace and love in his heart."[29] Thus, the solidarity that is a reality in which every person is immersed by virtue of human nature finds theological significance and a new horizon "in Christ." Moreover, this horizon is eschatological, because it is a possibility not yet fulfilled but already available for "ratification" in the commitment of the church to this social project.[30] The bishops make this assertion by way of explaining the laity's participation in mission: "The laity, like all Church members, *participate in the triple prophetic, priestly, and royal function of Christ, considering the fulfillment of their ecclesial mission*. But they specifically realize this mission in the sphere of the temporal, with respect to the construction of history, 'managing temporal matters and ordering them according to God.'"[31] In the same way, the priesthood's participation in mission is understood as solidarity: "It is of particular importance to underline that priestly 'consecration' is conferred by Christ with respect to the 'mission' of human salvation. This requires of every priest *a special solidarity of human service, which is expressed in a living missionary dimension*, that should cause one to put ministerial concerns at the service of the world with its grand progress and its humbling sins; and it is also an intelligent contact with reality, in such a way that its consecration results in *a special way of presence in the world*, rather than segregation from it."[32] In summary, the first sense of solidarity

---

28. Consejo Episcopal Latinoamericano, "Medellín," 92–93; emphasis added.
29. Consejo Episcopal Latinoamericano, "Medellín," 102–3; emphasis added.
30. Consejo Episcopal Latinoamericano, "Medellín," 158; emphasis added.
31. Consejo Episcopal Latinoamericano, "Medellín," 158 (quoting *Lumen gentium*); emphasis added.
32. Consejo Episcopal Latinoamericano, "Medellín," 167; emphasis added.

at Medellín—collaborative participation in the transformative mission of Christ—suggests that the agency of the Latin American church is (1) rooted in the fact of human solidarity ultimately made possible in Christ; (2) ratified through the collaborative commitment to the liberation, humanization, and development of the Latin American nations in history; (3) signified relationally by a holiness that induces presence in the world as it is; and (4) oriented eschatologically toward the world to come.

The second sense of solidarity as participation emphasizes the poverty of the Latin American church as the context of mission. Having surveyed the reality of this poverty, the bishops ground the church's solidarity with the poor in the example of Christ, who "not only loved the poor but 'being rich made himself poor,' lived among the poor, centered his mission on the announcement to the poor of their liberation and founded his Church as a sign of that poverty among his people." They add, "The poverty of so many brothers and sisters cries for justice, solidarity, testimony, commitment, effort, and overcoming for the complete fulfillment of the salvific mission entrusted by Christ."[33] These reflections move in two directions. On the one hand, the suffering of the church in poverty is a sign of Jesus's own salvific option for poverty. The poverty of the church is never valorized as such, because it is always that from which Christ liberates by becoming poor, but insofar as the church's poverty is a manifestation of a christological commitment to the poor, it remains Christ-signifying. On the other hand, the poverty of the church demands solidarity from those who are not poor. This is more than a demand for effective collaboration, however. The suffering of the poor cries out for the deepening of "commitment" according to Christ's option for poverty—the option to *suffer with* the poor for the sake of their liberation. Thus, "the poverty of the Church and its members in Latin America should be a sign and a commitment. A sign of the inestimable value of the poor person in God's eyes; a commitment of solidarity with those who suffer."[34] These two emphases—sign and commitment—lead the bishops to the germinal articulation of what becomes known as "the preferential option for the poor" in liberation theology. Under the subheading "Perferencias y solidaridad" (preferences and solidarity), they state: "The particular commandment of the Lord to 'evangelize the poor' should bring us to a distribution of the efforts and apostolic personnel that might give *effective preference* to the poorest and neediest and to those segregated for whatever reason,

---

33. Consejo Episcopal Latinoamericano, "Medellín," 191–92.
34. Consejo Episcopal Latinoamericano, "Medellín," 192.

encouraging and accelerating the initiatives and study that are already done to this end.... We must sharpen *conscience of the duty of solidarity with the poor*, to which charity bring us. *This solidarity means making their problems and struggles ours, knowing how to speak for them.*"[35]

Thus, the ethical duty of *Populorum progressio* combines with Freirean conscientization in the claim that "we must sharpen consciousness of the duty of solidarity with the poor," defined now in christological terms as "making their problems and struggles ours." This is what it means to have an "effective preference" for the poor in response to the Lord's command to evangelize the poor (Luke 4:18). This is solidarity as a sign and a commitment. In summary, the second sense of solidarity at Medellín—loving participation in the suffering of the poor—suggests that the poverty of the Latin American church is (1) the context in which to understand the church's role in Christ's mission; (2) the medium through which the church signifies the liberating intention of Christ's mission; (3) the demand for a preferential commitment to the poor; and (4) the suffering that love brings "us" to share.[36]

Medellín yields these two intertwined senses of solidarity: collaborative participation in the liberating mission of Christ and loving participation in the suffering of the poor. Beginning with Gutierrez's *A Theology of Liberation* (*Teología de la liberación* [1971]), liberation theology builds on these foundational conceptualizations of solidarity. In early liberation theology, participation in Christ's liberating mission and the suffering of the poor connect more fully with the praxeological epistemology that Freire advocated, resulting in a much clearer picture of solidarity as (1) practice, (2) virtue, and (3) theological method.[37]

---

35. Consejo Episcopal Latinoamericano, "Medellín," 192–93; emphasis added.

36. The "us" in "to which charity bring us" is important for understanding the conceptual tensions that mark poverty and solidarity from this point forward in Latin American liberation theology. The poverty of the church is a sign of the demand for solidarity from those who are also part of the church but not subject to its pervasive poverty. This maps roughly onto Freire's distinction between solidarity among the oppressed and the oppressor's solidarity with the oppressed.

37. This threefold division is my own way of organizing the uses of *solidarity* in the relevant literature, which follows the broad contours of the discussion unambiguously.

Solidarity as Participation in Liberation

For Gutiérrez, widely considered the father of Latin American liberation theology, solidarity is "participation in the process of liberation."[38] For Gutierrez, this is a missional proposition. The final words of *A Theology of Liberation* are these: "Only authentic solidarity with the poor and a real protest against poverty of our time can provide the concrete, vital context necessary for a theological discussion of poverty. The absence of a sufficient commitment to the poor, the marginated, and exploited is perhaps the fundamental reason why we have no solid contemporary reflection on the witness of poverty. For the Latin American Church especially, this witness is an inescapable and much-needed sign of the authenticity of its mission."[39] The intertwined solidarity of participation in Christ's liberating mission and the suffering of the poor articulated at Medellín resounds as solidarity and protest, but these have deepened and expanded in Gutiérrez's thought. In the following discussion I present his seminal articulations of solidarity as practice, virtue, and theological method, considering in turn how each ramified in subsequent liberation theology.

Solidarity as Practice

First, *protest* is shorthand for the practices of solidarity carried forward from Medellín, now explicated as "prophetic denunciation" of social injustices—a "prophetic task" that is "both constructive and critical and is exercised in the midst of a process of change"—"the determined, dynamic, and creative participation" in the process of liberation.[40] Further, the "call to struggle against oppressive structures and to construct a more just society" includes "conscientizing evangelization," intentional poverty, critique of inadequate church structures, and changes in the lifestyle of the clergy.[41] The emphasis of this practical vision of solidarity is social transformation in history. Gutiérrez develops the holistic soteriology in which "the radical incompatibility of evangelical demands with an unjust and alienating society" motivates participation in liberation.[42] Accordingly,

---

38. Gutiérrez, *Theology*, 32; see also 46, 75, 81, 106.
39. Gutiérrez, *Theology*, 173.
40. Gutiérrez, *Theology*, 69.
41. Gutiérrez, *Theology*, 69–70.
42. Gutiérrez, *Theology*, 81.

participation in the historical task of humanization (reflecting *Gaudium et spes* but also the broader humanism found in Freire, for example)[43] entails practical, political, justice-making work. Gutierrez strains against the dualism latent in the tradition: "To work, to transform this world, is to become a [hu]man and build the human community; it is also to save. Likewise, to struggle against misery and exploitation and to build a just society is already to be part of the saving action, which is moving towards its complete fulfillment. All this means that building the temporal city is not simply a stage of 'humanization' or 'pre-evangelization' as we held in theology until a few years ago."[44] In a phrase, *participation in the liberating work of God in history* is the practice of solidarity.

Attention to the historicity of God's work is key to the significance of solidarity as practice. Redolent of Lesslie Newbigin's "church as hermeneutic of the gospel," Ignacio Ellacuría, for example, says, "The Church must make clear the credibility of its mission. If it does not take note of the profound historical change involved in moving from the context of Christendom to the context of a missionary Church, it will not proclaim and carry out salvation in a historical way."[45] He explains: "The point, then, is that the sign of credibility which the Church is should be fleshed out in historico-social praxis. . . . Thus, salvation in history is the present-day sign of salvation history. This historicity takes at least three forms: 1) historicity as real-life authenticity; 2) historicity as effectiveness in history; 3) historicity as hope in an eschatological future."[46] Ellacuría conceives of this authentic, effective mission work as the struggle against injustice, which is "objectified sin," and as Christian love "concretely objectified in history."[47] But it is the eschatological dimension of his understanding that brings the historicity of praxis into striking alignment with my argument regarding participation and *theōsis* (recall the discussion of divine and human agency that weaves through chs. 2–3). First, the historicity of the church's mission as praxis is a function of God's own active presence in history: "God is the present

---

43. Gutiérrez, *Theology*, 91.

44. Alves, who might be considered the progenitor of Protestant liberation theology, offers a rich meditation in his seminal *Theology*, ch. 3, on the difference between "humanistic messianism" and "messianic humanism."

45. Ellacuría, *Freedom*, 87. See Newbigin, *Gospel*, ch. 18.

46. Ellacuría, *Freedom*, 93.

47. Ellacuría, *Freedom*, 112, 120.

future of history because he is the future present in history."⁴⁸ Second, the objectification of love in history leads to "the full divinization of the human world."⁴⁹ The church's loving presence in history ultimately unites with God's loving presence in history, and so the church's love objectified as work for justice in history is a sign of that future.

I will return to the theme of God's presence below. At this point, my focus is the eschatological aspect of solidarity as a concrete historical practice. Liberation theology's critique of European "theologies of hope" (aimed at theologians such as Johann Baptist Metz and Jürgen Moltmann) centers on this point.⁵⁰ As Enrique Dussel puts it: "It is not sufficient only to speak of hope beyond the status quo. Even though we say we are hoping for the kingdom, we are reaffirming and sacralizing the status quo by not risking all historically in a project for the future, by not becoming empirically through our praxis a dysfunctional factor within the system."⁵¹ This is the "revolutionary" disposition of liberation theology. Within a system bound in the absence of radical disruption to perpetuate the brutal fact of poverty, solidarity must be an effective practice bent on a disjunctive future. Accordingly, José Míguez Bonino states: "History, in relation to the Kingdom, is not a riddle to be solved but a mission to be fulfilled. That mission, one must hasten to add, is not a mere accumulation of unrelated actions, but a new reality, a new life which is communicated in Christ, in the power of the Spirit. How can we participate, act out, *produce* the quality of personal and corporate existence which has a future, which possesses eschatological reality, which concentrates the true history? We face the question of historical mediations for our participation in the building of the Kingdom."⁵² This es-

48. Ellacuría, *Freedom*, 123.

49. Ellacuría, *Freedom*, 118; see also 159.

50. See Alves, *Theology*, 55–68, for the opening salvo. See also Gutiérrez, *Theology*, 123–30.

51. Dussel, *Ethics*, 160.

52. Míguez Bonino, *Doing*, 143. See the reaction in Moltmann, "On Latin," 57–63. This conflict is particularly relevant to the conceptualization of participation in God's mission. It reflects the very concerns about the relationship of human agency to God's mission that arose in ch. 2, especially in Barth's theology. Sharing the experience of the same historical context (*viz.*, Nazi Germany), Moltmann is reticent to speak of "building the kingdom" in the full-throated way that Latin American liberation theology does. Missional theology, in the postcolonial context, is also gun-shy about overstating the eschatological significance of the church's work. As I have shown, this is precisely the point of developing a thick conception of participation in God's mission that rules out the church's missiological autonomy yet accounts fully for the church's agency in God's

chatological dimension is clarified in Míguez Bonino's subsequent work as "an eschatological ethics of justice, which assumes solidarity with the poor as its historical mediation."[53] Further, solidarity mediates this eschatological ethics over against the fact that "in the history of Christianity the eschatological symbols have been so cut off from this world, so individualized, and so exclusively related to God's power conceived as the negation of human participation that they have led to resignation and historical cynicism."[54] Human participation in God's eschatological action in history takes the form of solidarity with the poor in their concrete situation. Solidarity is, then, the practice of participation in liberation.

Solidarity as Virtue

Second, the voluntary poverty that is one of the practical entailments of solidarity as a practice has a special significance, which I call *virtue* in order to highlight its connection with issues of formation in my broader argument. Gutiérrez explains, "At Medellín it was made clear that poverty expresses solidarity with the oppressed and a protest against oppression. Suggested ways of implementing this poverty in the Church are the evangelization of the poor, the denunciation of injustice, a simple lifestyle, a spirit of service, and freedom from temporal ties, intrigue, or ambiguous prestige."[55] He is clear that "material poverty is a scandalous condition," not to be sought or admired. Yet this fact is in tension with the biblical notion of "spiritual poverty," which is "a spiritual attitude which becomes authentic by incarnating itself in material poverty."[56] The incarnation is the paradigm of solidarity that lives in this tension: "'For you know how generous our Lord Jesus Christ has been: He was rich, yet for your sake he became poor, so that through his poverty you might become rich' (2 Cor. 8:9). This is the humiliation of Christ, his *kenosis* (Phil. 2:6–11). But he does not take on the human sinful condition and its consequences to idealize it. It is rather

---

historical work. In my view, it is important to listen to the Latin American—and other liberationist—perspectives on this point, in order to understand how solidarity contributes to that conceptualization. As Alves, Míguez Bonino, and others write, the need is clearly to correct a theology of hope that is insufficiently historical from the perspective of the suffering of the poor.

53. Míguez Bonino, *Toward*, 44.
54. Míguez Bonino, *Toward*, 94.
55. Gutiérrez, *Theology*, 70.
56. Gutiérrez, *Theology*, 171.

because of love for and solidarity with others who suffer in it." Such solidarity "is a poverty lived not for its own sake, but rather as an authentic imitation of Christ."[57] *Imitatio Christi* is a function of spiritual poverty, "total availability to the Lord," also called "spiritual childhood—an ability to receive, not a passive acceptance."[58] This germinal understanding of solidarity as a spiritual attitude and an ability establishes the sense of solidarity in liberation theology as not only a practice but also a virtue.

Gutiérrez remains the principal exponent of the relationship between "spiritual poverty" and solidarity in Latin American liberation theology. In an essay interpreting the 1979 General Conference of the Latin American Episcopate in Puebla, Mexico, he returns to the notion that solidarity is a function of a certain spirituality. Commenting on §1156 of the Puebla document, which refers to "the evangelical demand of poverty, as solidarity with the poor and as a rejection of the situation in which the majority of the continent lives,"[59] he observes that "spiritual poverty permits one to live this solidarity, and all its consequences, in the insecurity of quest, and confidence in the Lord."[60] The rest of this passage refers to the poor church evangelizing the rich: "In the same way, the witness of a poor Church can evangelize the rich whose heart is attached to riches, converting and liberating them from that slavery and from their selfishness."[61] As the wider church is evangelized by the poor, their conversion results in "evangelical values" including solidarity.[62] In this sense, the capacity for solidarity is the function of a transformation that follows from an initial commitment.

Jon Sobrino's essay "Conllévaos mutuamente: Análisis teológico de la solidaridad cristiana" also emphasizes the mutuality of evangelization.[63] "A circular understanding of sending is an aid in carrying out missionary activity as solidarity—that is, as not only giving but also receiving. . . . It is from the vantage point of the poor that the missionary will best understand the content of evangelization and the best way to evangelize."[64] As a

57. Gutiérrez, *Theology*, 172.
58. Gutiérrez, *Theology*, 171.
59. Consejo Episcopal Latinoamericano, "Puebla," 469.
60. Gutiérrez, *Power*, 142.
61. Consejo Episcopal Latinoamericano, "Puebla," 469.
62. Consejo Episcopal Latinoamericano, "Puebla," 467.
63. The original title is translated "Bear with one another mutually: A theological analysis of Christian solidarity." See the translation, Sobrino, "Bearing," 1–41.
64. Sobrino, "Bearing," 21.

disposition of mutuality and a willingness to receive, the missional virtue of solidarity subverts the colonialist, triumphalist, and humanist demons that haunt Christian mission. And although the practice of solidarity forms one in the virtue solidarity, the experience inevitably brings to light the latter's stark limits. Gutiérrez advises that the church must "undertake this commitment [to the poor] although knowing in advance that the situation of the poor will almost certainly overstrain the human capacity for solidarity. The will to live in the world of the poor can therefore only follow an asymptotic curve: a constantly closer approach that can, however, never reach the point of real identification with the life of the poor."[65] This limit on the "human capacity for solidarity" is also a gift because it reminds us that just as the practice of solidarity is an imitation of Christ, so the virtue of solidarity is a gift of the Spirit and not a possession.

Solidarity as Theological Method

Third, the practice and virtue of solidarity become a theological method, referred to in Marxian fashion as *praxis*.[66] In a statement that is paradigmatic for the hermeneutical claims toward which I am working in the conclusion of this study, Gutiérrez says:

> Participation in the process of liberation is an obligatory and privileged *locus* for Christian life and reflection. In this participation will be heard nuances of the Word of God which are imperceptible in other existential situations and without which there can be no

65. Gutiérrez, *We Drink*, 126.

66. *Praxis* is often used as a synonym of *practice*, as we have seen in some quotations above, but its technical usage is distinct. The ambiguity arises once the technical explanation of praxis as a fusion of practice and theory in a hermeneutical circle becomes a claim that this is always already the case, so that every practice just is a part of one's praxis. The importance of this claim for critiquing the epistemological function of every human practice should not eclipse the usefulness of distinguishing practice from theory and therefore from praxis. As Boff, *Theology*, 193, notes, "Just as theory is constituted through a *breach* with praxis, to establish itself 'on its own'—in its own house, as it were—so also, in the opposite direction, the return from theory to praxis is reliable only through an analogous 'rupture,' *a leap in the opposite direction*. . . . No theory can replace practice. What theory can do is represent praxis (which, after all, is its definition)." Still, the distinction and unity of theory and praxis lead Boff to an evocative analogy: "If we look closely at the terms 'theory' and 'praxis,' taken separately, we shall observe that, on the one side as on the other, we find common elements or forms, constituting an area of coincidence in which these two spheres are in some fashion mutually inclusive. There obtains, then, a kind of *perichoresis* between theory and praxis" (210).

authentic and fruitful faithfulness to the Lord. If we look more deeply into the question of the value of salvation which emerges from our understanding of history—that is, a liberating praxis— we see that at issue is a question concerning *the very meaning of Christianity*. To be a Christian is to accept and to live—in solidarity, in faith, hope, and charity—the meaning that the Word of the Lord and our encounter with that Word give to the historical becoming of humankind on the way toward total communion.[67]

This is an innovative move beyond the basic epistemological function of solidarity in Freire's work. Solidarity as praxis is now a *locus theologicus* in which action and reflection, practice and theory, are indivisible. In solidarity, the church can perceive the Word of God uniquely in order to act faithfully, which gives rise to new understanding.

Solidarity is the essence of the praxis that liberation theology privileges epistemologically. Beyond general claims that all theology is subject to ideological commitments and that these are shaped by and serve practices is the more specific assertion that the preferential option for the poor embodied in solidarity is the practice that corresponds to Christian ideology. So Clodovis Boff says that liberation theologians' call for engagement with the poor "is not simply to be identified with the primary sociological *datum* . . . that all theology, and any theologian, is socially situated. They intend rather a position *taken*—a very determinate *option*."[68] The question, then, is why the option for the poor is a privileged *locus*. The answer is liberation theology's understanding of solidarity with the poor as being, in essence, solidarity *with Christ*. This "christological reading of solidarity with the poor"[69] has two primary expressions: solidarity with Jesus the liberator and solidarity with Jesus the liberated.

Solidarity with Jesus the Liberator. As I have already shown, the church in solidarity with the poor participates in the ongoing eschatological work of God. The point sharpens as we recognize that this is actually *solidarity with Jesus as Jesus is in solidarity with the poor* in the ongoing work of liberation. Following the Vatican II "Dogmatic Constitution of the Church" (*Lumen gentium*), Gutiérrez titles the twelfth chapter of *A Theology of Liberation* "The Church: Sacrament of History." Its core claim is: "The Church can be understood only in relation to the reality which it announces to

---

67. Gutiérrez, *We Drink*, 32.
68. Boff, *Theology*, 160.
69. Gutiérrez, *Power*, 65.

humankind. Its existence is not 'for itself,' but rather 'for others.' Its center is outside itself, it is in the work of Christ and his Spirit. It is constituted by the Spirit as 'the universal sacrament of salvation' (*Lumen gentium*, no. 48); outside of the action of the Spirit which leads the universe and history towards its fullness in Christ, the Church is nothing."[70] Accordingly, Ellacuría considers the church "the continuation of the principal sacrament which Jesus Christ is.... The proclamation and realization of salvation goes on continually today in Jesus Christ."[71] Hence, "the fullness of salvation that is proper to the Church requires a full-fledged incarnation in the radical historical variety that is lived by human populations.... Until this happens, Christ's incarnation, redemption, and resurrection will not attain their full measure."[72] Javier Jiménez Limón refers to such "passionate readiness to share his Messianic sufferings by identifying with those who suffer" as "transforming and kenotic solidarity."[73] All of these concepts—being centered in Christ and his Spirit; Christ's incarnation, redemption, and resurrection attaining their full measure; and sharing in Christ's messianic sufferings—convey that solidarity is not mere imitation of Jesus but, in a sense best represented by the theological notion of sacrament,[74] a real participation in his liberating work.

Solidarity with Jesus the Liberated. Jesus's solidarity with the poor cuts another direction, however. More than any other, liberation theology's consistent assertion that Jesus is present in the poor has constituted its unique contribution. Because Jesus is already in solidarity with the poor, the church's solidarity with the poor is solidarity with Jesus. Beginning with Gutiérrez, Matt 25:31–46 has been a primary point of reference for this idea. "The least of these who are members of my family" (Matt 25:40) is understood to be all of the poor, not just those of the church.[75] Gutiérrez can, therefore, speak of "relationship with God in solidarity with other persons."[76] Likewise, Leonardo Boff writes, "To accept a poor person as poor

70. Gutiérrez, *Theology*, 147.
71. Ellacuría, *Freedom*, 82.
72. Ellacuría, *Freedom*, 143.
73. Jiménez Limón, "Suffering," 707.
74. On conceiving solidarity as sacrament, see esp. Codina, "Analogía," 335–62.
75. Gutiérrez, *Theology*, 112. For similar uses of Matt 25, see Gutiérrez, *We Drink*, 38, 104; Gutiérrez, *Power*, 33; Boff and Boff, *Salvation*, 62; Sobrino, *Jesus*, 190–91; Ellacuría, "Crucified," 602–3.
76. Gutiérrez, *Theology*, 134.

is to accept the poor Jesus. He hides himself, he is incognito, behind each human face."[77] And Dussel says, "The Christian life is a daily putting into practice of certain categories that have been received from the Other (the other in this case being the God of revelation in the tradition of the church) through the summoning voice of the poor."[78] The parade of voices could go on. Scarcely a volume of liberation theology cited in this chapter does not make this claim in one form or another.[79] The conviction that Jesus is present in all the "crucified people"[80] of history grounds the expectation that the praxis of solidarity uniquely affords an encounter with God and, therefore, a deeper knowledge of God—and locates liberationist participation clearly in the debate about the extra-ecclesial work of God.

The sacramental analogy is at work in this claim as well. Citing Yves Congar's 1961 volume *The Wide World My Parish*, Gutiérrez contemplates "the sacrament of our neighbor."[81] This idea, too, becomes typical of liberation theology. Clodovis Boff and George Pixley explain: "It is in this sense that the poor are the sacrament of Jesus: the manifestation and communication of his mystery, the setting for his revelation and dwelling. So there is a coincidence between Christ and the poor, not just in a moral, but in a mystical sense, and so on the deepest level of reality. This does not mean that there is an abstract ontological identity (the poor = Christ), but that there is an actual identification (the poor *in* Christ)."[82] It is important to note, however, that "'the poor' do not go about with the words of revelation written all over their faces. 'The poor' are seen to be the 'sacrament of Christ' only by one who is attuned to this manifestation. And this is called 'faith.'"[83] This brings us full circle to Gutiérrez's understanding of his theological method in terms of Anselm's *Credo ut intelligam*.[84] Critically, however, faith is not mere belief but praxis: "faith from a point of departure in real, effective solidarity with the exploited classes, oppressed ethnic groups,

---

77. Boff, *Jesus*, 218.

78. Dussel, *Ethics*, 173.

79. E.g., see Ellacuría, *Freedom*, 116; Míguez Bonino, *Doing*, 151; Segundo, *Liberation*, 81; Gutiérrez, *Power*, 37–38, 106, 142–43, 211; Sobrino, *Spirituality*, 41–42; Boff and Pixley, *Bible*, ch. 5.

80. See Ellacuría, "Crucified," 580–603; Sobrino, *Jesus*, ch. 10.

81. Gutiérrez, *Theology*, 115.

82. Boff and Pixley, *Bible*, 113; see also Boff and Boff, *Salvation*, 62; Sobrino, *Jesus*, 21–22, 251.

83. Boff, *Theology*, 176.

84. Gutiérrez, *Power*, 55–56.

and despised cultures of Latin America, and from within their world."[85] Solidarity is *praxis seeking understanding*.

Solidarity with the poor, then, is possessed of a mutual sacramentality through which Jesus's unique presence for and in the poor constitutes praxis as a privileged theological locus. Indeed, Gutiérrez will go so far as to say that God "reveals himself only to the person who does justice to the poor."[86] Despite the problem this claim creates for the extension of liberationist solidarity into a wider missional conception of participation, the following pivot to an emerging Trinitarian vision of solidarity establishes the profound continuity of my understanding of solidarity with the liberationist understanding that is bound to the poor. Indeed, the missional implications of a Trinitarian conception of solidarity grow from the soil of liberation theology and are, therefore, inconceivable without the poor.

An Emerging Trinitarian Vision of Solidarity

The move from the christological reading of solidarity so essential for Latin American liberation theology to a Trinitarian reading of solidarity is quite natural, since both the claim that "in him all things hold together" (Col 1:17) and the claim that humanity is "in Christ," in distinct ways, already relate humankind perichoretically to the Triune God. The liberationist affirmation that Jesus is specially present among the poor is implicitly, therefore, a Trinitarian notion. Indeed, Gutiérrez affirms the Trinitarian missiology of *Ad gentes*: "Human beings are called together, as a community and not as separate individuals, to participate in the life of the Trinitarian community, to enter into the circuit of love that unites the person of the Trinity."[87] Still, despite the intuitive implications of participation in the Triune community for the conceptualization of solidarity, Trinitarian theology has been muted among liberationists. One might infer from the historical emphasis of liberationist Christology that this muting is a reflection of the desire to ground the preferential option for the poor in the more tangible reality of Jesus's ministry. Perhaps the more inclusive notion of "human beings" participating in Trinitarian community undercuts the claim that Jesus is specially present in the poor? But it is not obvious that

---

85. Gutiérrez, *Power*, 60. See also the discussion of the relationship between faith and ideology in the hermeneutical circle in Segundo, *Liberation*, ch. 4.

86. Gutiérrez, *Power*, 209.

87. Gutiérrez, *Theology*, 146; see also 113.

this is so. The relationship of humanity to the incarnate Son is epitomized in his presence among the poor, whose suffering he bore in the flesh of Jesus of Nazareth and among whom his Spirit moves in the liberating mission of God. But this is not an exclusive claim from a Trinitarian perspective, which not only allows for the recognition of the special character of God's presence among the poor but also incites the church to participate in God's mission precisely by discerning where in particular God is at work over against where God is not evidently at work.

Nonetheless, it is clear that a Trinitarian approach to solidarity pushes the concept back toward its broader usage in earlier Roman Catholic ethics. In the Puebla document, for example, the bishops correctly link Christ's solidarity with participation in Trinitarian communion. This vision, however, encompasses "all love and all communion."[88] Where the poor are concerned, the accent falls on "the eschatological liberation lived in the surrender to God and the new and universal solidarity with humankind."[89] Liberating solidarity is a practice of including the poor in humanity's communion with the Trinity, manifest in loving community in the present and consummated in the eschaton. Similarly, Pope John Paul II's encyclical *Sollicitudo Rei Socialis*—written in contemplation of liberation theology[90]—presents solidarity as an intensified human unity modeled on the "communion" of the Triune Persons. The link between the reality of Triune life and the practice of solidarity is even more tenuous here, however. The Trinity is a "model" that "inspires" solidarity, so that Christian communion reflects the life of God—which is different than *participating in* the life of God.[91]

Liberation theology insists, rather, that communion with God is not merely the possession of the church in which others might be included, much less that Christian communion is a mere reflection of the life of God. Rather, Christian communion is participation in the perichoretic fellowship of the Triune God who is *already* in solidarity with the poor. The possibility of integrating a liberationist understanding of solidarity with the church's missional participation in the Triune life comes to expression, if incompletely, in Leonardo Boff's *Trinity and Society*. Affirming that "human life is intrinsically bound up in the communion of the Trinity" and

---

88. Consejo Episcopal Latinoamericano, "Puebla," 298.
89. Consejo Episcopal Latinoamericano, "Puebla," 404.
90. See Beyer, "Meaning," 14.
91. John Paul II, *Sollicitudo*, 79.

that "the Trinity is present too in the course of history and the progress of society," Boff brings a liberationist understanding to bear: "Our faith, however, tells us that the Trinity is present in a specially close way in the struggles of the oppressed for their liberation."[92] Thus:

> When the oppressed unite, when interests converge for the common good, when men and women take heart to face up to the age-old threats to their lives and freedom, show solidarity and even identification with the cause of the oppressed, they are shot through with the hidden presence of the Spirit of life, prophecy and liberation. Human history does not cease to be human: its agents of change (and conservation), its conflicts, alliances, advances and setback are all human. But the Trinity lives in it, in a mysterious but nonetheless effective way, giving heart to the struggle that threatens these shoots of new life.[93]

In turn, the church's participation in mission is an extension of the Trinity's presence in the world: "The Trinity is present in a special way too in that section of humanity that the Spirit moves to accept Jesus as liberator and incarnate Son: the church. The two missions, those of the Son and the Holy Spirit, are carried out in the church. . . . In this life, the church lives on the communion of the Trinity; its unity derives from the perichoresis that exists between the three divine Persons."[94] Boff's liberationist Trinitarianism goes a long way toward the point at which I am driving. He does not, however, fully integrate (a) liberation theology's strong theological claims regarding the presence of Christ among the poor, including the correlate epistemological implications of liberationist solidarity, with (b) the claims about the church "carrying out" the missions of Son and Spirit and "living in" the perichoretic communion of the Trinity.

Following the trajectory that Boff has set, it seems correct to say that Christian communion is actualized through *mission as participation in God's perichoretic relationship to the poor*. I am interested in broadening this claim to account for God's perichoretic relationship with *the other* who may not be poor in the ways that concern liberation theology most (already suggested by Freire's interest in the liberation of both oppressor and oppressed).[95] At the same time, I want to retain liberation theology's con-

---

92. Boff, *Trinity*, 224–25.
93. Boff, *Trinity*, 125.
94. Boff, *Trinity*, 225.
95. Guitián, "Principio," 553–85, has extended the liberationist vision of solidarity.

crete, praxeological understanding of solidarity as virtue and practice. Both a broader vision of the other and the concreteness of praxis are indispensable dimensions of the claim at the heart of this chapter, that participation in God's Triune life in the world beyond the church is *missional solidarity*. There is, however, a tension between the two. In order to make this tension productive, the next section considers broader visions of solidarity, particularly in philosophical and theological ethics.

Toward a Theology of Missional Solidarity

On the way toward a theology of missional solidarity, I begin with the pivotal usage of solidarity language in the early work of feminist theologian Sharon Welch and its denouement in the *mujerista* theology of Ada María Isasi-Díaz. From there, I move to a review of *solidarity* in broadly feminist missiology, demonstrating its trajectory toward a postcolonial conception "beyond" early liberation theology's. This groundwork in place, I approach the need to conceive of the otherness with which one is in solidarity, appealing finally to additional philosophical and theological resources in order to arrive at my conception of solidarity as participation in God's mission.

Feminist Missiological Contributions

Solidarity in Feminist Discourse

The first feminist theologian to thematize solidarity was Sharon Welch. She insists, "The emphasis on solidarity means more than simply the discovery of another theme of theological reflection. This emphasis marks the manifestation of a new episteme."[96] This idea undergirds my recourse to

---

He affirms that "the ultimate foundation of solidarity is not mere common humanity, but the Trinity, in the mystery of God as Love, in the charity that communion engenders and is converted into the perfection of solidarity" (565; my translation) and combines this understanding with the christological specification that "we are responsible for others because we are brothers and sisters, and we are such because we all have the same Father, and we are called to be one in Christ by the Holy Spirit. Therefore, relationality decisively establishes solidarity" (570; my translation). In the end, then, "this solidarity is called to extend itself to *all humans* because the sacrifice brought about by Christ encompasses all humanity *at all times*" (572, emphasis added; my translation). Extension of liberation theology's praxeological epistemology to solidary relationships with all people remains an implication, however.

96. Welch, *Communities*, 46. It is necessary to address the perception that conceiving

solidarity as the final, practical category of analysis for participation in God's mission. It is not only the case that, following liberation theology, we may speak right of "the fundamental project of solidarity with all people"[97] but also that this project, which comprises the practices of participation in liberation, is epistemically privileged.

Welch's reflections are especially useful because she recognizes how fraught the definition of *liberation* becomes when, for example, it is applied not only to the poor of Latin America but also to wealthy, educated Western women. Reminiscent of Freire's original dichotomy, she says, "My own project is a theology of liberation; it is my attempt to develop a

---

of liberation more broadly—in terms of race or gender, to say nothing of colonialism and culture—is, for some, a betrayal of the materially poor. For example, Ivan Petrella argues the common label "contextual theology" fails to recognize that "liberation theologies are born from the struggles of the poor and the oppressed, struggles that were translated into an epistemological break with the whole of Western, wealthy, white, and male theological tradition; they are not one theological school among others in the canon" (Petrella, *Beyond*, 133). The idea that this epistemological break is at risk in the move beyond liberation theology's early socioeconomic concerns must be taken seriously. In particular, does the missiological conception of solidarity entail a "mission creep" that undermines the new episteme Welch extends to feminist theology and, by implication, other liberative practices?

Considering Freire's observation that the oppressed frequently become oppressors and Welch's sobriety about complex positionalities—and recalling solidarity of "the oppressor with the oppressed" (Isasi-Díaz) and "the former colonizer and the formerly colonized" (Dube)—one must wonder whether Petrella's rhetoric fails to represent the implications of solidarity. Surely perichoretic participation in Christ's own option for redemptive poverty (2 Cor 8:9) is paradigmatic. Indeed, I suggest that the attempt to conceive of solidarity in terms of a purely economic social location apart from the theological correlatives of participation as *theōsis* and embodied narrativity is a false path.

Granting the broadening of the concept of mission through *missio Dei* theology discussed in ch. 2, it is fair to say that mission is primarily concerned with the church's relationships with the rest of the world. The missiological discourse about solidarity helps us conceive of the church's relationships more broadly. This broadening cannot obscure liberation theology's axiomatic claim because the church finds itself in relationships whose socioeconomic imperatives solidarity cannot ignore. If participation in God's mission entails *theōsis* and embodied narrativity along with solidarity, God's presence and work among the poor necessarily calls the church into relationships that must bodily rewrite the story of mission. At the same time, these are not the only relationships in which God is at work. Participation as solidarity involves true mutuality across class, race, gender, nationality, culture, and every other type of relational barrier that divides humanity. The concrete practices of solidarity cannot be limited to economics, and each of them is party to the epistemic break that liberation theology identifies in relation to the materially poor.

97. Welch, *Communities*, 27.

liberating mode of theological reflection within my own situation, where I am both oppressor and oppressed."[98] She deals with this tension by embracing it: "Entanglement in power and particularity is not a condition to be avoided, but one to be understood. This becomes ironically clear as I realize that the very possibility of critique and of resistance is rooted not in a universal sense of justice, but in concrete, varied, tenuous experiences of resistance and liberation, that is, in my participation in different forms of power/knowledge."[99] The epistemic privilege of solidarity is its particularity, over against "universal" or "ontological"[100] claims. Thus, Welch navigates the extension of "solidarity" (*qua* participation in liberation) to a more complicated construal of the relationships purportedly constituted as "oppressed" and "oppressor" by refusing to define these in abstraction from the relationships themselves. There is a complex multiplicity of relationships through which—*in solidarity*—one might come to understand what sin, justice, reconciliation, hope, and so on really mean. In this way, Welch establishes the sense in which theologies that attend to relationships constituted in terms of race and gender (to mention prominent examples) have also fallen under the rubric of "liberation." Concomitantly, these theologies point to a wider, richer understanding of solidarity as the practices of participation in God's reconciling work.

No one has done more to develop the concept of solidarity theologically along these lines than *mujerista* theologian Ada María Isasi-Díaz. Through her experience as a missionary in Perú, Isasi-Díaz realized that "the goal is not to be like the poor and the oppressed (an impossibility), but rather to be in solidarity with them."[101] Isasi-Díaz rules out two misunderstandings of the term. First, solidarity is not mere "agreement with and sympathy for the poor and oppressed"[102] but instead "has to do with understanding the interconnections that exist between oppression and privilege, between the rich and the poor, the oppressed and the oppressors."[103] Second, therefore, it is not limited to the solidarity of the oppressed with each other. Rather, Isasi-Díaz envisions true "mutuality of the oppressor with the oppressed," in which oppressors become "friends"

---

98. Welch, *Communities*, 13.
99. Welch, *Communities*, 74.
100. See Welch, *Communities*, 38, 78.
101. Isasi-Díaz, *Mujerista*, 86; see also Isasi-Díaz, "Solidarity," 266–67.
102. Isasi-Díaz, *Mujerista*, 87.
103. Isasi-Díaz, *Mujerista*, 89.

of the oppressed. Accordingly, "the process of conversion that becomes an intrinsic part of the lives of the 'friends' . . . makes it possible for the 'friends' to participate with the oppressed in creating strategies for liberation, in deepening and clarifying the understanding of mutuality that is at the heart of liberation."[104] In turn, she connects these general specifications with the kingdom of God, so the identification of mutuality as the heart of liberation becomes theologically salient.

Isasi-Díaz writes: "From a Christian perspective the goal of solidarity is *to participate in the ongoing process of liberation through which we Christians become a significantly positive force in the unfolding of the 'kindom' of God*."[105] She coins the term *kin-dom* to avoid the patriarchal connotations of *kingdom* and to highlight the relational essence of God's reign. Liberation, then, is the process through which God's just rule unfolds—a process in which the Christian participates through solidarity. Again, following earlier liberation theology, she clarifies, "Our *participation in the act of salvation* is what we refer to as liberation."[106] Solidarity, whose heart is mutuality, is the means of Christian participation in the act of salvation. It is fair to say that what we have traditionally called "participation in God's mission" becomes "solidarity" in the work of Isasi-Díaz. This juxtaposition highlights the key idea—that the essence of participation in God's saving work is the kind of relational mutuality that deconstructs the oppressive relationships of colonialist missions. What the theology of *missio Dei* claims in Trinitarian (perichoretic) terms as a remedy to the failings of colonialist missions, *solidarity* specifies in terms of concretely relational practices.

Solidarity in Feminist Missiology

To what extent, then, does Christian missiology already define participation in God's mission in terms of solidarity? In chapter 2, the term appeared in reference (a) to ecumenical missiology's appropriation of liberationist themes and (b) to the practice of hospitality in the pneumatological relationship understanding of participation. In neither case does it play a definitional role. By contrast, like liberationist thinkers more broadly,

---

104. Isasi-Díaz, *Mujerista*, 97.

105. Isasi-Díaz, *Mujerista*, 89; emphasis added.

106. Isasi-Díaz, *Mujerista*, 90; emphasis added.

feminist and other postcolonial missiologies place solidarity at the heart of a redefinition of Christian mission.[107]

In service to the "urgent need to develop a feminist missiology,"[108] feminist theologian Letty Russell highlights the contributions of those whom African theologian Musa Dube calls "postcolonial subjects."[109] According to Dube, the term "describes both the former colonizer and the formerly colonized"—further complexifying the oppressor-oppressed dichotomy. Both are "a people whose perception of each other and of economic, political, and cultural relationships cannot be separated from the global impact and constructions of Western/modern imperialism, which still remain potent in forms of neocolonialism, military arrogance, and globalization."[110] An understanding of mission as solidary emerges from the feminist response to this challenge.

To begin, Mary Grey calls for "a conversion to a concept of mission as love-in-communication, which is more about listening, and responding to the needs of a context, than about a one-sided insistence on the superiority of Christianity."[111] Here, the necessary conversion is not that of the missionized but of the church's very conception of mission. As one of the doubly colonized, Mercy Amba Oduyoye, a Ghanaian Methodist, adds a significant perspective: "The mission of the church in Africa includes participating in the struggle against patriarchy in all its deadly forms. The interrelatedness and the complexity and variety of human existence on this earth must inform both the mission and the theology of the church. . . . This mission can hardly begin when the theology that it propagates is one developed in response to Euro-American Enlightenment and pietistic needs."[112] Couching the question in an African feminist theology, then, she too calls for

---

107. See Maluleke, "Postcolonial," 503–27; Santiago-Vendrell, "Not," 285–300; Longkumer, "Not," 297–309; Vähäkangas, "African," 170–85; Montero, "Contribution," 115–29; Clarke, "World," 192–206; Mainwaring, "Mutuality," 13–31; Padilla, "Globalization," 69–90; Reichard, "Mutually," 245–57.

108. Russell, "Cultural," 24. See also Russell, "God," 40. For an earlier assessment of feminist missiology, Kim has ably summarized these contributions in "Mission," 17–26.

109. Russell, "Cultural," 24; see Dube, *Postcolonial*, 15–16. Likewise, Heidemanns, "Missiology?," 115, states, "Postcolonial criticism can qualify the notion of relational consciousness particularly by means of the concept of postcolonial subjects, as introduced to feminist theology by Musa Dube."

110. Dube, *Postcolonial*, 15–16.

111. Grey, "'She Is,'" 204.

112. Oduyoye, "Church," 500–501.

a reappropriation and redefinition of mission according to the contextual realities of a postcolonial world. Kwok Pui-lan's entry on "Mission" in the *Dictionary of Feminist Theologies* provides an apt summary of feminist missiology at the end of the twentieth century:

> Mission is to proclaim the good news that God affirms life over death and that God acts among the poor, the majority of whom are women who are victimized in the globalization of the market economy and left out in decision-making processes. Mission is forming partnership, building bridges and coalitions, and strengthening grassroots movements to struggle for life and work for justice for all people. . . .
>
> In our multiracial and multireligious world, people of other faiths must not be treated as missiological objects but as partners in understanding the fullness of God and building solidarity across different faith traditions, for the welfare of the whole of humanity and the planet.[113]

The word *solidarity* in Kwok's final sentence encapsulates the redefinition of mission in postcolonial feminist missiology.

Russell connects this understanding with Trinitarian participation: "We need a feminist missiology that is life-giving for all as we participate in God's action of mending creation. Certainly that missiology should include a lot of work on our understanding of the Trinity and God's sending action, as we seek alternatives to patriarchal metaphors and traditions and make use of cultural hermeneutics to understand the metaphors and religious symbols that will best express God's welcome in multicultural and multifaith contexts."[114] Postcolonial subjects' participation together in the mission of God is the proper referent of mission language. Accordingly, Russell concludes, "In this recognition that there are many ways we are and are not oppressed is the possibility for *working together in solidarity* on concrete projects for change, including projects in which *theology itself is transformed*."[115]

Finally, Katja Heidemanns also commends attention to the perspectives of the postcolonial subjects who are actively engaged in God's work in their local contexts, which adds a critical dimension to the

---

113. Kwok, "Mission," 186. Kwok's work in feminist postcolonialism has proven noteworthy for its nuance, not least in regard to the complexities of assessing Christian mission's legacy. See, e.g., Kwok, "Image," 250–58.

114. Russell, "Cultural," 34.

115. Russell, "Cultural," 35; emphasis added.

Trinitarian theology that has invigorated missional theology since its inception. "Thus," she observes, "besides the claiming of a dialogical and reciprocal dynamic of missionary practice based on an understanding of God as a God of intrinsic relationality and communion, another critical function of feminist theology and ethics regarding an understanding of mission might consist in setting the context for an understanding of what enables solidarity and work for justice."[116] Such solidarity calls us to "a different kind of listening. This is a listening to the multifaceted movements of resistance and hope. This listening will challenge us to *redefine our understanding* of responsibility as it finally leads us to assume responsibility for the limitations of our own perspective and vision for this world. Such listening will also remind us that *what qualifies Christian practice as missionary practice* is to take the risk of living consciously in accordance with the mystery of God's ongoing presence to all creation and of embodying the promise we cannot yet capture with our very lives."[117] The redefinition of our understanding is the challenge that feminist postcolonial missiology consistently issues through its vision of solidarity.

The Dimensions of Missional Solidarity

My primary interlocutors in the chapter are liberation theology and feminist postcolonial missiology, but *solidarity* enjoys use in a wider context that impinges on the dialogue. In much of late modern Anglo-American philosophical discourse, *solidarity* refers to the collectivist end of the individual-social or private-public polarity at the heart of modern liberalism. In its socialist European uses, mentioned in connection with Catholic social theory and Marxian influences on early liberation theology, the term shares this frame of reference. *Solidarity* is the philosophical term of art for designating that which constitutes community in modern democracies.

For a variety of well-known reasons, modern democracies are fraught with difficulty when it comes to justifying the ethico-political bases of solidarity. Most urgent among them in the postmodern condition is the transition from mere plurality in the context of competing cultural hegemonies to radical cultural pluralism intensified by globalization. Modern conceptions of solidarity have been stretched to their limits, leaving philosophers to ponder what, if anything, might hold pluralistic societies together. Some

---

116. Heidemanns, "Missiology?," 109.
117. Heidemanns, "Missiology?," 118; emphasis added.

secularists, such as Richard Rorty, believe that solidarity has no foundational justification, divine or otherwise; it is a social construct of liberal democracies over against alternative forms of society.[118] Others, such as Richard Bernstein, find Rorty's "fideistic"[119] commitment to solidary unsatisfying, shifting the accent to the "dialogical encounter" of others through which solidarity is identified.[120] Notably, Bernstein's "engaged fallibilistic pluralism," which holds that "however much we are committed to our own styles of thinking, we are willing to listen to others without denying or suppressing the otherness of the other,"[121] cuts close to the contextual-dialogue and pneumatological-relationship types of missional participation discussed in chapter 2. Rorty and Bernstein's debate represents the conceptual milieu in which a missional understanding of solidarity moves—radical, globalized pluralism. Giles Gunn correctly identifies the need to address pluralism "not only in terms of our sense of solidarity with our own kind but also in terms of . . . our 'sense of fundamental kinship with the enemy.'"[122] He concludes that the otherness of the other—alterity—"is not one element of identity among others, nor is it merely that over against which identity supposedly constitutes itself. . . . Alterity is that which enables cultures, like selves, to learn from each other, to become constituents of each other's identity."[123] By insisting that this is so even in regard to the most conflictual

---

118. See Rorty, *Contingency*, 198, for whom the identification of a foundation for solidarity "seems to be impossible—a philosopher's invention, an awkward attempt to secularize the idea of becoming one with God." Throughout the argument, Rorty portrays the doomed search for the foundations of solidarity as a remnant of religious thinking. "The ideal form of liberalism would be one which was enlightened, secular, through and through. It would be one in which no trace of divinity remained, either in the form of a divinized world or a divinized self " (45). In this, he correctly sees that "secular ethical universalism has taken over the attitude of Christianity" (191) and that "such notions [as 'child of God,' 'humanity' and 'rational being'] have kept the way open for political and cultural change by providing a fuzzy but inspiring *focus imaginarius* (e.g., *absolute truth, pure* art, humanity *as such*)" (195). But he believes the usefulness of this imaginary has reached its limit. The enlightened now understand that there is only the "pragmatic" construction of solidarity.

119. Bernstein, *New*, 278.

120. Bernstein, *New*, 337.

121. Bernstein, *New*, 336.

122. Bernstein, *New*, 37, quoting Burke, "Four," 435. Perhaps unsurprisingly, the discussion of solidarity in the intervening decades seems not to have moved "beyond" this fundamental—and, from a Christian perspective, theological—issue.

123. Bernstein, *New*, 193–94. For Gunn, this conclusion is a move "beyond solidarity" in Rorty and Bernstein's terms, though it seems to be simply a better understanding of solidarity.

otherness with which globalized pluralism must contend, Gunn puts a finger on the question at the heart of secularist notions of solidarity: is it truly possible to overcome the depths of alterity?

I summarize, therefore, by sketching the dimensions of a missional solidarity that attends, from the theological perspective developed above, to a variety of tensions that characterize the depths of alterity. I label these tensions (1) theological-secular, (2) socioeconomic-integral, (3) asymmetrical-mutual, and (4) personal-systemic. Here, a theological vision of the other meets the concreteness of praxis identified at the end of section 1.

First, the theological-secular tension marks the difference between a solidarity that considers the universal nature of human relationships rooted in a theological account of the *imago Dei*, including both human-human and divine-human differences, and a secularist vision that limits solidarity to political terms. The question here is *Where is God at work?* Secularist solidarity highlights the depths of alterity that a theological definition may easily gloss with abstract claims.[124] Its pragmatism calls Christian theology to a renewed sobriety about the profound difficulty that faces grandiloquent affirmations of humanity's shared nature. But it also finds an ally in the theological affirmation of the ultimate difference—the essential otherness—between the human and the divine with which any Christian notion of solidarity must contend. Even the human *imago Dei* is an expression of alterity. For theological anthropology surely entails such difference not only in the human-divine distinction but also in the otherness that characterizes human-human relationships inasmuch as human alterity reflects the *imago Dei* in each that separates each from the humanity of the other.[125] Missional solidarity must, therefore, account for the depths of alterity in its human and divine dimensions. Trinitarian

---

124. I must note the outstanding account of pluralistic solidarity offered by Reynolds, *Broken*. Reynolds works with theological concerns in mind toward a tenable understanding of solidarity in relation to religious pluralism, but his method is philosophical, not theological. Here is an understanding of solidarity that builds from the pragmatic reality of pluralism that philosophy can profitably illuminate.

125. Mescher, *Ethics*, xi, puts it well: "Coming face-to-face with another person is an encounter with someone 'wonderfully made' (Ps 139:14) in the 'image and likeness' of God (Gn 1:26). In this way, encounters are sacraments—visible signs of God's invisible grace—such that encountering another person not only reveals the sacred in our midst but also bears an inexhaustible potential for greater discovery. Because God is love (1 Jn 4:8), encounters have the potential to be an experience of love, an invitation to share in the divine life: a Trinitarian communion of love that is offered, received, and returned. When we encounter others, we encounter God."

theology (*theōsis* and *perichōrēsis*) and liberation theology teach us that the divine at work in every human is both the ground of otherness (distorted by sin as it may be) and the basis of union.

Second, the socioeconomic-integral tension marks the difference between a solidarity that attends to the otherness created by virulent global systems of poverty and a solidarity that recognizes the multidimensional alterity that describes humanity beyond economics. This tension presses the question *What constitutes alterity?* We have noted the power dynamics that gender and race present. But contemporary theology also attends to another prominent otherness in our globalized context: religion.[126] The importance of religious otherness for missional theology highlights the need to conceive of solidarity integrally.[127] The many faces of alterity require of missional solidarity a holistic vision that comprehends the particular urgency of material poverty without ignoring the full scope of universal human otherness.

Third, the asymmetrical-mutual tension marks the difference between a solidarity that places particular burdens on the privileged and a solidarity that is fully mutual. As a practice, a virtue, and a theological method, solidarity requires the church to answer the question *Who is solidary?* From the perspective of missional theology, this question must be restated in other terms: whose agency is at work in God's mission? Without exception, the call to solidarity extends to the whole church—all classes, genders, races, and cultures. Certainly, the asymmetry of human relationships means the ethical burden of solidarity falls uniquely on the powerful and privileged.[128]

---

126. See esp. Min, "Dialectical," 587–604; Min, *Solidarity*, esp. ch. 9. Min's proposal of "the dialectical confessionalist pluralism of solidarity" ("Dialectical," 588) gives special attention to religious pluralism. Missional theology has recently begun attending to interreligious dialogue more robustly. See, e.g., Heo, "Revisiting," 169–82; Womack, "Converting," 183–98.

127. I borrow the term *integral* from evangelical iterations of liberation theology, represented especially by Padilla, "Globalization," 69–90. He calls for "the globalization of solidarity across national and ethnic borders" (84) with Christian partnership particularly in mind. Beyond the important focus of this article, the nature of integral mission calls the church to a comprehensive understanding of solidarity in keeping with liberation theology's core insight. God is at work in the other, whatever their alterity may be, and integral participation in God's mission entails holistic solidarity.

128. Peters, "Reflections," 225, for examples, argues that solidarity is "unapologetically, a first-world ethic for people of privilege. . . . The point of solidarity work is to ask particular questions about the ethical and moral status and responsibility of people with privilege who are complicit in or benefit from the current world order." So Rajendra, "Burdened," 109; Maruggi, "Disorienting," 37–47. Such understandings reduce solidarity

Yet, this imperative does not diminish the mutual agency that a Christian understanding of solidarity must affirm. All may participate equally in God's mission; all may enact solidarity as God works in the other.

Lastly, the personal-systemic tension marks the difference between a solidarity that emphasizes the responsibility of individuals to act in solidary ways and a solidarity that focuses on creating systems that serve solidarity. The question in this regard is *How does solidarity participate in reconciliation?* Neither a solely personal nor a solely systemic solidarity will suffice because alterity obtains at both levels.[129] The other is a neighbor, a stranger, an enemy; and otherness is a manifestation of economic, social, religious, political, and cultural systems. To suggest that participation in God's mission need only consider particular, personal relationships without regard for the systemic aspects of alterity is not only naïve but also a failure to see God as redemptively at work in social structures. Conversely, addressing systems of alterity without personal practices of solidarity, without the intimacy through which the virtue of solidarity comes to life, or without the contextual praxis of solidarity that generates theological reflection results in a failure to participate in concrete, perichoretic practices of personal bodies emplotted by the narrative of the *missio Dei*.

Together, four dimensions of a missional conception of solidarity as a practice, virtue, and theological method must account for (1) both the pragmatic and theological depth of human alterity; (2) the full scope of human alterity in a way that attends to the most problematic contextual challenges to mutuality, of which socioeconomic otherness is a primary but not exclusive manifestation; (3) the unique responsibility of the privileged

---

to "a way of describing the actions of persons and communities who seek to enact *social justice* in the world" (Peters, "Reflections," 227; emphasis added), which undergirds the use of the term in much of the recent theological literature on racism in the United States. See, e.g., Day, *Constructing*; and Swanson, *Rediscipling*. To the contrary, I agree with Copeland, *Enfleshing*, 93: "We need thoroughgoing, practical, genuine systemic change in the present global order. At the same time, we sense a need for something deeper and beyond the moral attention that social justice accords to the distribution of the material and cultural conditions for human living. That something deeper and beyond, I suggest, is solidarity." I am in pursuit of a more comprehensive understanding of solidarity that insists on the agency of the oppressed as participants in God's mission.

129. In this respect, I agree with Kelly, "Everyday," 416, who states: "Solidarity insists that moral change requires converting not only personal agents but also social structures. Consequently, solidarity indicates that an ethical approach to ordinary life cannot succeed by appealing to the formation of individual moral agents in isolation but must also encourage moral actors to take responsibility for the challenges and limitations of the social context that surrounds them."

and powerful without diminishing the fully mutual agency of every human participant in God's mission regardless of one's particular otherness; and (4) both the personal and systemic aspects of participation in God's redemptive work. Accordingly, the relationships in which the church embodies participation in the redemptive work of God's kingdom, which rightly reconstitute mission in the postcolonial world and occasion the epistemic break on which missional theology depends, are relationships possessed of a solidarity that is deep, wide, mutual, and holistic. What these relationships demand—what exactly the pursuit of God's kingdom entails—is a function of contextual particularity and, specifically, how God is at work in a given context. Solidarity is participation in God's mission, not merely in the achievement of preordained goods or ideological aims, precisely because the goods and aims of God's kingdom are to be discerned through the practice, virtue, and theological method of solidarity.

It remains, then, to bring these specifications into union with the Trinitarian understanding of solidarity to which liberation theology led us. I have argued that extending liberation theology's perception of the presence of Christ among the poor in conjunction with its Trinitarian claims that the church carries out the missions of Son and Spirit and lives in the perichoretic communion of the Trinity results in the conception of *mission as participation in God's perichoretic relationship to the other*. This is the essential meaning of solidarity as participation in God's mission. In this sense, the practice of solidarity is the church's loving presence in history perichoretically united with the Triune God's loving presence in history, expressed as an embodiment of the concrete practices of liberation integrally conceived on the basis of particular relationships to others. The virtue of solidarity is a spiritual attitude and a capacity—a deep, wide, mutual, holistic relational disposition toward the other—gifted by the Spirit through the practice of solidarity. And the theological method of solidarity is inhabitation of the theological locus that is communion with Jesus who is present in the other, an encounter with God that gives rise to new theological understanding.

Conclusion: Summing Up Participation in God's Mission

I began this exploration of the meaning of participation in God's mission by reviewing major understandings of it and establishing the status of the concept: it remains unclear what participation in God's mission is—too unclear, at least, for the concept to function cogently in my claim that participation in mission uniquely shapes readers of Scripture. This is so not merely because of the inevitable diversity of understandings but because significant aporias emerge from their comparison. In total, there persists a need for a Trinitarian account of how human and divine agency relate that gives way to a concrete conception of ecclesial, human action in relation to God's action in the world. Accordingly, I proposed an understanding of participation as *theōsis* that establishes the nature of human participation in the divine life in relation to the perichoretic union of Father, Son, and Spirit, then I proceeded to a corollary theological anthropology that combines the concepts of human embodiment and narrativity in order to clarify the nature of perichoretic participation in the Triune life, and finally I arrived at an understanding of participation that appropriates and extends the notion of solidarity in liberation theology in order to specify concretely the nature of the church's missional action. I recapitulate all three concepts here in order to integrate them in a working definition of participation in God's mission.

Recapitulating Participation in God's Mission

Theōsis designates an ontological union by which the church's works in Christ, through the Spirit, become participation in the saving work of God. *Perichōrēsis* further stipulates that human participation in the *missio Dei* involves an asymmetrical and incomplete yet truly reciprocal identification of human action with the divine movements of relationship subsisting in one event—the event of mission. This Trinitarian vision of participation maintains the distinction between the church's fallible missions and God's mission while indicating the sense in which the Triune movements of suffering, love, and reconciliation in the word include the church's work so as to instantiate a unity of human action and the Triune event of *missio Dei*.

Embodied narrativity clarifies the meaning of perichoretic participation in God's mission. In the hermeneutical circle of the read narrative and the life lived in the Spirit, the scriptural narrative is rightly mediated by Trinitarian doctrine, which is the grammar by which the church coauthors its embodied, narratival participation in the *missio Dei*. Correlatively, embodied narrativity is the ontological status through which humanity is capable of being taken up into the divine life thrown open for the world's redemption. The twofold dynamic of self-narration and Spirit-narration that describes embodied narrativity entail a hermeneutic spirituality that constitutes the divine-human synergy of perichoretic participation in God's mission.

Solidarity is the perichoretic relationality that characterizes human action in union with the Triune event of *missio Dei*. This is the practice, virtue, and theological method through which the church embodies participation in the redemptive work of God's kingdom. The deep, wide, mutual, holistic relationships of solidarity give rise to contextually specific discernment about cooperation with God's work in the other. And through the embodied, narrative practices of solidarity with the other, the church is perichoretically united with the Triune God's loving presence in history, thereby enacting the hermeneutic spirituality of missional self-narration and Spirit-narration and placing the church bodily in communion with God in the other so as to engender new theological understanding.

A Definition of Participation in God's Mission

Participation in mission is participation in the Triune God's perichoretic relationship to the other, in union with Christ, through solidary action that embodies the scriptural narrative of missio Dei *and cooperates in the work through which the Spirit writes the church into the story of God's mission.*

God's perichoretic relationship to the other means that *theōsis* takes place in missional relationship to the other. The other is the locus of God's reconciling work in which the church may participate. The mode of participation is embodied solidary action discerned and specified concretely through relationships that span the depths of human alterity in its personal and systemic expressions mutually and holistically. Through this cooperative action, the church's narrative identity is perichoretically transformed as the church's work joins with the *missio Spiritus* in the storied event of mission.

Recall that my thesis is that *the church is epistemically constituted as an interpretive community through participation in the ongoing* missio Dei *because that participation occasions a reconfiguration of human embodied narrativity in conformity with the life of the Triune God revealed in Scripture.* In order to explain theologically why it is the case that participation in God's mission epistemically constitutes an interpretive community in this way, it was necessary, first, to clarify the meaning of the phrase "participation in God's mission." In the course of devising a theological definition of participation in God's mission, I have indicated the significance of other key terms in the thesis. The praxeological dimension of solidarity as a theological method—namely, the epistemic break it occasions—explains the sense of *epistemically constituted*. Further, *a reconfiguration of human embodied narrativity* signals the perichoretic relationship of human narrativity with the *missio Dei*. Finally, *the life of the Triune God revealed in Scripture* refers to a Trinitarian account of the perichoretic relationships of Father, Son, and Spirit thrown open through the divine *opera ad extra* manifest as the historical event of *missio Dei*.

With a definition of participation in God's mission established, I return to the remainder of the thesis—the hermeneutical component. In chapter 6, I first extend my conception of missional participation to the interpreted text through a theological and philosophical reflection on the hermeneutics of participation. The final dimension of the argument is a concluding conceptualization of readerly formation through participation in God's mission that locates my thesis within the missional hermeneutics discourse and indicates what my theological account of the formation of missional readers contributes to theological interpretation of Scripture.

CHAPTER 6

The Hermeneutics of Participation

> "Theologically a hermeneutic of an *embodied* text reflects an incarnational Christology, in which revelation operates through the interwovenness of word and deed. It also coheres with a theological account of the role of the community in which their actions and witness give credibility to, and facilitate understanding of, the word which is spoken and read." —Anthony Thiselton[1]

To BRING MY DEFINITION of participation in God's mission to bear on readerly formation in missional hermeneutics, it is necessary to draw the connection between missional participation and the phenomena of textual interpretation. The discussion of embodied narrativity in light of Moltmann's theological anthropology began in this direction already, and the affinity with Ricoeur established there will prove to be of further significance. Ricoeur is among the foremost luminaries of the twentieth-century "hermeneutic turn" in philosophy.[2] Because Ricoeur's body of

---

1. Thiselton, *New*, 75.

2. The phrase "hermeneutic turn" characterizes a broad and diffuse shift of interest among continental philosophers. Martin Heidegger's *Being and Time* (first published in German, 1927) is the central pivot point, though the turn can be traced from the phenomenology of Edmund Husserl through Heidegger's existentialism to the overtly hermeneutical work of Hans-Georg Gadamer and Paul Ricoeur. See Noé, "'Hermeneutic,'" 117–28; Risser, "After," 71–88; Hoy, "Heidegger," 177–201; and especially Ricoeur's programmatic essay "Existence," 3–24.

work uniquely encompasses embodied narrativity and textual interpretation, his insights provide the hinge on which my thesis pivots. Yet, missional participation is a theological concept that calls for a wider vision of hermeneutics than Ricoeur's work alone can provide.

In the interest of this wider vision, section 1 follows Ricoeur's understanding of the relationship between the critical project of philosophical hermeneutics and "faith" to stipulate methodologically how general hermeneutics and theological interpretation relate in the present argument. Section 2 briefly locates the discussion of participatory hermeneutics in relation to the recent development of "carnal hermeneutics" by one of Ricoeur's protégés, Richard Kearney, to develop Ricoeur's insights about the relationship between embodiment and interpretation into a model of embodied textual hermeneutics. Finally, section 3 extends this model through my definition of participation in God's mission.

General Hermeneutics and Theological Interpretation

In a 2003 interview, Ricoeur commented: "It's true that I have changed in the last fifty years. I have read lots of new books, and the whole philosophical climate has altered in all kinds of important ways. I began in an era of existentialism, traversed structuralism, and now find myself before a 'post-I-know-not-what,' deconstruction, etc."[3] Ricoeur's post-I-know-not-what landscape has not become any easier to characterize in the intervening years, but in the realm of biblical hermeneutics with which Ricoeur so often engaged, a distinctive horizon has emerged in the discourse called theological interpretation of Scripture (see ch. 1). I argue that the encounter between Ricoeur and theological interpretation takes place on a landscape that is, to use Ricoeur's famous expression, "beyond the desert of criticism."[4] Here, the horizon is filled with postcritical faith that need not—indeed, should not—be bracketed in the return to the biblical text. In order to suggest what biblical hermeneutics beyond the desert might entail, this section (1) briefly recapitulates in Ricoeurian terms the characterization of theological interpretation given in chapter 1, (2) describes "the specific nature and singularity of the encounter"[5] between

---

3. Kearney, *Debates*, 46.
4. Ricoeur, *Symbolism*, 349.
5. Kearney, *Debates*, 46.

theological interpretation and Ricoeur, and (3) indicates how Ricoeur and theological interpretation fruitfully challenge each other.

A Ricoeurian Recapitulation of Theological Interpretation of Scripture

To adapt a schema familiar to students of Ricoeur, theological interpretation is animated by sets of interests behind, in, and in front of the text.[6] *Behind the text*, the interest is, in a word, God. Karl Barth's influence is tangible here, though arguably theological interpretation shifts the accent from Barth's view of the *Sache* of Scripture as the Word of God mediated by the text to the very Triune God who speaks the word presently through Scripture. As Joel Green says, "Theological interpretation is concerned with encountering the God who stands behind and is mediated in Scripture."[7] *In the text*, theological interpretation is interested in approaching the text as canon, which typically entails either intertextual or narrative reading practices. The underlying issue, however, is that taking the text as canon both delimits the field of intertextuality by stipulating that other texts are not canonical (viz. authoritative) and correlates the text's narrative unity with the Rule of Faith that emerged with and from the process of canonization. Theological interpretation elevates the faith commitments that determine which texts constitute the Bible in the first place to the level of hermeneutical guidelines for reading those texts together, intertextually and narratively. *In front of the text*, theological interpretation is interested in the theological constitution of the reading community through both theological traditions and the ongoing practices of the believing community. The emphasis here falls on the concern of the present study—the theological formation of readers, especially as an ecclesial community. Together these three sets of interests behind, in, and in front of the biblical text sketch the meaning of approaching the biblical text *as Scripture* and suggest the ground on which theological interpretation might encounter Ricoeur.

---

6. Ricoeur, "Hermeneutical," 86. See Vanhoozer's use of this schema in "Introduction," 23.

7. Green, "Rethinking," 163.

Ricoeur and Theological Interpretation

Theological interpretation has been strongly influenced by some of Ricoeur's major interlocutors, particularly Karl Barth and postliberal theology, and Ricoeur's work has itself influenced theological interpretation.[8] Furthermore, the narratival construal of the biblical canon, on which Ricoeur had a decisive influence, has become an indispensable dimension of theological interpretation. Yet, resistance to theological interpretation of Scripture has arisen among some advocates of theological hermeneutics in such a way as to place Ricoeur's contribution in serious doubt. New Testament scholar Stanley Porter, for example, proposes "a fundamental distinction must be made between theological hermeneutics and theological interpretation."[9] Theological interpretation, complains Porter, lacks "a coherent methodological center" and "some type of larger interpretive construct."[10] In other words, by resisting the methodological priority of general hermeneutics over theological hermeneutics, theological interpretation forfeits the philosophical rigor of proper hermeneutics. This problem is compounded by theological interpretation's retrieval of premodern or precritical interpretation, which may proceed without the critical consciousness entailed by the hermeneutical turn to which Ricoeur was a major contributor.

It is true that many proponents of theological interpretation are wary of granting a general hermeneutics control over theological interpretation. Stephen Fowl summarizes the concern well:

> If one's interpretive practice is governed by a general hermeneutical theory (of any type), then it is very hard to avoid the situation where theological interpretation of Scripture becomes the activity of applying theological concerns to interpretation done on other grounds. It seems all too easy to allow a general theory of textual meaning to provide the *telos* of theological interpretation. The key to interpreting theologically lies in keeping theological concerns

---

8. For example, Kevin Vanhoozer was among the earliest of advocates of theological interpretation to engage Ricoeur extensively. See Vanhoozer, *Biblical*. Likewise, Dan Stiver, a member of the editorial board of the *Journal of Theological Interpretation*, is a major exponent of Ricoeur's significance for theology. See Stiver, *Theology*; Stiver, *Ricoeur*. Concepts such as distanciation, the surplus of meaning, and the world of the text have helped theological interpreters escape the stranglehold of historical-critical methods on biblical studies. See, e.g., Toffelmire, "Scripture," 97–112; Bennett, "Ricoeur," 211–30; Bell, "Interpreting," 70–93; Pidel, "Ricoeur," 193–212.

9. Porter, "Biblical," 37; see also Porter, "What?," 234–67.

10. Porter, "Biblical," 42, 43.

and ends primary to all others. In this way, theology becomes a form of scriptural interpretation, not simply its result.[11]

This resistance to "other grounds" or another *telos* reflects the theological academy's experience with historical criticism. Founded on Ernst Troeltsch's principles of historical inquiry (doubt, analogy, and correlation), historical criticism entails what Murray Rae calls "methodological atheism"[12] (apparently borrowing Peter Berger's use of the phrase to describe "bracketing" religious experience in the social sciences).[13] Attempts to use the methods of historical criticism without assuming its operating principles have foundered because (to invoke Wittgenstein once more) Troeltsch's principles are the rules of the language game in which those methods are moves—so the game determines their explanatory sense.[14] The same might ostensibly apply to general hermeneutics, because both historical criticism and general hermeneutics stand on the Enlightenment assumption that the Bible should be interpreted "like any other book."[15]

The possibility that historical criticism and general hermeneutics should be critiqued on the same grounds is further complicated by the fact that some of the most vociferous opponents of general hermeneutics reserve a place for historical-critical tools once they have been relocated within a theological framework that rules out naturalism. Such reframing, by some lights, does not apply to general hermeneutics, dooming it alone to play by the rules of methodological atheism. Darren Sarisky's volume *Reading the Bible Theologically* is the foremost example of this disparity.

---

11. Fowl, *Theological*, 39. John Webster is one of the most avid critics of general hermeneutics along these lines. See his *Holy*, 28–29; see also 36–37, 48, 92. Interestingly, Webster aims his critique at "virtue" approaches like Fowl's on the same basis (see Webster, *Holy*, 43–45, 69–70, 88).

12. Rae, *History*, 38. This is practically identical with the term *methodological naturalism* that Sarisky, *Reading*, 354, prefers, as well as Mark Bowald's "operational" deism (Bowald, *Rendering*, 33). Each of these author's discussions illuminate the diagnosis further (Sarisky adds an insightful commentary on Spinoza and Bowald on Kant), though I think the language of "atheism" hits the mark most squarely.

13. See Porpora, "Methodological," 57–75.

14. Heringer, "Worlds," 189, is right: "The gears of the historical method turn with the grease of naturalism—or as Troeltsch said, the whole system works together and cannot be taken piecemeal. If naturalism is removed, the gears come to a screeching halt and what used to be a smoothly functioning method seizes."

15. For a historical review and contemporary assessment of this slogan, see Moberly, "'Interpret?,'" 91–110.

Sarisky's project is far-reaching, but the heart of his argument is that a properly theological account of both the theological reader and the scriptural text allows for a "via media" between the naturalism of critical methods on the one hand and the anti-historicist overcorrection of some theological interpreters on the other hand.[16] While he marshals a strong critique of naturalism, he is equally concerned by the suggestion that historical-critical tools as such are to be rejected.[17] The latter, he believes, can be "recontextualized" by theological categories.[18] This claim is animated by the conviction that textual mediation of the theological realities of the economy of salvation is irreducibly historical.[19] Therefore, a theological understanding of history is necessary, not a rejection of "historical consciousness" as such.[20] The Gadamerian phrase "historical consciousness" signals that Sarisky is willing to deploy at least some insights of general hermeneutics, yet, curiously, he does not seek a recontextualization of general hermeneutics that is coextensive with that of historical criticism. One is forced to read between the lines to account for the disparity. It appears that, for Sarisky, historical-critical tools are ultimately indispensable for careful attention to the text, whereas hermeneutical theories (excepting those related to historical distanciation?) are not.[21] The implication is that, whereas historical-critical methods can be recontextualized theologically, general hermeneutics are, in some sense, inherently opposed to a

---

16. Sarisky, *Reading*, 361. See also 56–63, 155–59, 242–67. The argument corresponds to Webster's call for "neither naturalism nor supernaturalism" but rather "balance" (Webster, *Holy*, 21).

17. Sarisky, *Reading*, 298–99.

18. Sarisky, *Reading*, 224–25.

19. Sarisky joins his voice to those who warn against a "docetic" view of history (*Reading*, 248–49n19). His view is that "the one economy of salvation" (226) constitutes the reality of which the historically mediated text is a sign and in which readers discern their "participation" (288).

20. The phrase appears throughout. See esp. Sarisky, *Reading*, 63, 239, 304, 329–30.

21. Notably, Sarisky's appropriation of "*explicatio*" includes three interests: "First, to what extent does the interpretation fit with the text's historical backdrop? . . . A further question is how well a reading accords with the passage's local and global literary context. . . . A final query is to what extent a reading has a theological focus, seeking to determine what the passage in question says about God" (Sarisky, *Reading*, 307). This is the phase of interpretation in which theologically recontextualized historical-critical tools find use, but no comparable appeal to general hermeneutics obtains. Nor does his discussion of the subsequent phases, *meditatio* and *applicatio*, make recourse a theological recontextualization of general hermeneutics, though passing references to Ricoeur and Gadamer are footnoted.

doctrinally informed explanatory scheme.[22] My contention is, inversely, that some historical-critical methods are endemically naturalist, whereas much of general hermeneutics is essentially agnostic and, therefore, more fit than historical criticism for playing the interpretive game without methodological atheism.[23] More to the point here is the possibility of recontextualizing even the avowedly critical dimensions of Ricoeur's hermeneutics. I agree with Sarisky that "the reader should be discussed because the specifics of the interpreter's identity shape the whole approach to reading," but whereas he adds that "the reader is stressed for the sake of emphasizing the interpreter's theological identity," I insist that the explanatory resources of

---

22. Sarisky sets up an initial dichotomy in which his project "aims to base itself on an articulation of theology's role that takes theological commitment on its own terms, rather than transposing it into a register determined by generic explanatory language" (*Reading*, 37). Ricoeur is a key representative of the problem (66n139, 110n12), mediated in exemplary fashion through the theological work of David Tracy, with reference to which Sarisky concludes: "Biblical hermeneutics thus becomes a local application of an entirely general scheme, without that application involving any substantial modification to fit the specific textual content under consideration. This sort of theory is procedural, not in the sense that it is fixated on questions of method, but in that it does not assume commitment to a particular set of substantive (theological) beliefs. *Theologians can employ this sort of theory only if they are willing to set their theological convictions aside*" (194–95; emphasis added).

23. See Green, "Rethinking," 160–61, for a nuanced delineation of distinct conceptions of "historical criticism": reconstruction of the past ("historical criticism 1"), reconstruction of the events of the Bible's textualization ("historical criticism 2"), and study of the historical context that informs the biblical materials ("historical criticism 3"). Green points out that the first two are methodologically beholden to the atheistic assumptions and attitudes that theological interpretation must reject. Consequently, the search for a *via media* between anti-historicism and historical consciousness, which I affirm, requires that *ad hoc* use of either historical-critical methods (even those of Green's historical criticism 3) or general hermeneutics involve caution as to their theological viability in specific cases. It is not obvious that any given method can survive theological recontextualization, and one must make the case in each instance. Marshall, "Absorbing," 69–102, provides a helpful discussion of the justificatory process of "absorbing" discourses foreign to the normed linguistic world of the Christian community. On the one hand, "interpretation is closely bound up with assessment, testing for meaning with testing for truth. Specifically, the interpretive process of 'absorbing the world' employs something along the lines of the 'principle of charity' which, so Donald Davidson argues, we must invoke if we are to account for how we are able to understand sentences spoken in an initially unfamiliar natural language" (Marshall, "Absorbing," 75). On the other hand, "sometimes the best available interpretation, applying the principle of charity, may still require that a certain discourse or even whole worldview be rejected; there may be no plausible interpretation on which that discourse is even minimally coherent with the scripturally normed web of Christian belief and practice" (Marshall, "Absorbing," 77).

general hermeneutics, deployed in dialectical relationship with theology, may further illuminate that theological identity.[24] Thus, I contend, Ricoeur deepens our understanding of how the "*embodied practice* of reading" that Sarisky seeks is theologically constituted.[25]

As I have noted, Ricoeurian concepts in particular have helped theological interpretation to subvert the dominance of historical-critical methods. But it is still necessary to ask: to what extent are Ricoeur's phenomenological observations about reading texts entrenched in the atheistic language game that treats the Bible like any other text by bracketing faith and, therefore, bracketing the hermeneutically productive theological commitments of theological interpretation—not least, participation in God's mission? To answer this question, I suggest that the critical moment in Ricoeur's hermeneutical arc[26] be *critiqued* in view of the social context in which he felt compelled to bracket faith and *refigured* in view of the "post-I-know-not-what" context—the philosophical climate change occurring by the end of his career. Some sectors of the theological academy have begun to emerge from the desert of criticism, called again, and the desert is more evidently not a destination but a discrete moment in the continuing hermeneutical spiral. Ricoeur, in other words, provides a model for understanding the hermeneutical reconstitution of the theological academy as a whole.

Ricoeur describes his context as "a contemporary intellectual culture which still wants people to say whether they are 'philosophers' or 'theologians' and is uncomfortable with overlaps."[27] When he goes on to admit that the practice of "conceptual asceticism" by which he kept his philosophical thought separate from religious and biblical issues is no longer tenable, he links this asceticism directly with "the tendency of modern French thought."[28] There are interesting questions here about how Ricoeur's own

---

24. Furthermore, it is not clear that Sarisky's claim goes far enough. The reader's identity seems irrelevant to *explicatio* in his interpretive process.

25. Sarisky, *Reading*, 196.

26. Ricoeur's hermeneutical arc includes a movement from explanation to understanding to appropriation. In other words, "To explain more is to understand better" (Ricoeur, *Time*, 1:x). At the same time, the arc characterizes his movement from first naïveté to critique to second naïveté, discussed at length below. This coincidence is essential to Ricoeur's hermeneutics. Critique involves both explanation and understanding, and second naïveté requires appropriation—an appropriation of the new self made possible by the text.

27. Ricoeur in Kearney, *Debates*, 43.

28. Ricoeur in Kearney, *Debates*, 45.

faith was always already at work in his hermeneutical vision, but my focus is instead on the fact that his secularized context determined his construal of "explanation" in the hermeneutical arc. "We are in every way children of criticism," he declares at the end of *The Symbolism of Evil*; therefore, the only way "beyond criticism" is "by criticism."[29] Ricoeur criticizes Bultmann's demythologization precisely because Bultmann's modernism disposed of myth without remainder, but Ricoeur's alternative still conceives the critical moment according to the exigencies of modernism: "Modern man can neither get rid of myth nor take it at its face value. Myth will always be with us, but we must always approach it *critically*."[30] The implication is that his hermeneutical arc figures the language game of a specifically modernist hermeneutics. This comes to the fore in Ricoeur's essays in *The Religious Significance of Atheism*. "Atheism opens a new path to faith" that, unlike the prophetic preacher, the philosopher must travel slowly, because "he belongs to a time of desiccation and thirst in which Christianity as a cultural institution is truly 'a Platonism for the people' and a 'law' in the Paulinian sense." Further, "the process of nihilism has not reached its end"; therefore, "the philosopher thinks in this intermediary time."[31] There is a glimpse here of the whole culture, not just the individual reader, passing through critique to a postcritical faith. What happens, though, once faith emerges from the desert? If the hermeneutical arc is actually a spiral, does the second naïveté always become a newly credulous naïveté that must pass forever through the desert? Moreover, how do we conceive the hermeneutical arc once we can no longer say we are children of criticism in every way because Ricoeur and others have helped us see a path beyond the desert?

It seems to me that theological interpretation of Scripture represents a postcritical faith that is itself a new hermeneutical context. Many corners of the theological academy have passed through what Jon Levenson calls "suspecting the hermeneutics of suspicion"[32] and embraced, among some theologians and biblical scholars at least, a postcritical "hermeneutics of trust."[33] Accordingly, the hermeneutical arc is refigured so that modernism's naïve atheism (call this "immediacy of unbelief")[34] becomes the context of

29. Ricoeur, *Symbolism*, 350.
30. Ricoeur in Kearny, *Debates*, 120.
31. MacIntyre and Ricoeur, *Religious*, 69–70.
32. Levenson, *Hebrew*, 116.
33. Hays, "Salvation," 218.
34. To modify Ricoeur's phrase "immediacy of belief" in *Symbolism*, 351.

initial understanding, and theology takes the place of critical explanation. We might say: *postmodern persons can neither get rid of criticism nor take it at its face value. Criticism will always be with us, but we must always approach it theologically.* This is akin to Dan Stiver's contention that "one can think of theology especially as a dimension of the second stage of the hermeneutical arc that reflects critically on primary sources of faith such as the Scripture, experience, and tradition."[35] Systematic theology is, then, "a form of critique."[36] In the remainder of this section, I highlight some implications of theology assuming the role of critical explanation beyond the desert of modernist criticism.

Theological Interpretation Beyond the Desert

How, then, does theological interpretation of Scripture extend Ricoeurian hermeneutics in the encounter beyond the desert? First, whereas Ricoeur claims we wish to be called again, theological interpretation specifies by whom. Mark Wallace is right that Ricoeur demonstrates ambivalence regarding the subject matter of the Bible. "The problem is that Ricoeur appears to define the biblical world in three different ways: as human reality; as a new world or new covenant, and as God."[37] Systematic theology brings confessional resources to the explanatory moment that help clarify the experience of the world opened in front of the text. These theological resources are, of course, no more or less prejudicial than the atheological explanations indigenous to the desert of criticism.

Second, theological interpretation contends that Ricoeur's insistence on the primacy of originary (i.e., precanonical) expressions of faith over against theology is itself naïve. Although Ricoeur eventually set aside the "diachronic"[38] approach of historical criticism in favor of more narratival and final-form methods of interpretation, his contrast of "the most *originary* expressions of a community of faith"[39] in the biblical text with theology as a second order discourse ultimately still plays the game of prioritizing a faith ostensibly excavated from the accretions of later theology. This fails to account for the function of the Rule of Faith in relation to the

35. Stiver, *Ricoeur*, 55.
36. Stiver, *Ricoeur*, 38.
37. Wallace, *Second*, 100.
38. Ricoeur, *Figuring*, 171.
39. Ricoeur, *Figuring*, 37; see also 228 and esp. Ricoeur, "Toward," 1–37.

formation of canon. To reiterate Robert Jenson's position: "The function of neither 'canon'/'Scripture' nor 'creed' can be grasped without reference to the other.... Their alienation from one another in some modern scholarship and in the consciousness of some parts of the church is, ironically, blatantly ahistorical."[40] Ricoeur's idea of returning to "the fluidity of the hermeneutical situation of the precanonical period"[41] undermines the basis for narratively and intertextually interpreting the Bible as such. That basis is what the church calls the Rule of Faith.

Third, theological interpretation highlights the fact that the Bible was, for Ricoeur, always more than a regional application of general hermeneutics precisely because Ricoeur was a "listener to Christian preaching."[42] Liberated from the taboos of a desert-dwelling critical culture, this ecclesial posture of listening becomes hermeneutically fruitful in a way that Ricoeur does not seem to recognize. And Ricoeur's own anthropology explains why such listening is inevitably hermeneutical: the interpreter who listens to sermons is not a disembodied brain but a bodily participant in the practices of faith. Others have already observed that Ricoeur's own notion of narrativity undermines the attempt to bracket faith.[43] As I will explain further below, in Ricoeur's hermeneutical arc, the moment of postcritical appropriation is *a wager of embodied praxis*. For theological interpretation, the ecclesial character of this praxis shapes theological criticism in the return to the text beyond the desert.

How, in turn, does Ricoeur enrich theological interpretation in the encounter beyond the desert? The fact that, as Stiver puts it, "Ricoeur has undermined the notion of a detached reason that is cut off from attestation" and "has thrust faith into the hermeneutic spiral where it continually meets the analysis of such a reason" means that his hermeneutics is open to theological appropriation in a way that the methodological atheism of historical criticism is not.[44] Yet, I think Ricoeur uniquely offers more than a toolkit of concepts for *ad hoc* use, significant though these are. Arguably, the major issue in a postcritical culture is the dialectic of pluralism and public discourse, and this is no less so for theology. Levenson rightly asks, "What common conceptual framework will ground this new discourse

---

40. Jenson, *Canon*, 18.
41. Ricoeur, *Figuring*, 70.
42. Ricoeur, *Figuring*, 217.
43. Stiver, *Ricoeur*, 34; Wierciński, *Hermeneutics*, 309.
44. Stiver, *Ricoeur*, 143.

once historicism has been relegated to another item within it?"[45] Boyd Blundell has ably rehearsed the difference between liberal and postliberal appropriation of Ricoeur, identifying the contrast between the two in terms of "*relevance* to the wider public" and "*integrity* of theological discourse." One might hope that relevance and integrity are not mutually exclusive, but of course Blundell is right insofar as his point is that postliberal theology tends toward "sealing off theological discourse."[46] The wide diversity of scholars engaging in theological interpretation indicates that it embraces far more than just postliberals. Nonetheless, the confessional and ecclesial commitments of many theological interpreters, because they are articulated over against the public rationality of the critical desert, make their theological interpretation prone to the same sort of isolationism. It seems to me that Ricoeur offers theological interpretation as a model of the relationship of theological criticism and wider public discourse—particularly if, as I have suggested, the hermeneutical arc is refigured in view of a postcritical starting point.

Charles Taylor's *A Secular Age* renders a thick description of the context in which the Western church understands the text in the first place. This "immanent frame" *is* the naïveté Western readers brings to the critical work of theological interpretation.[47] Consequently, for theological interpreters interested in resisting the public irrelevance of a closed or essentially incommensurable theological discourse, the "second naïveté"[48] that emerges beyond the desert is an immanent frame reconfigured through theological criticism. Call it a worldview, a social imaginary, a life world, a fused horizon—or perhaps just a new world in front of the text. In any case, Taylor indicates the plausibility of such transformation, since the immanent frame already "spins"[49] toward openness to transcendence—no surprise to Ricoeur, who always expected "faith" to endure the desert. No matter if he perhaps overestimated the endurance of modern criticism.

For my purposes, the upshot of this post-theological refiguration of the hermeneutical arc is that, through it, theological interpretation stands to maintain both its integrity and its relevance: *integrity* because the explanatory moment of theological critique unfolds under the guidance of

45. Levenson, *Hebrew*, 124.
46. Blundell, *Paul*, 52.
47. Taylor, *Secular*, ch. 15.
48. Ricoeur, *Symbolism*, 351–52. An extended discussion of the term appears below.
49. Taylor, *Secular*, 549–56.

Christian theology's own conceptual tools; *relevance* because theological interpreters start from and return to a shared world and a public discourse. Wallace and Blundell have both demonstrated that postliberalism's critique of Ricoeur fails because he never considered general hermeneutics to subsume or to serve a foundational role for Christian theology.[50] Blundell in particular foregrounds the dialectical relationship between theological and philosophical hermeneutics in terms of Ricoeur's "pattern of detour and return."[51] Yet, because Blundell sets postliberal integrity over against liberal relevance, he does not seem to recognize that Ricoeur's dialectical approach to theology and philosophy is isometric with integrity and relevance. The dialectic means, in other words, that just as philosophy does not subsume theology, so relevance does not subsume integrity. What is more, the inverse applies to the theological critique through which theological interpretation engages the preunderstanding of the immanent frame. Ricoeur's general/regional (i.e., philosophical/theological) dialectic encourages theological interpretation not to absolutize its explanatory resources. Instead, as the hermeneutical arc passes beyond the desert of modern criticism, Ricoeur's hermeneutics becomes for theological interpretation of Scripture a model of discourse—a public "conflict of interpretations,"[52] just as the church's public witness requires it to be.

These observations serve to stipulate methodologically how Ricoeur's general hermeneutics and theological interpretation relate in the present argument. In the following section, I explore the specific aspects of Ricoeur's thought that bear on the hermeneutical dynamics of readerly formation through participation in God's mission. This requires not only a careful reading and synthesis of insights generated throughout his long career but a theological "recontextualization" of their implications, specifically in terms of the understanding of missional participation I have developed in the preceding chapters. I offer, in other words, a theological critique of the general hermeneutical processes that Ricoeur illuminates by locating it in the world in front of the biblical text read missionally, in which both the agency of the Triune God in the world and the participation of the church in God's mission is assumed.

---

50. Wallace, *Second*, 40–45, 96–103; Blundell, *Paul*, throughout and esp. chs. 2 and 6.

51. Blundell, *Paul*, 3.

52. This phrase is taken from a compilation of essays: Ricoeur, *Conflict*. See therein 19, 62, 66–67, 317–26, and 496 for Ricoeur's own references to interpretive conflict.

On the way to a theological account of Ricoeurian hermeneutics, it is necessary to pass briefly through the contemporary discussion of "carnal hermeneutics," in which Richard Kearney comments on the "return" to embodiment at the end of Ricoeur's career (already explored in ch. 4). Having critiqued Kearney's reading of Ricoeur, I proceed to develop an alternative understanding of Ricoeur's overall vision of embodied textual hermeneutics that gives rise to a model of missional readerly formation.

The Ineluctable Incarnation of Textual Hermeneutics

Carnal Hermeneutics

If the hermeneutic turn in continental philosophy elucidated the deeply problematic relationship between the text and the minds of its author and reader, the philosophical re-embodiment of the mind transposes those problems to the relationship between the text and the *bodies* of its author and reader. In this sense, the development of "carnal hermeneutics" cannot cease to be the development of hermeneutics "in the technical sense of the interpretation of texts."[53] Yet, Richard Kearney's recent "carnal hermeneutics" proposals proceed on the assumption of a "rift between a hermeneutics of texts, on one hand, and a phenomenology of affectivity, on the other" in Ricoeur's work.[54] Kearney contends that Ricoeur's participation in the hermeneutic turn was "an embrace of language at the expense of body."[55] Granting the inextricably phenomenological nature of Ricoeur's hermeneutical explorations, Kearney claims: "Yet there is no denying that the linguistic turn to the text was often construed as a turning away from the flesh—in practice if not in principle. And one of the main purposes of this volume is to suggest ways of undertaking a return journey. Ways which might help us recover the body as text and the text as body: to restore hermeneutics to phenomenology and vice versa, making explicit what was implicit all along."[56] Thus, to plot the course of Ricoeur's career, Kearney's language calls to mind Ricoeur's well-known tendency to structure his reflections as "detour and return." The bodily concerns of *Freedom and Nature* (1950) and *Oneself as Another* (1990) bracket a long period of seemingly disembodied

---

53. Ricoeur, "On Interpretation," 14.
54. Kearney, "Wager," 49.
55. Kearney, "Wager," 16.
56. Kearney, "Wager," 17.

textual philosophy, and this may be seen as a grand detour from and return to the body. Kearney thereby already imagines the "turning away" of textual hermeneutics as something more continuous than a "rift"—it is a path that can be traversed back to the body.

The return trip appears, however, to have left textual hermeneutics in the rearview mirror. For Kearney's carnal hermeneutics, the text is a different destination than the body.[57] The detour metaphor leaves the body and the text at an essential distance from one another. Thus, we have difficulty asking what the body has to do with the text, for one always seems to be a "turning away" from the other. What, then, does the embodiment of the author and the reader mean for textual hermeneutics? My contention is that the hermeneutic turn in Ricoeur's philosophy should not be seen as a detour of disembodiment from which he began to return at the end of his career but as part of a grand dialectic of incarnate existence and linguistic mediation that spans his work.[58]

After a brief word about Maurice Merleau-Ponty's *Phenomenology of Perception*, I will sketch two indices that support my claim. The first index is the dialectic relationship of Ricoeur's well-known hermeneutical second naïveté with his original, incarnate second naïveté in *Freedom and Nature*. The second index is Ricoeur's narrative mediation of incarnate intentionality in *Oneself as Another*. The progression of these two indices traces the emergence of the grand dialectic that constitutes the ineluctable incarnation of Ricoeur's textual hermeneutics.

A Prefatory Word on the Aporia of Embodied Expression in *Phenomenology of Perception*

Kearney insightfully observes the parallel between the course of Ricoeur's work and his praise for Merleau-Ponty's own linguistic turn, but Kearney

---

57. Kearney, "What?," 101, defines carnal hermeneutics as "a mode of understanding that helps us 'diacritically' discern between diverse kinds of embodied beings; a method for reading between gaps and discriminating, distinguishing, and differentiating between selves and others—and others in ourselves." It seems fair to say that the text is not in view here.

58. I owe the hypothesis that led to my reading of Ricoeur to Stiver, *Ricoeur*, 93: "Because Ricoeur has not particularly focused on embodiment since [*Freedom and Nature*], it is an important dimension of his overall thought as it also does not appear that he rejected it or left it behind. Rather, he seems to have assumed it."

perceives therein a symptom of disembodiment.[59] Yet, if one takes Merleau-Ponty's linguistic and cultural explorations of structuralism as an index of the inextricably linguistic mediation of embodied persons, then a vision of the body-text dialectic emerges as a result of his soundings in *Phenomenology of Perception*. Moreover, Ricoeur's "grafting" of hermeneutics onto his early, incarnational phenomenology mirrors this trajectory.[60] Both move forward from their phenomenologies of embodiment to the linguistic dimension of embodied existence, which comes to its greatest ambiguity through *the inscription of embodied expression in the text*. This aporia is a motive for the exploration of language and, ultimately, textual hermeneutics. The fact that linguistic expression is that of an incarnate existence demands a hermeneutical encounter with texts, which seem to disembody expression. For Merleau-Ponty, the speaker's *embodied* perception is a "mental landscape" that can be sketched out by a verbal "gesture."[61] The question is whether language can effectively mediate between two instances of embodied being-in-the-world (the author's and the reader's) in the same way that a gesture in shared physical space does. Thus, in his later structuralist writings, Merleau-Ponty was in search of a theory of language that would hold firmly to the author's embodied perception as the world her work expresses. His linguistic turn was not a turn away from the body but toward the aporia of *being-in-the-world expressed in language*—toward a phenomenology of embodied language sprouting from a phenomenology of embodied existence. This initial index of the body-text dialectic echoes in Ricoeur's own hermeneutical turn. In the early endeavor to "graft" hermeneutics onto phenomenology, Ricoeur poses the question: "In expressing itself, how can life objectify itself, and, in objectifying itself, how does it bring to light meanings capable of being taken up and understood by another historical being, who overcomes his own historical situation?"[62] This

---

59. Kearney, "Wager," 49.

60. Ricoeur, "Existence," 3–24. This is significant because of the role Merleau-Ponty plays in carnal hermeneutics: "One of the aims of our carnal hermeneutics project is to bring Merleau-Ponty's radical phenomenology of flesh (working forwards to a diacritical hermeneutics with his notion of diacritical perception) with Ricoeur's hermeneutics of the text (working backwards to his early phenomenology of embodiment in light of his later hermeneutic reflections on flesh as paradigm of 'oneself as another')" (Kearney, "Wager," 326n132).

61. See Merleau-Ponty, *Phenomenology*, 189–92, for discussion of the "verbal gesture."

62. Ricoeur, "Existence," 5.

question, on the assumption that historical being is *incarnate*, establishes the body-text dialectic in Ricoeur's hermeneutics.

The foregoing definition of missional participation sharpens the question. How does participation in God's mission understood as *theōsis*, embodied narrativity, and solidarity form readers who engage specifically with the text of the Bible? In what sense does missional participation constitute the "overcoming" of one's historical situation in relation to Scripture? The following discussion develops a Ricoeurian model of the body-text dialectic that begins to make sense of the formative effects of participation.

Ricoeur's Two Second Naïvetés

The "second naïveté" is a well-known aspect of Ricoeur's hermeneutics. The term commonly refers to the postcritical understanding that comes on the other side of interpretive explication in his "hermeneutical arc."[63] Yet, even though the arc ends in a potentially practical "appropriation" that is "applied to human things" in the "final act of personal commitment,"[64] the second naïveté remains vulnerable to the accusation of disembodiment. This is because it is part and parcel of the "most fundamental hermeneutical problem," which has the appearance of disembodiment, namely, the alteration of reference through distanciation.[65] With the fixation of discourse in the text, it loses its dialogical character and, hence, the ostensive reference "determined by the ability to point to a reality common to the interlocutors."[66] For the ear attuned to carnal hermeneutics, the phrase "point to" resonates with Merleau-Ponty's bodily "gesture," and one rightly wonders whether the loss of the interlocutor is not the loss of the incarnate other and, concomitantly,

---

63. See Ricoeur, "What?," 121, 124; Ricoeur, "Model," 164. Although Ricoeur's concern is the hermeneutical "circle" in his original hermeneutical discussion of second naïveté, the later "arc" better typifies the relatively linear movement that presumes the impossibility of a return to "primitive naïveté." See Ricoeur, *Symbolism*, 351–52. Notably, the claim that this circle is not vicious is echoed in the later defense of "the circle of mimesis," in regard to which Ricoeur "would rather speak of an endless spiral." Ricoeur, *Time*, 1:72. Cf. the conflation of "hermeneutical circle" and "spiral" in Ricoeur, "Metaphor," 171.

64. Ricoeur, "Model," 167.

65. Ricoeur, "Hermeneutical," 86. For Ricoeur, distanciation refers to the objectification of speech as text by separating (1) the event of speech from its meaning, (2) the intention of the author from what is said, (3) what is said from a specific recipient, and (4) author and reader from a shared circumstance.

66. Ricoeur, "Hermeneutical," 84–85.

the body. Indeed, if distanciation makes irrelevant the author's subjectivity, the inextricable corporeality of that subjectivity becomes equally irrelevant.[67] Put succinctly, if "the theory of 'understanding' is no longer tied to the understanding of others, but becomes a structure of being-in-the-world,"[68] how then does Ricoeur's early, explicitly corporeal conception of being-in-the-world relate to the "world in front of the text"? The text appears to be a product of disembodiment in which the hermeneutical phenomena of sense and reference exist apart from the body and, in turn, naturally invite explanation and understanding without reference to the body. For why should the interpreter's exercise of explanation and understanding need a body if the meaning of the text exists without one?

Ricoeur's *original* portrayal of "second naïveté" is a critical early index of the body-text dialectic. Before the famous deployment of the phrase at the end of *Symbolism of Evil*, the first chapter of *Freedom and Nature* had already made use of "second naïveté."[69] Let us call this original (postreflective) usage *second naïveté1* and the later (postcritical) usage *second naïveté2*. *Freedom and Nature*'s major concern is the exploration of the human will as an embodied phenomenon. He later calls the book his "phenomenology of the project."[70] Ricoeur uses the word *project* in a technical sense to designate the "object of a decision—the willed, that which I decide."[71] The project is essentially purpose-oriented (teleological). Further, *Freedom and Nature* develops a theme that marks all of Ricoeur's work: consciousness of the self. From the beginning, Ricoeur is concerned with the *identity*

---

67. It is necessary to connect this question with theological interpreters' broad refusal to locate meaning in "authorial intent"—in large part following Ricoeur's sustained critique of Romantic hermeneutics. For an overview of the problems with authorial intent, see Vanhoozer, *Is?*, ch. 2; Westphal, *Whose?* Regarding theological interpretation specifically, see, e.g., Fowl, "Role," 71–87. Thiselton, *New*, 69, notes that the loss of the author through Ricoeurian distanciation raises the question: "Does this therefore imply, as Ricoeur and others might seem to suggest in their theories of textuality, that the written text becomes a disembodied voice, detached from the author and the author's situation, and no longer constituting an act of inter-personal communication?" The present argument seeks, without returning to a Romantic notion of authorial intent, to confirm and explain Thiselton's affirmation: "*The text is more than a 'docetic' or disembodied system of signifiers*" (75).

68. Ricoeur, "Hermeneutical," 86.

69. Ricoeur, *Freedom*, 76 and 140. See also the corresponding use of "naïveté" in conjunction with "hyper-reflection" on p. 83. The argument regarding reflection and the loss of naïveté unfolds in pp. 72–84.

70. Ricoeur, *Oneself*, 86.

71. Ricoeur, *Freedom*, 43.

that a philosophical understanding of the self entails: "I meet myself in my project, I am involved in my project, the project of myself by myself. Self-consciousness is thus at the basis of the identity which is prior to judgment and conditions it, a presence of *projecting* subject and *projected* myself. We can understand reflexive judgment precisely by starting out with this prereflexive imputation of myself in my projects."[72] Finally, Ricoeur writes *Freedom and Nature* after the "rediscovery of incarnation."[73] His fascination is the "projecting of the project" as "intentionality"[74]—but specifically, *incarnate intentionality* or "the project of the body."[75] Thus, purpose, identity, and embodiment converge in *Freedom and Nature*.

Putting these three ideas together, Ricoeur argues that one's identity can become trapped in the "bad infinite of reflection"[76]—a crippling state of anxiety in which the project of incarnate intentionality is suspended and delayed in an ethical "hyper-reflection" on goals and values.[77] He explains, "When I reflect on the value of the project, I partially set aside its thrust. Thus valuation is a drawing back to question the legitimacy of my project and my own value because *the project is myself.*"[78] The result of this continual valuation is, consequently, an identity crisis rooted in the loss of the responsibility for and commitment to the project. There may be an ethical determination of the *telos*, but this remains an abstraction, not a true object of incarnate intentionality. Ricoeur states, "If ethics and practice cease to form a circle, both the one and the other become corrupted. Thus ethics is possible only as a reflection on the valuation entailed by the thrust of the project, and yet this reflection becomes impossible and founders in bottomless anxiety if it cuts the umbilical cord which ties it to the thrust."[79] The solution, therefore, is to move beyond reflection stuck in a "disembodied, cerebral" mode of hesitant reflection. "We must constantly return to a *second naïveté*, suspend the reflection which itself suspends the living relation between valuation and project."[80] Figure 2 represents this process:

72. Ricoeur, *Freedom*, 60.
73. Ricoeur, *Freedom*, 15.
74. Ricoeur, *Freedom*, 58.
75. Ricoeur, *Freedom*, 54.
76. Ricoeur, *Freedom*, 76.
77. Ricoeur, *Freedom*, 83.
78. Ricoeur, *Freedom*, 73; emphasis added.
79. Ricoeur, *Freedom*, 77.
80. Ricoeur, *Freedom*, 140.

Figure 2: The Ethics-Practice Circle

To reiterate, whereas second naïveté2 is a move beyond suspicion and critical inquiry through a hermeneutically mediated postcritical faith, second naïveté1 denotes the recovery of decision and commitment beyond a "disembodied, cerebral" mode of hesitant reflection. Nonetheless, there is a correlation between Ricoeur's textual hermeneutics and his phenomenology of the project. The connection is clearest in regard to his notion of "distanciation," which deals with the loss of intentionality in a written text (often referred to in terms of "authorial intent"),[81] and the abstraction of the project (in terms of the text's subjectless "projection" of a world). The text's projection of a world is a kind of mirror in which the reader's self (or project) discovers itself: the self (the *cogito*) is "recaptured in the mirror of its objects, of its works, and, finally, of its acts." Ideally, however, hermeneutical reflection on the distanciated text becomes interpretation in the step *beyond* the "vain truth" of the self.[82] Still, the interpreter may become Narcissus, enthralled by the spectacle of this mirror, that is, of a self-understanding that is not yet a commitment and a project. In other

---

81. See n. 67 above. Because Husserlian intentionality is such a critical part of *Freedom*, it is important to note that, for Ricoeur, "authorial intent" and "intentionality" are not merely cognates in Romantic hermeneutics but synonymous: "After 1900 Dilthey relied on Husserl to give consistency to the notion of interconnection. During the same period, Husserl established that mental life is characterized by intentionality, that is, by the property of intending an identifiable meaning" (Ricoeur, "Task," 60).

82. Ricoeur, "Existence," 17; cf. Ricoeur, "Hermeneutics," 327.

words, juxtaposing the two second naïvetés highlights the tension between the bodily project and the hermeneutical experience. In the hermeneutical experience, *a disembodied hermeneutical circle may constitute the bad infinite of reflection*. In this case, the interpreter may come to second naïveté2 in which understanding becomes belief but not the action of second naïveté1. *Such interpretation results in postcritical faith, as it were, without works.* Figure 3 captures this dynamic:

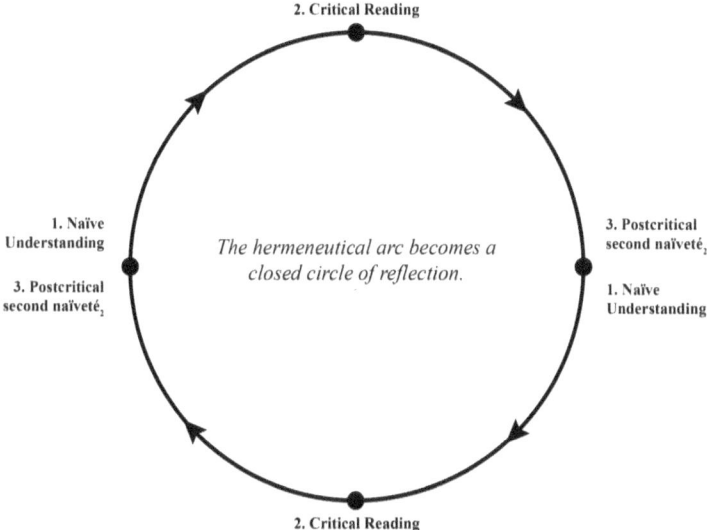

Figure 3: The Bad Infinite of Disembodied Hermeneutical Reflection

Yet, if the hermeneutical arc brings one to the projection of one's "ownmost possibilities"[83] in the world in front of the text, the two second naïvetés coincide in a striking way. In particular, if, through the hermeneutical experience of reflection, one receives from the text "the conditions for a self other than that which first undertakes the reading,"[84] this may be, beyond new understanding, the reception of the postreflective self of second naïveté1. Prior to recoil, reflection, and hesitation, "the self is not complete in itself. In particular it does not will itself in a void, but in its projects. I affirm myself in my acts. This is precisely what the feeling of responsibility teaches us: this action is myself. . . . Prior to all reflection about the self which I project, the myself summons itself, it inserts itself

83. Ricoeur, "Model," 86.
84. Ricoeur, "On Interpretation," 17.

into the plan of action to be done; in a real sense it becomes *committed*."[85] Potentially lost in reflection is the "thrust of the project" that "is myself."[86] The "hermeneutical variation of phenomenology"[87] stands to mediate the recovery—more, the transformation—of the self newly capable of responsibility, commitment, and action. Furthermore, Ricoeur's language suggests he saw the connection between the "gamble" of commitment in *Freedom and Nature* and the need to break out of the hermeneutical circle in *The Symbolism of Evil*: "How shall we get beyond the 'circle of hermeneutics'? By transforming it into a *wager*."[88] The project outlined in the text, the project that myself may become, can entail "a mission confided in me," the response to which is not a "stupid gamble"[89] but the sober wager of a "new hermeneutical ontology."[90] The wager of bodily, ethical commitment of second naïveté1 emerges on the basis of (and nearly in conjunction with) the significance of the being-in-the-world one encounters in second naïveté2. Together, the corporeal project and the hermeneutical mediation of the self form a dialectic that takes the shape of an infinity loop. The hermeneutical process renders identity beyond crisis, and reflection on and production of committed action renders meaning:

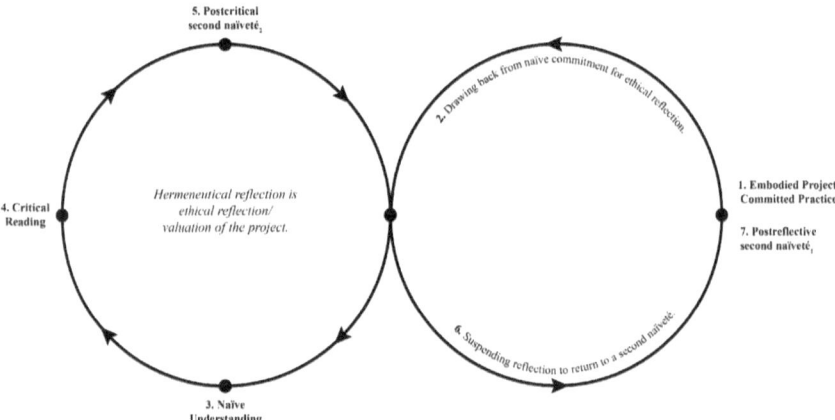

Figure 4: The Good Infinite of the Incarnate Hermeneutic

85. Ricoeur, *Freedom*, 59.
86. Ricoeur, *Freedom*, 73.
87. Ricoeur, "On Interpretation," 12.
88. Ricoeur, *Symbolism*, 355.
89. Ricoeur, *Freedom*, 81.
90. Ricoeur, "On Interpretation," 19.

I call this the good infinite of the incarnate hermeneutic. In it, identity emerges from the dialectic of the embodied commitment and the hermeneutical mediation of the conditions for a new self. On the one hand, the hermeneutical experience consists of the reflection necessary for the reception and valuation of the mission confided in the reader: to understand a text is to inhabit the world it projects. On the other hand, the identity of the reader enters a crisis if she becomes trapped in a circle of hermeneutical reflection without bodily commitment.

Still, the recovery of corporeal commitment does not yet address the loss of the author's intentionality, and Ricoeur's rhetoric at this early stage is so bent on overcoming Romantic hermeneutics that the search for a solution here is bound to be fruitless.[91] The aporia of embodied expression remains. Despite the ostensible recovery of the project after reflection, the question must be restated: if "what we understand first in a discourse is not another person but a project, that is, the outline of a new being-in-the-world,"[92] then what has become of Ricoeur's phenomenology of the project, in which is imputed a self that is both intentional and corporeal? It remains to be seen how a project disembodied through distanciation could be appropriated by a bodily reader.

Narrative Mediation of Incarnate Intention

Turning once more to *Oneself as Another*, the body-text dialectic comes into focus at the point where three ideas considered in the definition of missional participation converge: the narrative self, the body, and the other. First, although *Oneself as Another* is virtually unconcerned with textual hermeneutics per se, focusing instead on "the hermeneutics of the self," its narrative ontology implicitly sets limits on the meaning of the hermeneutical mediation of the self discussed in the previous section. That is, the self is a matter of narrative identity, which suggests that the world of the text, if it is to provide the conditions for a new self, must do so in narrative terms.

Second, the assumption that the self is incarnate moves to the foreground once more. Ricoeur recapitulates many of the themes of *Freedom and Nature* in another bid to defeat the subject-object duality that haunts Western philosophy. This time, its apparition is initially the polarity of *idem*

---

91. Ricoeur is evidently aware of this issue as early as his essay "Model," 148. See also Stiver, *Ricoeur*, 39–40.

92. Ricoeur, "Model," 148.

and *ipse* within the ontology of the self.[93] The point for the present study is to note that the body is a dimension of this polarity, which the theory of narrative identity serves to reconcile. The narrative hermeneutics of the self is at once a narrative ontology of the body—embodied narrativity.

Third, another manifestation of the subject-object duality is the return to the question of intersubjectivity. Ricoeur proceeds almost linearly from the establishment of "intention" as the possibility of responsible agency, through the teleological plot structure of narrative identity, then through the ethical basis for understanding oneself as another, and finally to an ontology in which the fleshly self is a bodily other. Again, I underscore a single implication: narrative intersubjectivity, described as the "competition between narrative programs,"[94] now explicitly coincides with bodily intersubjectivity.

The philosophical convergence of the narrative self, the body, and the other draws the eye back to the text, not merely because the wager of "appropriation" now more than ever has *bodily* ethical stakes but because the aporia of the incarnate other mediated through the world of the text becomes the heart of the body-text dialectic. Ultimately, the ontology of the self is undiscoverable without the bodily other, which places in doubt the possibility of the textual hermeneutical mediation of the self unless the text remains in relationship with the body of the author as well as the reader. The body-text dialectic must not be limited to the pole of a reading self, lest the self mediated by the text fail to be oneself as another. But once it is clear that the bodily intention is a narrative self, Ricoeur's narrative hermeneutics suggest how the bodily other might be inscribed meaningfully in the text. The narrative program (the projection of a storied being-in-the-world) that the reader encounters in the text is an *inscribed narrative self*—not the author's personal intentionality necessarily[95] but at

---

93. This polarity corresponds in significant ways to the involuntary and the voluntary, where the sameness of *idem* is semantically derived from the discourse of agentless action, leaving the self in the position of the passive basic particular; and the sameness of *ipse* is pragmatically derived from speech act theory, finding the self to be the intentional agent of willing that Ricoeur specifically correlates with the phenomenology of the project in *Freedom*. See Ricoeur, *Oneself*, studies 1–3.

94. Ricoeur, *Oneself*, 157.

95. Not the author's personal intentionality necessarily but *potentially*, depending on genre and (following Merleau-Ponty) style—the possibility of which is not a problem once the bogeyman of Romantic hermeneutics is banished. In this regard, it is important that Ricoeur reconceives "intention" in *Oneself* explicitly over against Husserlian "intentionality" (67) but retains its connection with the essential ingredients of the phenomenology

least the intentional horizon of the author's ownmost possibilities as an embodied "configuration."[96]

In the final analysis, the hermeneutics of oneself as another subsumes the hermeneutical mediation of the self through the text as a species of the encounter of embodied narratives or narrative bodies. Thus, the grand dialectic of incarnational existence and linguistic mediation that spans Paul Ricoeur's philosophy confirms that it is indeed hermeneutics all the way down, but this can only mean that it is embodiment all the way down. Though the body-text dialectic emerges with greater clarity in the course of Ricoeur's work, his textual hermeneutics never entails a turn from the body. The wager of corporeal commitment, both precritical and postcritical, always anchors the hermeneutical arc in incarnate existence. And the hermeneutical significance of the bodily other always means that "every hermeneutics is thus, explicitly or implicitly, self-understanding by means

---

of the project in *Freedom and Nature* (85-86). That which incarnate intention projects—the project—can be inscribed as a narrative world in the text, and this can be the author's projection without risk of the psychologism of Diltheyan appropriation of Husserlian "intentionality" (see n. 81 above). The distinction is vital given that theological interpreters of Scripture widely reject the location of textual "meaning" in authorial intent (see n. 67 above). The present argument does not intend to return to a hermeneutics concerned with authorial intent. Critiques of Romantic intentionality stand, and a further complication should warn biblical readers away from such notions: Many biblical texts are the product of multiple human authors, as well as being full of intertextuality, making it impossible to say whose intention would count. Moreover, I have affirmed key contentions of theological interpretation: "behind" the text is the Triune God who speaks the word presently through Scripture, and "in" the text is the canonical narrative that correlates to the Rule of Faith, neither of which should be mistaken for a reconstructed authorial intent, human or divine. Nonetheless, the inscribed narrative selves of both the human and divine authors of Scripture represent non-Romantic intentionalities with which readers engage hermeneutically as other. Inscripturated being-in-the-world, in other words, is not an objectified meaning but a set of linguistically mediated gestures that does not cease to be irreducibly embodied and whose "meaning" can, therefore, only be produced through the embodied narrativity of readers "in front of" the text.

96. Ricoeur uses *configuration* in two related ways that both lend themselves to the notion of an inscribed narrative self. First, configuration is the second stage of mimesis, which relates to Ricoeur's "obstinacy in trying to discover in the poetic uses of language the referential mode appropriate to them and through which discourse continues to 'say' Being" ("On Interpretation," 19). Second, configuration is a synonym for an author's unique "style": "The singular configuration of the work and the singular configuration of the author are strictly correlative" ("Hermeneutical," 82). Given the correlation of "gesture" and "style" in Merleau-Ponty's work, Ricoeur's latter usage is particularly suggestive for my argument.

of understanding others."[97] By the end of Ricoeur's career, narrative illuminates the mode in which the text mediates this encounter between the bodily self and the inscribed incarnate other, and the hermeneutical nature of the circle from reflection to ethics becomes evident. We find here not a return to the body but a full view of the body-text dialectic—the ineluctable incarnation of Ricoeur's textual hermeneutics.

I have delved deeply into this analysis of Ricoeur's general hermeneutics because, on one level, there is (to my knowledge) no reading of his textual hermeneutics that combines his early and late work so as to yield this model of the body-text dialectic. Though it is an original reading, I believe it correctly represents a major, if unappreciated, Ricoeurian contribution to philosophical hermeneutics, namely, a more thoroughly conceived vision of the hermeneutical circle. And, on another level, I am interested in the unique explanatory power of the good infinite of the incarnate hermeneutic for the purposes of my thesis. The primary upshot of this synthesis of Ricoeur's thought, therefore, is that the good infinite of the incarnate hermeneutic offers a model of the hermeneutics of missional participation. I highlight three implications.

First, participation in God's mission (conceived as *theōsis*, embodied narrativity, and solidarity) is the embodied project/committed practice from which missional hermeneutical reflection draws back for critical reading of Scripture and to which it returns postcritically and postreflectively. Second, participation in God's mission recontextualizes the body-text dialectic theologically by stipulating not only the missional quality of the reader's and the textual authors' embodied narratives but also the incarnate narrative identity of the divine author with whom the reader of Scripture engages in both reading and mission. Third, solidarity with the other in missional participation expands the concept of critical reading theologically to include reading with the other in whom God is at work. The final section of this chapter elaborates these implications.

Incarnate Hermeneutics and Missional Participation

To borrow a Ricoeurian idiom, the burden of this chapter's conclusion is to "graft" missional hermeneutics onto the good infinite of the incarnate hermeneutic. I have argued for the feasibility of using Ricoeur's general hermeneutics beyond the desert of criticism by breaking the immanent frame with

---

97. Ricoeur, "Existence," 17.

a vision of the relationship of divine and human agency that accords with missional theology. In effect, I endeavor to recontextualize Ricoeur's body-text dialectic theologically in order to explain the formative effects of the wager of missional participation beyond the desert. This movement entails both an affirmation of Ricoeur's own expectation that faith will survive the critical moment and a theological critique of the critical moment itself. The affirmation and the critique together gesture toward a theological reconfiguration of naïveté, embodied interpretation, and oneself as another.

Missional Naïveté

Participation in mission represents both the precritical naïveté from which hermeneutical reflection proceeds and the postreflective second naïveté2 to which it returns. That is, the practices of missional participation are an embodied-narrative commitment that constitutes the being-in-the-world whose horizon fuses with that of the biblical text through critical hermeneutical reflection, engendering the new hermeneutical ontology that returns to the wager of missional commitment.[98] In view here is the being of the missional church, considered as the hermeneutical being of the reading community.

Missional theology holds that the constitution of the church's being is inconceivable apart from the *missio Dei*.[99] In conversation with Ricoeur, missional hermeneutics adds that this missional ontology exists in a state of perpetual reconstitution as the church moves unceasingly from participation in God's mission to scriptural interpretation and back to participation. The new hermeneutical ontology of the reading church emerges neither from the de facto theological status of having been sent as participants in God's mission nor from the mere engagement with Scripture as a missional narrative and an instrument of missional formation but rather from the hermeneutics of participation.

Theōsis understood as perichoretic participation in the redemptive work of the Triune God is the theological context that encompasses the

---

98. Underlying the language of "fusion" is the contention that Gadamer and Ricoeur can be combined helpfully in this regard. Gadamer did not conceive of "the fusion of horizons" narratively. For a helpful discussion of this omission, see Arthos, "Where?," 119–41. For another discussion of the relationship between Ricoeur's narrative hermeneutical arc and Gadamer's fusion of horizons, see Stiver, *Theology*, ch. 2.

99. See ch. 2.

entirety of the good infinite of the incarnate hermeneutic. Accordingly, the ontological union with Christ in which the church's works become, through the Spirit, participation in the saving work of God frames not only the original naïveté of the church's fallible, asymmetrical participation in God's mission but also its critical engagement with Scripture in light of the experiences of this participation and the purposes for which it reads and to which it returns in the postcritical, postreflective commitment of second naïveté. What *theōsis* contributes theologically to biblical hermeneutics on this account is more than an abstractly spiritual reading in union with Christ or for union with Christ. Framing the good infinite of the incarnate hermeneutics in terms of perichoretic participation in God's mission revisions the entire body-text dialectic as a process of becoming from which emerges a hermeneutical ontology that is inextricable from either the church's being in the act of missional participation or the church's reading as the body of Christ caught up in the event of the Triune movements of suffering, love, and reconciliation in the world.

Hermeneutics is missional, then, when the first and the second naïvetés that exist in relationship to the biblical text are expressions of *"becoming a faithful embodiment"*[100] of the gospel through participation in the perichoretic movements of the *missio Dei*. When reading Scripture in union with God is a dimension of *theōsis* so conceived, participation in God's mission is not merely the precondition of missional hermeneutics nor merely its result. That is, the formation of readers can be reduced to neither the preunderstanding generated by hermeneutically naïve participation in mission nor the functions of biblical "equipping" for mission or "absorption" by the missional narrative of Scripture. The missional formation of readers is, rather, the production of a new hermeneutical ontology in union with Christ through the dialectic of embodied missional commitment and textual interpretation.

Interpretation in the Flesh

Embodied narrativity further reconfigures the body-text dialectic, theologically specifying the nature of both the reader's missional commitment and the reader's engagement with the text. To reiterate a conclusion drawn in chapter 4, as the ontological status through which humanity is capable of being taken up into the divine life thrown open for the world's

---

100. Gorman, *Becoming*, 36.

redemption, embodied narrativity describes a hermeneutical spirituality that constitutes the divine-human synergy of perichoretic participation in God's mission. This hermeneutical spirituality locates the coherence of embodied practice and embodied interpretation principally in the Holy Spirit, who fosters the narrative unity of the church's life by co-narrating its missional participation in conjunction with its interpretation of the biblical story of God's mission. Here, however, I wish to re-accent the anthropological dimension of co-narration. The concept of embodied narrativity, once grafted onto the good infinite of the incarnate hermeneutic, elicits further explanation of the coherence of practice and interpretation in terms of human participation in God's mission.

To this end, John Sanders's volume *Theology in the Flesh* offers a fresh perspective. Sanders brings the insights of cognitive linguistics to bear on theological reflection, including biblical interpretation. His primary contention is that "our human conceptual structures are all we have to understanding anything, including God," and cognitive linguistic findings serve to confirm and explain that claim.[101] "Human knowing is situated embodied knowing,"[102] avers Sanders, referring to the twin contextual determinants of meaning construction, embodiment and culture. Embodiment is a universal human experience with cognitive linguistic implications that are "panhuman (common to all normally functioning humans) across languages and cultures because they are basic to the way humans interact with our environment."[103] Referring to Mark Johnson and George Lakoff's "embodied realism," Sanders affirms the assumption that "there is a real world that we come to know through our interaction with it as embodied agents."[104] At the same time, "once developed beyond basic concepts, there is tremendous cultural variation" in the conceptual systems that arise from the shared truths constrained by embodiment.[105] Here too, cognitive linguistics has explanatory power. For example, regarding moral reasoning, "there seem to be some panhuman moral sensibilities that are quite general in nature. These general moral precepts manifest considerable cultural variation due to different prototypical scenarios (e.g., whether anger is appropriate) and which cognitive metaphors, cultural frames (e.g., honor-shame versus

---

101. Sanders, *Theology*, 3.
102. Sanders, *Theology*, 23.
103. Sanders, *Theology*, 48.
104. Sanders, *Theology*, 88; quoting Johnson and Lakoff, "Why," 245–64.
105. Sanders, *Theology*, 93.

guilt-based), and idealized cognitive models are used."[106] These broad strokes are sufficient to establish the dialectic of embodiment and culture out of which Sanders, with the help of cognitive linguistics, brings forth numerous hermeneutical insights, especially regarding interpretive difference across cultures. In what follows, I consider two implications of his findings for conceiving of embodied commitment and critical reflection missionally in the good infinite of the incarnate hermeneutic.

To quote the book's subtitle, *Theology in the Flesh* accounts for "how embodiment and culture shape the way we think about truth, morality, and God." To recast this shaping in terms of readerly formation, I am interested in the light his cognitive linguistic tools might cast on the ecclesial formation—and, specifically, the missional formation—of readers. Sanders is concerned primarily with what we might call the de facto formation of humans as embodied cultural thinkers. Embodiment establishes the panhuman categories, metaphors, and frames that cultural specificity mediates in biblical interpretation. Can we understand theological formation through the embodied commitment of missional participation—which is decidedly not panhuman—in the same way? I think so. Consider the two key implications of Sanders's argument present in his account of "making meaning in community": "In the cases of biblical writers revising earlier biblical texts and in the cases of Christians selecting which teachings to revise and which to reject, they generally tried to keep two things in mind. First, they sought to be *faithful to the overall story of God in the Bible* and, second, they practiced *innovation in order to envision what to do in the present moment*."[107]

First, what does faithfulness "to the overall story of God in the Bible" mean here? The presumption of "embodied realism" raises the question With *which* reality are embodied humans engaged? What is the "real world"? Sanders mounts an apology for thinking of God as an agent, concluding that "cognitive scientific research ought to inhibit critics of divine agency from simply dismissing the vast majority of religious believers around the world as duller folk mired in the muck of so-called anthropomorphic God concepts."[108] But this is not a claim about the "real world": "it only shows that thinking of God as agent is natural and the default position for humans."[109] The relationship between such thinking and the reality of

---

106. Sanders, *Theology*, 170.
107. Sanders, *Theology*, 137; emphasis added.
108. Sanders, *Theology*, 273.
109. Sanders, *Theology*, 272.

God remains a question. Sanders notes that "religious instruction, worship, and devotional practices reinforce the ideas of God as an agent. . . . By participating in religious practices, we come to take the existence of God for granted."[110] In this sense, missional participation is an ecclesial practice that builds on the "natural" position, reinforcing the perception of God as a certain kind of agent, one who collaborates, even unites, with humans for the purpose of redemption. In relation to biblical hermeneutics, this reinforcement is more than an arbitrary religious assertion. Rather, it constitutes the "background frames shared by" biblical writers and interpreters.[111] In other words, the embodied narrativity of participation in God's mission represents not a panhuman experience of embodiment but a theologically mediated pantemporal experience of engagement with the reality of the *missio Dei*. This experience of embodied faithfulness to "the overall story of God in the Bible," as much as any other experience of "embodied realism," results in basic category formation.

For the purpose of grafting missional participation onto the good infinite of the incarnate hermeneutic, call this experience of embodied narrative encounter with the God of mission the committed practice of naïve understanding. Not only the cognitive schemata that underlie human construal of God as agent but also those that arise from the theologically mediated experience of embodied narrative participation in God's mission compose the cognitive frame that draws back from naïve commitment for hermeneutical reflection. The formation of this background frame is hermeneutically generative in that its cognitive categories constrain and make possible the ensuing critical engagement with the biblical narrative. The hermeneutical spirituality of missional interpretation depends on the formative effects of embodied narrativity. Sanders's cognitive linguistic account of human formation allows us to stipulate that this is so because participation in God's mission is the engagement with reality that generates the particular preunderstanding that well-formed interpreters bring to the text of Scripture. Embodied narrativity, conceived missionally, is faithfulness to the overall story of God in the Bible. Such faithfulness configures the embodied narrative self that meets the inscribed narratives selves of the biblical authors and the divine author of Scripture.

Second, what does "innovation in order to envision what to do in the present moment" mean? Sanders notes that "wherever Christianity has

---

110. Sanders, *Theology*, 271–72.
111. Sanders, *Theology*, 127.

gone, Christian communities have debated exactly how it should be indigenized with the beliefs, values, and practices of the receptor audience."[112] In missiological parlance, indigenization has long been referred to as cultural contextualization.[113] From a missiological perspective, Sanders's observations are rudimentary. For example: "There is no simple way to transcribe the values and virtues of biblical texts to new cultural settings and languages with different cultural frames and metaphors."[114] This is a missiological given that much of *Theology in the Flesh* reiterates. Nonetheless, the book's constructive contribution to contextualization is considerable, and this bears directly on the missional reframing of the good infinite of the incarnate hermeneutic. The cognitive-linguistic lens uniquely identifies the sense in which the critical moment of Ricoeur's hermeneutics is the encounter of the reader's embodied narrativity with the inscribed narrativity of the textual authors, human and divine.[115]

On the one hand, the biblical text communicates through embodied categories. "When we read biblical texts, we are encountering the work of minds that naturally used cultural frames that can be considerably different

---

112. Sanders, *Theology*, 134.

113. Other prominent terms for this operation historically deployed in mission studies include *accommodation, adaptation, inculturation,* and *identification* (see Gilliland, "Contextualization," 226). This shift from *indigenization* to *contextualization* took place in the 1970s amid considerable missiological debate and development, which has not much abated in the intervening decades. For the most comprehensive survey of contemporary contextualization theory available, see Moreau, *Contextualization*. Notably, despite the vast literature on cultural contextualization in relation to biblical translation and hermeneutics, Sanders's only missiological interlocutor is Paul Hiebert (Sanders, *Theology*, 199–200), the progenitor of "critical contextualization" (see Hiebert, "Critical," 287–96; Hiebert, "Critical," 104–12). Yet, Sanders simply borrows Hiebert's development of set theory for modeling cultural diversity, demonstrating no awareness of the extent to which Hiebert attends to matters such as ethnosemantic analysis of category formation (see, e.g., Hiebert, *Transforming*, 33–37; 91–97).

114. Sanders, *Theology*, 168.

115. To speak of the embodied narrativity of the divine author casts the hermeneutical encounter with divine authorship in christological terms. As the inscription at the head of this chapter states: "theologically a hermeneutic of an *embodied* text reflects an incarnational Christology" (Thiselton, *New*, 75). The doctrine of the incarnation places the embodiment of God in Jesus of Nazareth in a typological relationship to divine authorship in the biblical text as an accommodation to human language. In this sense, by reference to the inscribed narrativity of the divine author, I understand all revelatory accommodation to the cognitive-linguistic—and, therefore, embodied—parameters of human comprehension as a type of the incarnation.

from the ones we use today."[116] To understand these frames in cognitive-linguistic terms is to admit that they signify according to the embodied experiences of biblical authors, shared with all humanity and mediated through cultural variation. The hermeneutical upshot is that the inscribed narrativity of biblical authors is not best conceived as disembodied: despite textualization, distanciation is not disembodiment but the inscription of embodiment, or better, of embodied narrativity.

On the other hand, interpretive "care" is a phenomenon of the embodied encounter of oneself with another. Discussing conceptual metaphors, Sanders states that "biblical writers used this cognitive structure to understand various topics in their experience. There is nothing exceptional about the metaphors they used to think about God, morality, and spirituality." All biblical metaphors arise from the same human experience of embodiment. Yet, "it is important to understand how cultures used a particular metaphor since the same metaphor can have variation in meaning."[117] Drawing back from naïve commitment to God's mission for hermeneutical reflection, therefore, involves the care of critical reading, because our common embodied experiences are contextually variable. For example, Sanders observes that "culture deeply shapes our understanding of what is meant by emotions, what causes them, how they are to be displayed, and how they are evaluated. Hence, care is needed not to read our English psychological categories into the biblical text."[118] Because participation in God's mission as I've defined it heightens our awareness of this cultural variation, such careful reading typifies the critical moment in cultural contextualization.

Well-formed readers of Scripture, then, are shaped for careful, contextual reading of the biblical text by faithful embodiment of the biblical story through participation in God's mission. Like biblical interpreters in the New Testament, "the innovators, those who reinterpreted the mission of God," contemporary readers of Scripture engage the biblical story critically in order to embody its "common values and virtues" anew in relation to their own faithful embodied narrativity.[119] The missional reconfiguration of the body-text dialectic entails both the category formation that follows from the embodied realism of participation in the *missio Dei* shared with biblical authors and the innovation of contextualization that attends to

---

116. Sanders, *Theology*, 207.
117. Sanders, *Theology*, 226.
118. Sanders, *Theology*, 232.
119. Sanders, *Theology*, 169–70.

the careful negotiation of cultural difference between reader and text. The reader draws back from the naïve commitments of missional participation in order to engage the textual encounter of culturally diverse, embodied-narrative commitments to the reality of God's mission.

Interpretation with the Other

Finally, the embodied project of missional participation defines the committed practice of the good infinite of the incarnate hermeneutic as the *praxis* of solidarity that engenders the epistemological break—the reconstitution of knowledge through relationship with the other in whom God is at work—after which the church reads Scripture anew. In mission, the church encounters the other, and God in the other, in the depth, breadth, mutuality, and multidimensionality of alterity. As a consequence, the "critical reading" of hermeneutical reflection is further recontextualized theologically as reading Scripture in solidarity with the other. For missional hermeneutics, then, withdrawal from naïve commitment is not a withdrawal from the relationships that, in Ricoeur's terms, constitute oneself as another. Instead, the relationships that comprise participation in God's mission reconfigure the reading self as a self-in-communion and the critical moment as reading-in-communion.

Stephen Fowl and L. Gregory Jones's landmark volume *Reading in Communion* argues persuasively that interpretation of Scripture for the purpose of ethical discernment depends on the formation of interpreters' character through the friendships and practices that pertain to socially embodied traditions.[120] They claim that the "political constitution" of the Christian community gives rise to the "interpretive interests" or "aims" necessary to interpret the Bible wisely.[121] That is to say, the "practical reasoning" of wise interpreters depends on the "friendships and practices" through which proper interpretive aims—and the virtues that accompany them—arise.[122] The question that follows is, of course, Which friendships and practices? Written in 1991, *Reading in Communion* represents a mainline Protestant ecclesiology unmarked by missional theology. Thus, when the authors state

---

120. Fowl and Jones, *Reading*. See ch. 1 for the contours of the argument.

121. Fowl and Jones, *Reading*, 15–16.

122. Fowl and Jones, *Reading*, 29. The phrase "friendships and practices" is key to the argument. See also pp. 2, 34, 36, 67, and the extended discussion of friendship with God and strangers (67–80, 117–29).

that "wise interpretation of Scripture both requires and occasions the virtues of Christian discipleship embodied in and through particular Christian communities," *discipleship* betokens neither the disciple-making agenda of evangelical missions nor Lesslie Newbigin's participatory kingdom theology but rather the recovery of "a common life among disciples of Jesus Christ" over against the individualism that plagues late-modern Western churches.[123] Nonetheless, Fowl and Jones grapple with two issues that are central to the question of readerly formation through missional solidarity: the practice of hospitality and friendship with "strangers."

The suggestion that friendship with strangers should shape the church's reading of Scripture develops on the horns of a dilemma. Fowl and Jones are at pains to preserve the integrity of a faithful Christian community, which compels them, borrowing the language of Jas 4:4, to construe friendship with God (faithful discipleship) in contradistinction from friendship with "the world."[124] They overcome an initially facile construal of this dichotomy, clarifying that "to be a friend of the 'world' is to see things the way the 'world' does, to define my identity on the 'world's' terms."[125] And, ultimately: "Even in cases where we initially seem to encounter true aliens, the familiarity that comes with the passage of time and the extension of interpretive charity may cause us to reconsider these aliens as outsiders or even friends."[126] These friendships, then, are not friendship with the world in the sense that threatens the integrity of the Christian community. Yet, Christian identity must be shaped in isolation from and prior to friendship with outsiders, lest these friendships become the friendship with the world that corrupts Christian identity. Accordingly, "one way of serving the world is to live apart from it so that . . . those who do not know God can see what it means to live in friendship with God."[127] The sequence of separation in order to demonstrate friendship with God thus characterizes the authors' vision of "recovering the centrality of Christian communities . . .

---

123. Fowl and Jones, *Reading*, 61–62; 64. Notably, they suggest that "even such acts as working in a soup kitchen can provide a 'hidden space' [their term for formative environments] where Christians begin to discern more clearly what God is calling us to be and do" (32). This concession ("even"), made in terms of the prototypical mainline social program (a soup kitchen), represents well the nonmissional imagination to which the argument is addressed.

124. Fowl and Jones, *Reading*, 67–71.

125. Fowl and Jones, *Reading*, 68.

126. Fowl and Jones, *Reading*, 126.

127. Fowl and Jones, *Reading*, 75.

by reclaiming the mission to serve in the world."[128] Like many who advocate communitarian ecclesiology, Fowl and Jones remain captive to an imagination inherited from Christendom in which the church—or faithful discipleship or Christian identity—could be conceived of apart from its ontological constitution by participation in the *missio Dei*.[129] So they can state as a mat-

128. Fowl and Jones, Reading, 76. Against my portrayal of this "sequence," the authors insist that "it is not a matter of first recovering a distinctive sense of the eschatological context of Christian community and subsequently asking about strangers, their needs and the question of hospitality.... Only by being the kind of people open to receiving strangers as friends of God do we discover what it means to be a community bearing witness to the openness and graciousness of God's inbreaking Kingdom. *By welcoming strangers into our midst, we are transformed and welcomed into a new life*" (73; emphasis added). I am in agreement with this statement, but how it coheres with the rest of their argument eludes me. Their polemic against friendship with the world clearly entails the formation of Christian identity in isolation from "the world." Only subsequently, "when we serve and work in particular social settings we are to do so *as followers of Jesus Christ*" (77)—an identity already established *prior to and without* such service.

129. Stanley Hauerwas, the most iconic representative of the communitarian perspective, states: "The Bible is not and should not be accessible to merely anyone, but rather it should only be made available to those who have undergone the hard discipline of existing as part of God's people" (*Unleashing*, 9). Though Hauerwas considers communitarianism an antidote to the failures of Christendom ecclesiology, he has, in my view, never convincingly responded to the criticism that his alternative community amounts to a sectarian withdrawal that is inimical to Christian mission despite his emphasis on "witness." I think the reason he ultimately cannot deny this charge is that, despite his intentions, Christendom still sets the terms of the discussion. Hauerwas reduces the question of the church's relationship to the world to either faithful alterity (the church community as "alternative linguistic community" [Hauerwas, Work, 29]) or unfaithful accommodation (the Christendom church as a distorting translation of "our fundamental linguistic habits" into the idiom of an incommensurate politics, e.g., liberalism [Hauerwas, Work, 30]). Consequently, he dismisses works of missional ecclesiology such as Frost and Hirsch's *Shaping*: "I have little sympathy for Frost and Hirsch's call to contextualize our language and worship" (Hauerwas, Work, 119). With characteristic belligerence, he adds in a footnote that he is relying on a third party account of Frost and Hirsch's work because, he says, "I quite simply find such books painful to read" (Hauerwas, Work, 118n22). His dismissiveness toward missional contextualization is a symptom of a compound error. By reducing the difference between Christendom and authentic Christian community to "translation" and then equating the linguistic infidelity of such "translation" with contextualization, he misapprehends both the problem of Christendom and the nature of missional contextualization. For missional theology, Christendom represents a loss of participation in God's mission in the sense that God is at work redemptively in ways that call the church outside of itself, beyond its established cultural, institutional, and ideological limits. In turn, missional ecclesiology posits that the practices of missional contextualization represent the church's response to a perception that God is doing a new thing in a new time and place—that Christian linguistic fidelity in the Wittgensteinian sense is, therefore, inherently the responsive, adaptive fidelity of participation. In sum, to

ter of course, "It is less clear that we should be interested in conversing with outsiders who are complete strangers to us"—a sentence that is problematic for missional theology.[130] To their credit, they argue "nevertheless" that Christian should be so interested, which leads to their discussion of hospitality and friendship with strangers. The problem is that they cannot go far enough because of the way they frame the argument. Their effort to protect the integrity of the community renders a church that *may* participate in God's mission but essentially exists without it. Consequently, "reading in communion" is not reading in communion with God in mission, and participation in God's mission does not, therefore, constitute the identity—the hermeneutical self—of the reading community.

I suggest that Fowl and Jones are on the right heading, especially regarding friendship with "strangers" as a hermeneutical imperative for the church. This foundational insight begins to indicate how the Christian practice of hospitality expands the notion of communion and, in turn, theologically reshapes the committed practice of the good infinite of the incarnate hermeneutic as *reading with*. Missional hermeneutics insists, however, that *reading with* is an aspect of the missional church's solidary *praxis* as it participates in the Triune God's redemptive work. As a dimension of the participation in God's mission that constitutes the very being of the church, this solidary reading is not an engagement before which the church becomes a faithful community, a conversation of questionable interest, nor much less an optional, ancillary ecclesial practice. This readerly solidarity with "the world" constitutes the church that is missional by nature and, therefore, forms the hermeneutical self that the church brings to Scripture.

"Reading with" is a concept that liberation and intercultural hermeneutics scholars have developed in recent years.[131] Gerald West has focused especially on the interaction between "trained" and "ordinary" readers, interrogating the nature of supposedly "critical" readings. His interest is not to dismiss the usefulness of critical tools but to assess what happens

---

mistake the situation of the post-Christendom church in this way leads communitarians to continue speaking, in unison with Christendom, as though the church can be a faithful community apart from participation in God's mission.

130. Fowl and Jones, *Reading*, 117. "Less" here is in comparison with other kinds of "outsiders": Scripture itself, the resurrected Christ, estranged church members (e.g., homosexuals), and Jews (Fowl and Jones, *Reading*, 111–16).

131. Cf. "congregational hermeneutics," or "empirical hermeneutics," which likewise focus on "ordinary" readers, though not necessarily with the liberationist emphasis on social engagement that I highlight here. See, e.g., Rogers, *Congregational*.

when they are made accessible to ordinary readers in settings of mutual, dialogical interpretation: "Our task . . . in contextual Bible study is not to do the reading for ordinary readers, nor to simply uncritically accept their readings. Rather, our task is to read the Bible *with* ordinary readers. This requires that we vigilantly foreground our respective subject positions, and that we become explicit concerning the power relations implicit in the reading process."[132] Conversely, trained readers are transformed by this mutuality: "Our subjectivities as trained and ordinary readers are differently constituted, and so the effect that the corporate reading has on our subjectivities will be different. However, and this is extremely important, we will have been *partially constituted by each other's subjectivities*. And this should always be a constituent element of the contextual Bible study process: a desire to be partially constituted by those from other communities."[133] This partial constitution of the critical reader is a function of the epistemic break that solidarity engenders, discussed in chapter 5. But West's work has the virtue of moving beyond the individual commitment to liberative *praxis* to the hermeneutical practice of reading with the other.[134]

Furthermore, the practice of reading with the other reconfigures the critical hermeneutical moment. The varieties of liberationist hermeneutics are already counted among the critical methodologies of scholarly reading, applying the hermeneutics of suspicion to sociological and ideological critique. But, as Hans de Wit argues, "The position represented by genitive hermeneutics makes genuine, profound interaction difficult." That is, the positionalities of poor Latin Americans, women, and so on often treat alterity as hermeneutical incommensurability. By contrast, "intercultural hermeneutics invites genitive hermeneutics to take a critical look at its expressions of exclusion and unwillingness for real interaction. Here, interaction and self-criticism will have a complementary relationship: true interaction will also expose possible ways of exclusion."[135] This "critical look" makes intercultural hermeneutics a dialogical approach to the text that is itself a form of critique—"a rich, never-ending process, a continuous

---

132. West, "Constructing," 66.

133. West, "Constructing," 67; emphasis added. See also West, "Being," 44–53.

134. "For socially engaged biblical scholars like myself 'reading with' requires more than specifying my identity and social location; it requires relocating and becoming partially constituted by the other I read with" (West, "Constructing," 52).

135. De Wit, "Intercultural," 481.

interaction."¹³⁶ Of course, "reading with" in the work of scholars such as West and de Wit assumes that ordinary readers are Christians interested in reading Scripture rather than the "outsiders who are complete strangers" of Fowl and Jones's argument. Why else should they engage in reading the biblical text? Yet, de Wit correctly asserts that intercultural Bible reading can be seen as "a new missionary practice that is related critically to institutionalized practices and attempts to do justice to the eschatological dimension of missions."¹³⁷ Certainly, evangelistic engagement with the biblical text is one dimension of "reading with" the religious other, but the practice of missional solidarity involves a broader *dialogue* that reshapes the church's critical engagement with "institutionalized practices" of critical hermeneutics. Not all the dialogue partners of missional solidarity have the "scriptural attitude" that is essential to theological interpretation of Scripture, nor do they even necessarily read Scripture "with" the church in a literal sense.¹³⁸ Yet, the dialogical mutuality of missional solidarity reshapes the church's critical reading just as profoundly.

In this sense, I agree with West that "intercultural biblical hermeneutics has the potential to take our discussion beyond the current terms of 'a hermeneutics of trust' versus 'a hermeneutics of suspicion,' for both the ordinary and the scholarly reader."¹³⁹ Missional hermeneutics bridges the gap between suspicion and trust by reconfiguring the critical moment of the good infinite of the incarnate hermeneutic through "reading with" the other. Participation in God's mission entails the dialogical mutuality of solidarity that reconfigures hermeneutical reflection on Scripture.

---

136. De Wit, "Intercultural," 490.

137. De Wit, *Empirical*, 83. The "eschatological dimensions of mission" refers to "pluralism, globalization, contextuality, and culture. These are movements and phenomena that bear in themselves references to and longings for something else, something new: finally a redeemed and liberated humanity, a deep and complete mutual acknowledgement among people, and a successful communication in which all of humankind is involved—'reconciled variety'" (De Wit, *Empirical*, 81).

138. De Wit identifies a "scriptural attitude" as a vital component of intercultural hermeneutics: "Having a scriptural attitude means reading as if one were walking on sacred ground—not as a conqueror in full marching kit, but carefully, gropingly, with shoes removed. This is ground on which the other is welcome, for the simple reason that it is not one's own but belongs to an Other" (De Wit, *Empirical*, 61).

139. West, "Locating."

Conclusion: The Emergent Hermeneutical Ontology of Missional Readers

By grafting missional theology onto Ricoeur's good infinite of the incarnate hermeneutic, I have claimed that the theological reconfiguration of naïveté, embodied interpretation, and oneself as another according to my definition of participation in God's mission renders a model of the hermeneutics of participation. The argument has developed in stages, depending first on the methodological viability of such "grafting" given the difficult relationship between theological interpretation of Scripture and philosophical hermeneutics. Taking on board Sarisky's notion of theological "recontextualization" of methodologically atheistic hermeneutical resources, I argued that Ricoeur's hermeneutics is particularly open to a theological critique of the critical moment in his hermeneutical arc. Accordingly, I proposed that theological interpretation of Scripture represents a postcritical faith that is a new interpretive context in which Ricoeur's hermeneutical phenomenology proves no less fruitful. Indeed, as the hermeneutical circulation of the reading church continues, his unique insights into the relationship between readerly commitment and hermeneutical reflection, analyzed in relation to the anthropological status of embodied narrativity, suggest a model of the body-text dialectic through which the formative effects of missional participation may be understood, namely the good infinite of the incarnate hermeneutic. Specifically, I concluded that reconfiguring this model by extending its theological recontextualization through my definition of participation in God's mission explains multiple dimensions of readerly formation.

Primarily, the initial, hermeneutically naïve embodied commitment of participation in God's mission, as well as the return to the bodily project after critical reflection, are reconfigured by reference to the ontological union of the church with God in missional participation. This union is a theological account of the encounter with reality through which the embodied narrativity of the reading church is shaped to perceive, understand, and return to the shared world of the biblical text. Readerly formation, then, is the constitution, through the solidary relationships that comprise participation in God's mission, of the hermeneutical self of the church that reads Scripture. The missional conception of solidary indicates that these formative relationships include both God and other humans, engaged in the mode of embodied narrativity through perichoretic participation in the redemptive work of the Father, in Christ, through the Spirit.

Secondarily, the moment of hermeneutical reflection on Scripture is reconfigured because the hermeneutical spirituality of embodied narrativity encounters in the biblical text recognizable, culturally diverse embodied-narrative commitments to the reality of God's mission. The alterity that readers engage in the critical moment includes both the textualized embodied narrativity of the human authors of Scripture and that of the divine author. Careful reading, therefore, attends to the shared embodied reality of God's mission mediated through cultural particularity that, in turn, reshapes the self of the reading church that returns to the committed practices of missional participation. Further, in missional interpretation, the church reads in solidarity with hermeneutical others. Dialogical mutuality transforms the missional church's hermeneutical reflection on Scripture, so that the church reads with eyes of postcritical faith partially constituted by the vision of others.

This missional recontextualization of the good infinite of the incarnate hermeneutic renders a model of missional interpretation of Scripture that foregrounds the dynamics of readerly formation in front of the text. Ricoeur's textual hermeneutics focuses especially on "the conditions for a self other than that which first undertakes the reading"—a "new hermeneutical ontology." My appropriation of Ricoeur, expanding as it does on the body-text dialectic that comes into view through a synthesis of concepts that develop across his career, shifts the focus to a broader conception of emergent hermeneutical ontology as the circulation of the good infinite of the incarnate hermeneutic moves from participation in God's mission to textual interpretation and back to participation. Certainly, it remains useful to observe the new hermeneutical ontology that emerges from the critical moment of reflection. Setting aside the thrust of missional participation for textual interpretation is still an evaluative moment, a drawing back to question the legitimacy of the church's project and the church's "own value" because the church has no self apart from its project—God's mission. And Scripture remains "the mirror of [the church's] objects, of its works, and, finally, of its acts," in which its self is recaptured. So the theological recontextualization of the process that engenders this new hermeneutical ontology—the scriptural reconfiguration of the missional church through interpretation—is an indispensable aspect of readerly formation in missional hermeneutics. But it is equally important to consider the missional constitution of the self that undergoes this hermeneutical renewal to return to participation, which is in turn the hermeneutical self formed by ongoing participation in God's mission.

Such a vision of readerly formation emphasizes the hermeneutical self of the church constantly renewed through participation in God's mission and missional interpretation of Scripture. It does not offer a method for the production of meaning. Rather, it conceives of an emergent hermeneutical ontology that corresponds to a theological understanding of participation. The meaning of Scripture is rendered *through* the being of the missional church as a reader whose ownmost possibilities—those of embodied-narrative *theōsis* ongoing in the perichoretic solidarity of reconciling relationships—take up residence in the world in front of the biblical text. And the meaning of Scripture is rendered *as* the being of the missional church whose inhabitation of the world in front of the text transforms its ownmost possibilities into a missional self newly capable of responsibility, commitment, and action.

The upshot of this conception is the epistemic reconstitution of the missional church's theological interpretation of Scripture: theological interpretation, insofar as it is the practice of the church constituted through the hermeneutics of participation, becomes missional interpretation of Scripture. The final chapter concludes by returning to the conjunction of theological interpretation and missional hermeneutics introduced in chapter 1 to specify how my understanding of readerly formation in missional interpretation of Scripture bears on the ecclesial commitments, narrativity, and virtues that shape well-formed readers.

CHAPTER 7

Conclusion: The Formation of Missional Readers

THE QUESTION THAT HAS guided my research is why the theological formation of the reading community should be conceived missionally. More specifically, why does participation in God's mission form better readers of Scripture? The presupposition of this question is that the theological formation of the reading community through the ecclesial practices commonly identified in the discourse called theological interpretation of Scripture produces "better" readers. The hypothesis that accompanies this question is that the conjunction of theological interpretation of Scripture and the discourse called missional hermeneutics entails a reorientation of the theological commitments, narrative configurations, and hermeneutical virtues that comprise readerly formation in theological interpretation. Therefore, beyond the inclusion of ecclesial participation in God's mission among the hermeneutically formative practices of theological interpretation, missional hermeneutics understands participation in God's mission to be the proper *locus theologicus* of theological interpretation of Scripture.

To substantiate this hypothesis, I proposed that the church is epistemically constituted as an interpretive community through participation in the ongoing *missio Dei* because that participation occasions a reconfiguration of human embodied narrativity in conformity with the life of the Triune God revealed in Scripture. Defense of this thesis required, first, a theological understanding of participation in God's mission. Chapter

2 surveyed the aporias of participation in God's mission in the literature of missional theology on which the missional hermeneutics discourse depends. I concluded that the concept of participation in God's mission needs theological clarification. Consequently, chapters 3–5 offered a multidimensional account of missional participation. Therein I argued that participation in God's mission should be understood in terms of *theōsis*, embodied narrativity, and solidarity. The following definition resulted: *participation in mission is participation in the Triune God's perichoretic relationship to the other, in union with Christ, through solidary action that embodies the scriptural narrative of* missio Dei *and cooperates in the work through which the Spirit writes the church into the story of God's mission.* Based on this definition, I proceeded in chapter 6 to construct a model of readerly formation through missional participation in conversation with the hermeneutical phenomenology of Paul Ricoeur. I concluded that participation in God's mission reconfigures the hermeneutical self of the reading community as well as the hermeneutical encounter of the missional church with the text of Scripture. Accordingly, the hermeneutics of participation illuminates the epistemic reconstitution of the missional church's theological interpretation of Scripture.

My contention is that the epistemic constitution of the ecclesial community through the reconfiguration of its embodied narrativity in conformity with the life of the Triune God revealed in Scripture justifies a reconceptualization of theological interpretation's ecclesial commitments, narrative configurations, and hermeneutical virtues. This chapter brings my findings to bear explicitly on these three aspects of readerly formation in theological interpretation. I begin by confirming that my understanding of participation in God's mission as theological interpretation's proper *locus theologicus* should reorient the notion of readerly formation toward the argument I have developed in the preceding chapters. Second, I recapitulate the implications of the hermeneutics of participation in relation to the perceptions, approaches, and dispositions of theological interpretation. Finally, I conceive of the formation of missional readers in terms of works seeking understanding.

CONCLUSION: THE FORMATION OF MISSIONAL READERS

Missional Interpretation of Scripture

In *Becoming the Gospel: Paul, Participation, and Mission*, Gorman asserts that "missional hermeneutics is a form of theological interpretation."[1] This is a significant statement given that *Becoming the Gospel* is the first major scholarly monograph to emerge from the missional hermeneutics movement associated with the Gospel and Our Culture Network. Gorman claims that missional hermeneutics is a form of theological interpretation and undertakes his own missional exegesis of Paul's letters conscious of the fact that both missional hermeneutics and theological interpretation are contested practices. Although theological interpretation has attained relatively clear contours, its definition remains open to the challenge of missional hermeneutics. The critical aspects of missional hermeneutics are present inchoately in various discussions of theological interpretation, corroborating Gorman's assertion. Yet, these aspects remain less-than-indispensable for the definition—which is to say, the *essential practice*—of theological interpretation. Missional hermeneutics challenges theological interpretation to cultivate these germinal dimensions into constitutive elements of its definition and practice.

The context of Gorman's claim that missional hermeneutics is a form of theological interpretation is a response to Barram, who asks, "Now that we have large, viable, and respected spaces available for 'theological interpretation' in service to the church, do we really need missional hermeneutics? Are we simply duplicating efforts that others are already engaged in—and to greater effect?" Barram's answer is that "what distinguishes these two lines of interpretation is the *conscious* and *consistent emphasis* on the church as a 'sent' community that undergirds each of the four streams within missional hermeneutics. . . . The missional 'sent-ness' of the interpretive community of faith has become pretty close to a *sine qua non* for ecclesial hermeneutics." He continues, "Missional hermeneutics may be a necessary enterprise, therefore, precisely because its focus on the 'sent-ness' of the interpretive community may, in some cases, enable it to go beyond forms of 'theological interpretation' that lack this emphasis."[2] To this Gorman responds: "I would, however, still maintain that missional hermeneutics is a form of theological interpretation, even while granting

---

1. Gorman, *Becoming*, 53; see also Gorman, *Elements*, 155–58. Much of this section is taken from McKinzie, "Missional," 157–79.

2. Barram, "Reflections."

Barram's claim that theological interpretation as a whole needs to make the missional identity of the church a more explicit and central feature of its approach to scriptural interpretation."[3]

Gorman is right to see Barram's claim as a challenge to theological interpretation to become more explicitly missional, not a move "beyond" theological interpretation; theological interpretation is not definitionally unmissional, nor should it ultimately lack an emphasis on God's mission. At the same time, Gorman underestimates the force of Barram's claim that "sent-ness" is a *sine qua non* for ecclesial hermeneutics. Gorman's own self-identified exercise in missional theological interpretation consciously engages only the "more text-centered" streams of missional hermeneutics, leaving Barram's and James Brownson's contextual approaches for later—as "the ultimate goal of a missional hermeneutic." Gorman seems to recognize that this is reminiscent of a linear meant-means sequentialism, for he immediately points out that his text-centered approaches "are not 'merely' exegetical and historical in orientation," because they already assume theologically "that there is a continuity in the biblical narrative; that there is in fact a *missio Dei*; that the biblical writings exist, at least in part, to invite and summon us to participation in that divine mission; and so on."[4] The problem is that this misses the point of Barram's claim that the church's participation in God's mission "undergirds" the other streams: all of the church's theological assumptions are already constituted by participation.[5] Barram refers to mission as the "social location" of the church that shapes the "located questions" of missional hermeneutics—"questions that

---

3. Gorman, *Becoming*, 53.

4. Gorman, *Becoming*, 56.

5. Gorman's portrayal of missional hermeneutics in *Becoming* parallels his discussion of the practice in *Elements*. To the benefit of theological interpretation, he highlights the importance of missiological attention to "the questions and perspectives on scriptural texts from people of diverse cultures" (Gorman, *Elements*, 158). Unfortunately, he conflates cultural location and "social location." Thus, his discussion of missional hermeneutics does not suggest that mission itself is a social location with hermeneutical implications. Granted, Gorman does state that "mission must become the governing framework within which all biblical interpretation takes place" (Gorman, *Elements*, 156). Yet, he consistently characterizes missional hermeneutics as questions readers ask about God's mission in order to participate in God's mission. Considering participation in God's mission as that which shapes the questions readers may ask is nowhere in view. This is not surprising, since he says that "the final goal of exegesis is actualization, or embodiment—living the text" (Gorman, *Elements*, 160). Participation is, for Gorman, a "final goal"—a result. Following Barram, I suggest instead that embodied participation in mission is not simply a result of but a constitutive element of a missional hermeneutic.

we ask of the text—and more importantly, questions that the text may ask of us." He states:

> At this point, I would define a missional hermeneutic as an approach to the biblical text rooted in the basic conviction that God has a mission in the world and that *we read Scripture as a community called into and caught up by those divine purposes*. This affirmation, which is at once disarmingly simple and dauntingly comprehensive, provides the requisite missional framework and context for asking critical questions. Christian congregations caught up in the *missio Dei* read the Bible from a social location characterized by mission. From this "location," every interpretative question becomes a "missional" question.[6]

Participation, in other words, is not just one hermeneutical stream alongside the others but is the *locus theologicus* of the church that rightly perceives the subject matter of Scripture, that approaches the canonical narrative of God's mission rightly as the church's ongoing story, and that rightly understands the purpose for which it is formed and equipped by Scripture. From this perspective, there is no ecclesial interpretation except that of the sent church—the church constituted by the *missio Dei*.

The obvious difficulty with this assertion is that the church frequently interprets Scripture without reference to, much less participation in, God's mission. That is the reality missional theology decries. It seems, therefore, to be a simple misapprehension to say that participation in God's mission is constitutive of the church's theology. To the contrary, the challenge missional hermeneutics issues to the church is to *recognize* that if the church is, according to its own Trinitarian confession, caught up in the mission of God, then the church's participation *or failure to participate* is hermeneutically determinative.

J. Todd Billings's notion of "functional theology" can be applied helpfully here: "Everything the church does and does not do points to its functional theology, the theology that is exposed by the actions (and omissions) in the lives of its members."[7] He continues: "Theological reasoning is inescapable because action is inescapable . . . . One of the concrete skills of theological hermeneutics is learning how to discern the specificity of one's own theological hermeneutic."[8] Billings is ultimately writing about theo-

---

6. Barram, "'Located'"; emphasis added; see also Barram, "Bible," 42–58.
7. Billings, *Word*, 15.
8. Billings, *Word*, 16.

logical interpretation, so the point is not unidirectionally that observing the church's actions will reveal its theology but that *the theology with which the church approaches Scripture is inevitably embodied*. His emphasis falls on the idea that "the rule of faith provides guidance for our functional theology,"[9] but the corollary is unavoidable: if the Rule of Faith does not become the church's functional theology—if the church does not embody the Rule of Faith—then it is not *actually* the church's theology. Concomitantly, only the church's functional, embodied faith—its participation—constitutes the theology that actually rules theological interpretation.

Theological hermeneutics accepts the fact that theological commitments (conscious or not) always already determine interpretive results. That is, the objectivity of historical criticism is an illusion. Analogously, the church's participation (or failure to participate) in God's mission always already determines interpretive results. That is, unembodied interpretation is an illusion. Therefore, just as theological interpretation embraced the inevitability of theological commitments and had to ask what those commitments *should* be in order to read the text as Scripture, so theological interpretation that embraces the inevitability of embodied commitment must also ask *which* embodied commitments are necessary in order to read the text as Scripture.[10] Missional hermeneutics assumes that the *missio Dei* guides the church toward the answers to both questions. To read the text of the Bible as Scripture, the church should be theologically committed to a Trinitarian understanding of God's mission, and this theological commitment *is* embodied participation in God's mission. If, therefore, missional hermeneutics is a form a theological interpretation, it is a form that pushes theological interpretation to understand the church's participation in God's mission to be an interpretive *sine qua non*. The reason this is so is what my argument has substantiated: participation is an interpretive *sine qua non* because readerly formation is a function of the reconfiguration of the interpretive community's embodied narrativity in union with God. This epistemic constitution happens in the *locus* of the perichoretic movements of solidarity. "Better" readers are formed in the missional location of the good infinite of the incarnate hermeneutic.

Thus, Lesslie Newbigin's poignant description of "the congregation as hermeneutic of the gospel"[11] carries an implication that is often overlooked.

9. Billings, *Word*, 22.
10. Cf. Barram, "Bible," 58.
11. Newbigin, *Gospel*, ch. 18.

Newbigin is clearly developing an answer to his question, "How is it possible that the gospel should be credible, that people should come to believe that the power which has the last word in human affairs is represented by a man hanging on a cross?" His concern is the church's public witness in pluralist Western society, and he concludes: "I am suggesting that the only answer, the only hermeneutic of the gospel, is a congregation of men and women who believe it and live by it."[12]

One may also ask, if the congregation is the hermeneutic of the gospel for society, what is the hermeneutic of the gospel for the congregation? As Newbigin says elsewhere:

> The gospel is not a set of beliefs that arise, or could arise, from empirical observation of the whole human experience. It is the announcement of a name and a fact that offer the starting point for a new and life-long enterprise of understanding and coping with experience. It is a new starting point. To accept it means a new beginning, a radical conversion. We cannot side-step that necessity. It has always been the case that to believe means to be turned around to face in a different direction, to be a dissenter, to go against the stream. *The church needs to be very humble in acknowledging that it is itself only a learner, and it needs to pay heed to all the variety of human experience in order to learn in practice what it means that Jesus is the King and Head of the human race.*[13]

Guder calls this "the essential fact of the gospel-centered community: It is itself experiencing continuing conversion. Its own evangelization is constantly going on. The evangelizing congregation is continuously being evangelized."[14] Regarding Scripture's role in this conversion process, Guder says, "The Holy Spirit shapes God's people for mission through the continuous encounter with the Scripture. Continuing conversion happens as the community 'indwells' Scripture."[15] And, as it happens, Guder takes the language of "indwelling" from Newbigin's postliberal hermeneutic. Guder, however, presents a more cognitive picture of what indwelling the narrative of Scripture entails than Newbigin does. This is because, though Newbigin works with a postliberal framework (explicitly Hans Frei at this point), he blends it with Michael Polanyi's epistemology and Peter Berger's notion of

---

12. Newbigin, *Gospel*, 227.
13. Newbigin, *Foolishness* 48–49; emphasis added.
14. Guder, *Continuing*, 151.
15. Guder, *Continuing*, 160.

"plausibility structures." Accordingly, Newbigin clarifies his claim that the Christian community indwells the biblical story:

> I am suggesting that to live in this way means to inhabit an alternative plausibility structure to the one in which our society lives. A plausibility structure is not just a body of ideas but is necessarily *embodied in an actual community*. It cannot exist otherwise. In this case the community is that company of people who have been chosen and called by God in continuity with those who have gone before from the very beginning of the story. A plausibility structure is *embodied in an actual historical community* among all human communities, one which carries forward a tradition of rational discourse and argument as ever new situations have to be met and coped with, and it is therefore something which is always changing and developing.[16]

The congregation's own continuing conversion depends on an encounter with the gospel through Scripture that is also mediated hermeneutically by the congregation's embodiment of the biblical narrative.

Thus, I suggest the overlooked implication of Newbigin's claim that the congregation is the hermeneutic of the gospel is this: the congregation's lived faith is also the hermeneutic of the gospel for the congregation itself. In other words, the church's life is the embodied interpretation of the gospel, but this does not mean the church's life is the application of an already interpreted gospel or a previously determined theology. Rather, embodied interpretation of the gospel is constitutive of the church's theology. Embodiment is not how the church presents an already interpreted gospel to the world but how the gospel is interpreted both for the world *and for the church*. Missional (participatory) ecclesiology is an interpretive process, not an interpretive result. Through this process, the church too learns the meaning of the gospel. To be the hermeneutic of the gospel is not merely to put on display interpretive results but to be the embodied *locus theologicus* in which interpretation takes place—and through which theology takes shape. In short, participation in God's mission is constitutive of the theology that guides the church's theological interpretation.[17]

---

16. Newbigin, *Gospel*, 99; emphasis added.

17. As Derek Taylor puts it in his bracing exploration of missional hermeneutics through the lens of Dietrich Bonhoeffer's theology, "It is not the call to mission but the ensuing movement that gives the church eyes to read her story—indeed, to know her gospel and her Lord—in new ways. Mission itself is hermeneutically transformative" (Taylor, *Reading*, 225).

CONCLUSION: THE FORMATION OF MISSIONAL READERS

Implications of the Hermeneutics of Participation for Theological Interpretation

Missional hermeneutics specifies theologically that the Christian church's embodied commitments are participation in God's mission. Thus, missional hermeneutics is theological interpretation that envisions the complex practice of "approaching Scripture with eyes of faith" in light of the theologically constitutive nature of participation in God's mission. In particular, a distinctly missional understanding of the theological commitments, narrative configurations, and hermeneutical virtues that I outlined in chapter 1 has come into view. I have considered each of these dimensions of readerly formation, as well as the three dimensions of my definition of participation in God's mission, separately for heuristic purposes. Yet, readerly formation and missional participation alike, though multidimensional, are more or less integrated phenomena. Therefore, rather than continuing to treat each component of these phenomena discretely, in the following two subsections I offer constructive reflections in a more integrative fashion. In conclusion, readerly formation arises from the missional church's embodied narrative practices of perichoretic solidarity with God through the other that account for human agency in the process of *theōsis*. Given the definition of participation and the model of missional hermeneutics I have developed, readerly formation through participation in God's mission epistemically constitutes the interpretive community. This account of readerly formation explains the reconfiguration of human embodied narrativity in conformity with the life of the Triune God revealed in Scripture.

Stephen Fowl's basic contention that the convictions, practices, and concerns of the church shape interpretation is correct. I introduced this contention by arguing, however, that Fowl's discussion of these ecclesial commitments reflects an ecclesiocentrism born of two mistakes: an appeal to Trinitarian theology without the *missio Dei* and ecclesial practices (including hospitality) that do not participate in the *missio Dei* beyond the church. Additionally, the presumptive narrativity of ecclesial readers in theological interpretation—represented especially by theologians such as Joel Green, Robert Jenson, and J. Todd Billings, whose understanding of Scripture's and the Rule of Faith's formative effects function in relation to Scripture in narrative terms—correctly identifies the anthropological dynamic at the heart of readerly formation. While missional hermeneutics has added to these perspectives an overt understanding of God's mission as the plotline of Scripture, I argued that a corollary conception of human narrativity would further illuminate the nature of readerly participation in the biblical drama of the *missio Dei*. Finally, the hermeneutical virtues that theological interpretation advocates correctly designate the character of good readers. As Fowl notes, ecclesial practices engender these virtues. I suggested that here as well, however, formative practices should be conceived missionally as those of communities engaging their local contexts to discover and take part in the redemptive work of God, so that participation in the ongoing narrative of God's mission determines the habits of wise perceiving and living that readers bring to Scripture. Together, theological interpretation's notions of readerly commitments, readerly narrativity, and readerly virtues indicate *that* embodied participation in God's purposes shapes the reading community hermeneutically. The definition of participation in God's mission as solidary, embodied-narrative *theōsis* clarifies, in turn, *why* commitments, narrativity, and virtues should be understood missionally. To say that the *locus theologicus* of theological interpretation is missional is to understand the epistemic constitution of the church in terms of *theōsis*, embodied narrativity, and solidarity.

The doctrine of *theōsis* indicates that ecclesial practices shape readers by placing the church in the social location of the Triune God's work in the world. The missional church's social location is perichoretic participation in God's Triune redemptive work. Moreover, the practices of the missional church are rooted in the anthropological fact of embodied narrativity. The nature of readerly formation entails human co-narration in the story of God's mission and the teleological praxis of meaningful agency that comprise the hermeneutical spirituality of missional interpretation of Scripture. Further still, missional solidarity is the practice that embodies and gives rise to the virtue with which the church theologically engages Scripture. The relationships in which the church perichoretically embodies participation in the redemptive work of God's kingdom represent the depth of the alterity of the other and God in the other that occasion the epistemic break at the heart of missional interpretation of Scripture.

Together, these dimensions of missional participation account for the particular nature of the hermeneutical dialectic in which the church exists. The missional church moves from the embodied-narrative commitments of perichoretic solidarity to the hermeneutical encounter with the narrative of Scripture in solidarity the other and with God at work in the other. This movement constitutes the church as a reading community in the ongoing

CONCLUSION: THE FORMATION OF MISSIONAL READERS

process of "becoming the gospel," rendering the church's embodied narrative participation in the life of the Triune God thrown open to the world as a hermeneutic of the gospel both for the world and for itself.

Therefore, the social location of the *missio Dei* entails more than a set of contextual interests or questions. The reading church's "absorption" by the biblical story, its conscription in the divine drama, is an embodied participation in the narrative of God's ongoing mission. In the relationship between the biblical narrative and the solidary, embodied narrativity of readers in local contexts—the good infinite of the incarnate hermeneutic—the missional church becomes one with the Triune God and returns to read Scripture anew. Becoming the gospel is an ontological transformation of readers' embodied narrativity—not a spiritual abstraction but solidary participation in the *missio Dei*, an embodiment of union with the life of God revealed in the narrative of Scripture as redemptive movement beyond the inner communion of Father, Son, and Holy Spirit.

Accordingly, participation in God's mission epistemically constitutes the interpretive community by reconfiguring human embodied narrativity in conformity with the life of the Triune God revealed in Scripture. The commitments, narrativity, and hermeneutical virtue rendered through missional participation represent the ontological transformation of the reading community. Thus, the missional church reads Scripture with the character forged by the "habits of perceiving and living in the world" that correspond to participation in God's mission—preeminently, the deep, wide, mutual, holistic relationships of solidarity that give rise to contextually specific discernment about cooperation with God's work in the other. This forging of character is not a self-transformation, of course. Although participation in God's mission requires human agency to *cooperate* with divine agency, although the consequent reconfiguration of ecclesial embodied narrativity is a matter of *co-narration*, and although solidarity is the church's redemptive *collaboration* in pursuit of God's inbreaking kingdom, missional theology maintains the primacy of the *missio Dei*. The mission is God's. *Participation* represents an ontological union with God by which the church's works in Christ, through the Spirit, may share—asymmetrically and incompletely—in the divine movements of relationship subsisting in the event of mission. This becoming cannot, therefore, be an act of hermeneutical self-constitution, as though the virtue of well-formed readers were the fruit of some sort of interpretive works righteousness. Rather, through participation in God's mission, by the grace of God's own will to union, the church created *capax Dei* becomes *capax interpretationis*. Only in this sense do the works of the missional church find their proper place in the process of readerly formation, as the eyes of faith belong to a body whose works seek understanding.

Works Seeking Understanding: The Formation of Missional Readers

Missional hermeneutics issues a challenge to the whole complex practice of theological interpretation to place the church's participation in God's mission front and center as a hermeneutical *sine qua non*. What is ultimately at stake in this challenge is an epistemological shift without which the church's eyes of faith remain half blind. Recall Hays's definition of theological interpretation as "a complex *practice*, a way of approaching Scripture with eyes of faith and seeking to understand it within the community of faith." He describes these "eyes of faith" as "the epistemological precondition" and then compares biblical scholarship to the blind man in Mark 8:22–26 who requires a second touch from Jesus to see clearly.[18] In the comparison, of course, theological interpretation is the second touch. Importantly, theological interpretation generally assumes that faith is embodied. There are, in other words, some things the church can only see from a position of embodied faith. Extending the point, missional hermeneutics contends that the practices of participation in God's mission are the particular embodiment of faith that constitutes the epistemological precondition for approaching Scripture faithfully. The eyes of faith are the eyes of the church-in-mission.

Theological interpreters are accustomed to the need to make rather obvious observations: among others, Scripture belongs to the church, God is the subject matter of Scripture, and well-formed readers have better sensibilities than unformed readers. Missional hermeneutics adds another: embodied faith is participation in God's mission. The need for this observation is unsurprising because the misconstrual of faith is virtually as old as the church. Faith without works, James needed to write, is dead (2:14–26). There is no faith without works, and to the interpreter who attempts to show James eyes of faith without works, James replies, "I will show you my faith by works" (2:18).

---

18. Hays, "Reading," 6.

CONCLUSION: THE FORMATION OF MISSIONAL READERS

In this sense, missional hermeneutics accepts that the complex practice of theological interpretation is "a way of approaching Scripture with eyes of faith and seeking to understand it within the community of faith" but insists that faith seeking understanding is *works seeking understanding*. Consider Gustavo Gutiérrez's clarification of Anselm's *credo ut intelligam*:

> Discourse about God comes second because faith comes first and is the source of theology; in the formula of St. Anselm, we believe in order that we may understand (*credo ut intelligam*). For the same reason, the effort at reflection has an irreproachable role, but one that is always subordinate to a faith that is lived and receives guidance within the communion of the church.
>
> The first stage or phase of theological work is the lived faith that finds expression in prayer and commitment. To live the faith means to put into practice, in the light of the demands of the reign of God, these fundamental elements of Christian existence. Faith is here lived "in the church" and geared to the communication of the Lord's message. The second act of theology, that of reflection in the proper sense of the term, has for its purpose to read this complex praxis in the light of God's word.[19]

Prayer and commitment as the expression of faith determine the meaning of faith seeking understanding. This is the genius of the praxeological hermeneutic that liberation theology pioneered. As my elaboration of liberationist solidarity has indicated, missional hermeneutics operates with the same basic assumption, which can be stated more starkly as *works seeking understanding*. This entails both commitment to embodied participation and intentional practices of reading and theological reflection in light of those experiences of God's mission. Brian Russell summarizes the point well:

> *Missional* reading of Scripture needs to arise out of our *missional praxis*. As we (re)learn the Bible as a means of (re)aligning with God, we will discover that the practice of mission will enhance our understanding of Scripture. There is no way forward unless we are actively and intentionally present in the world.
>
> As we seek to implement a missional reading of the Bible, it is imperative that we actively engage in missional activity. There is something of a hermeneutical circle in this process. A missional

---

19. Gutiérrez, *Theology*, xxxiii–iv.

reading ought to fuel the actual practice of mission; the practice of mission brings the Church back to the Scriptures.[20]

Participation in God's mission is not merely a call the text makes on the church through a missional reading but is the *locus theologicus* that finally occasions a missional reading because participation occasions a reconfiguration of human embodied narrativity in conformity with the life of the Triune God revealed in Scripture. The church's "work of faith and labor of love and steadfastness of hope in our Lord Jesus Christ" (1 Thess 1:3) should become works seeking understanding—a missional hermeneutic of embodied participation that is an epistemological precondition of theological interpretation. In this location, in this pursuit, the church's eyes may be opened as its faithful work is joined to God's, and through this union God transforms the church's hermeneutical self. In the hermeneutics of participation, God forms better readers of Scripture through missional faithfulness.

---

20. Russell, *(re)Aligning*, 180.

Bibliography

Althouse, Peter. "Towards a Pentecostal Ecclesiology: Participation in the Missional Life of the Triune God." *JPT* 18 (2009) 230–45.

Alves, Rubem. *A Theology of Human Hope*. New York: World, 1969.

Anderson, H. George, et al., eds. *The One Mediator, the Saints, and Mary*. Lutherans and Catholics in Dialogue 8. Minneapolis: Augsburg Fortress, 1993.

Arthos, John. "Where Is *Muthos* Hiding in Gadamer's Hermeneutics? Or, the Ontological Privilege of Emplotment." In *Gadamer and Ricoeur: Critical Horizons for Contemporary Hermeneutics*, edited by Francis J. Mootz III and George H. Taylor, 119–41. Continuum Studies in Continental Philosophy. New York: Bloomsbury, 2011.

Augustine. *On the Trinity*. Translated by Arthur West Haddan. In *The Church Fathers: The Complete Ante-Nicene and Nicene and Post-Nicene Church Fathers Collection*. London: Catholic Way, 2014.

Bargár, Pavol. "Christian Identity as an Embodied Story: A Perspective of Narrativist Theology." *Studia Universitatis Babes-Bolyai Theologia Orthodoxa* 61 (2016) 93–104.

———. "Narrativity as a *Locus Hermeneuticus* for Ecumenical Theology: Culture, Koinonia, and Transformation." *Transformation: An International Journal of Holistic Mission Studies* 35 (2018) 30–43.

Barram, Michael. "The Bible, Mission, and Social Location: Toward a Missional Hermeneutic." *Int* 61 (2007) 42–58.

———. "'Located' Questions for a Missional Hermeneutic." Paper presented at the Annual Meeting of the Society of Biblical Literature, GOCN Forum on Missional Hermeneutics, Washington, DC, November 2006.

———. "Reflections on the Practice of Missional Hermeneutics: 'Streaming' Philippians 1:20–30." Paper presented at the Annual Meeting of the Society of Biblical Literature, GOCN Forum on Missional Hermeneutics, New Orleans, LA, November 2009.

Barram, Michael, and John R. Franke. *Liberating Scripture: An Invitation to Missional Hermeneutics*. Studies in Missional Hermeneutics, Theology, and Praxis. Eugene, OR: Cascade, 2024.

BIBLIOGRAPHY

Barth, Karl. *Church Dogmatics*. Vol. 4/1, *The Doctrine of Reconciliation, §§57–59*. Translated by G. W. Bromiley. Study Edition 21. New York: T&T Clark, 2009.

———. *Church Dogmatics*. Vol. 4/1, *The Doctrine of Reconciliation, §§61–63*. Translated by G. W. Bromiley. Study Edition 23. New York: T&T Clark, 2010.

———. *Church Dogmatics*. Vol. 4/2, *The Doctrine of Reconciliation, §§67–68*. Translated by G. W. Bromiley. Study Edition 26. New York: T&T Clark, 2009.

———. *Church Dogmatics*. Vol. 4/3.2, *The Doctrine of Reconciliation, §§70–71*. Translated by G. W. Bromiley. Study Edition 28. New York: T&T Clark, 2010.

———. *Church Dogmatics*. Vol. 4/3.2, *The Doctrine of Reconciliation, §§72–73*. Translated by G. W. Bromiley. Study Edition 29. New York: T&T Clark, 2010.

Bauckham, Richard J. "Colossians 1:24 Again: The Apocalyptic Motif." *EvQ* 47 (1975) 168–70.

———. "Reading Scripture as a Coherent Story." In *The Art of Reading Scripture*, edited by Ellen F. Davis and Richard B. Hays, 38–52. Grand Rapids: Eerdmans, 2003.

Baudzej, Julia. "Re-Telling the Story of Jesus: The Concept of Embodiment and Recent Feminist Reflections on the Maleness of Christ." *FemTh* 17 (2008) 88.

Behr, John. *The Formation of Christian Theology*. Vol. 1, *The Way to Nicaea*. Crestwood, NY: St. Vladimir's Seminary Press, 2001.

Beldman, David J. H., and Jonathan Swales. "Biblical Theology and Theological Interpretation." In *A Manifesto for Theological Interpretation*, edited by Craig G. Bartholomew and Heath A. Thomas, 149–70. Grand Rapids: Baker Academic, 2016.

Bell, Allan. "Interpreting the Bible on Language: Babel and Ricoeur's Interpretive Arc." In *Ears That Hear: Explorations in Theological Interpretation of the Bible*, edited by Joel B. Green and Tim Meadowcroft, 70–93. Sheffield: Sheffield Phoenix, 2013.

Bellini, Peter J. *Participation: Epistemology and Mission Theology*. Asbury Theological Seminary Series in World Christian Revitalization Movements 2. Lexington, KY: Emeth, 2010.

Belousek, Darrin W. Snyder. *Atonement, Justice, and Peace: The Message of the Cross and the Mission of the Church*. Grand Rapids: Eerdmans, 2012.

Bender, Kimlyn J. "Søren Kierkegaard and Karl Barth: Reflections on a Relation and a Proposal for Future Investigation." *IJST* 17 (2015) 296–318.

Bennett, Thomas Andrew. "Paul Ricoeur and the Hypothesis of the Text in Theological Interpretation." *JTI* 5 (2011) 211–30.

Bernstein, Richard J. *The New Constellation: The Ethical-Political Horizons of Modernity/Postmodernity*. Cambridge: Polity, 1991.

———. *Praxis and Action: Contemporary Philosophies of Human Activity*. Philadelphia: University of Pennsylvania Press, 1971.

Bevans, Stephen B. "A Prophetic Dialogue Approach." In *The Mission of the Church: Five Views in Conversation*, edited by Craig Ott, 3–20. Grand Rapids: Baker Academic, 2016.

———. "A Theology of Mission for the Church of the Twenty-First Century: Mission as Prophetic Dialogue." In *Contextual Theology for the Twenty-First Century*, edited by Stephen B. Bevans and Katalina Tahaafe-Williams, 99–108. Missional Church, Public Theology, and World Christianity. Eugene, OR: Pickwick, 2011.

Bevans, Stephen B., and Roger P. Schroeder. *Constants in Context: A Theology of Mission for Today*. ASMS 30. Maryknoll, NY: Orbis, 2004.

———. *Prophetic Dialogue: Reflections on Christian Mission Today*. Maryknoll, NY: Orbis, 2011.

Beyer, Gerald J. "The Meaning of Solidarity in Catholic Social Teaching." *Political Theology* 15 (2014) 7–25.
Bigwood, Carol. "Renaturalizing the Body (with the Help of Merleau-Ponty)." In *Body and Flesh: A Philosophical Reader*, edited by Donn Welton, 99–114. Malden, MA: Blackwell, 1998.
Bilgrien, Marie Vianney. *Solidarity: A Principle, an Attitude, a Duty?—or the Virtue for an Interdependent World?* American University Studies. New York: Lang, 1999.
Billings, J. Todd. *Union with Christ: Reframing Theology and Ministry for the Church*. Grand Rapids: Baker Academic, 2011.
———. *The Word of God for the People of God: An Entryway to the Theological Interpretation of Scripture*. Grand Rapids: Eerdmans, 2010.
Bingle, E. J. "The World Mission of the Church: A Survey." In *Missions Under the Cross: Addresses Delivered at the Enlarged Meeting of the Committee of the International Missionary Council at Willingen, in Germany, 1952; with Statements Issued by the Meeting*, edited by Norman Goodall, 181–84. New York: Friendship, 1953.
Bloor, Joshua D. A. "New Directions in Western Soteriology." *Theology* 118 (2015) 179–87.
Blowers, Paul M. "The *Regula Fidei* and the Narrative Character of Early Christian Faith." *ProEccl* 6 (1997) 199–228.
Blundell, Boyd. *Paul Ricoeur Between Theology and Philosophy: Detour and Return*. Bloomington: Indiana University Press, 2010.
Boersma, Hans. *Violence, Hospitality, and the Cross: Reappropriating the Atonement Tradition*. Grand Rapids: Baker Academic, 2004.
Boff, Clodovis. *Theology and Praxis: Epistemological Foundations*. Translated by Robert R. Barr. Maryknoll, NY: Orbis, 1987.
Boff, Clodovis, and George V. Pixley. *The Bible, the Church, and the Poor*. Translated by Paul Burns. Maryknoll, NY: Orbis, 1989.
Boff, Leonardo. *Jesus Christ Liberator: A Critical Christology for Our Time*. Translated by Patrick Hughes. Maryknoll, NY: Orbis, 1978.
———. *Trinity and Society*. Translated by Paul Burns. Eugene, OR: Wipf & Stock, 1988.
Boff, Leonardo, and Clodovis Boff. *Salvation and Liberation: In Search of a Balance Between Faith and Politics*. Translated by Robert R. Barr. Maryknoll, NY: Orbis, 1984.
Bokedal, Tomas. "The Rule of Faith: Tracing Its Origins." *JTI* 7 (2013) 233–55.
Bordo, Susan. "Bringing Body to Theory." In *Body and Flesh: A Philosophical Reader*, edited by Donn Welton, 84–97. Malden, MA: Blackwell, 1998.
Bosch, David J. *Transforming Mission: Paradigm Shifts in Theology of Mission*. ASMS 16. Maryknoll, NY: Orbis, 1991.
Bowald, Mark Alan. *Rendering the World in Theological Hermeneutics: Mapping Divine and Human Agency*. Studies in Historical and Systematic Theology. Bellingham, WA: Lexham, 2015.
Boyd, Brian. *On the Origin of Stories: Evolution, Cognition, and Fiction*. Cambridge: Belknap, 2009.
Briggs, Richard S. *The Virtuous Reader: Old Testament Narrative and Interpretive Virtue*. STI. Grand Rapids: Baker Academic, 2010.
Bright, William, ed. *The Orations of St. Athanasius Against the Arians: According to the Benedictine Text*. Cambridge Library Collection. Cambridge: Cambridge University Press, 2014.
Bruner, Jerome. *Actual Minds, Possible Worlds*. Cambridge: Harvard University Press, 1986.

BIBLIOGRAPHY

Burke, Kenneth. "Four Master Tropes." *Kenyon Review* 3 (1941) 421–38.
Butler, Judith. "Bodies That Matter." In *Body and Flesh: A Philosophical Reader*, edited by Donn Welton, 71–83. Malden, MA: Blackwell, 1998.
———. *Bodies That Matter: On the Discursive Limits of "Sex."* New York: Routledge, 1993.
———. "Gender Trouble." In *Body and Flesh: A Philosophical Reader*, edited by Donn Welton, 27–44. Malden, MA: Blackwell, 1998.
Campbell, Constantine. *Paul and Union with Christ: An Exegetical and Theological Study*. Grand Rapids: Zondervan, 2012.
Chandran, J. Russell. "The Christian Mission and the Judgement of History." In *Missions Under the Cross: Addresses Delivered at the Enlarged Meeting of the Committee of the International Missionary Council at Willingen, in Germany, 1952; with Statements Issued by the Meeting*, edited by Norman Goodall, 95–100. New York: Friendship, 1953.
Chia, Roland. "Salvation as Justification and Deification." *SJT* 64 (2011) 125–39.
Christensen, Michael J., and Jeffery A. Wittung, eds. *Partakers of the Divine Nature: The History and Development of Deification in the Christian Traditions*. Grand Rapids: Baker Academic, 2007.
Clandinin, D. Jean, and F. Michael Connelly. *Narrative Inquiry: Experience and Story in Qualitative Research*. San Francisco: Jossey-Bass, 2000.
Clark, Meghan J. *The Vision of Catholic Social Thought: The Virtue of Solidarity and the Praxis of Human Rights*. Minneapolis: Fortress, 2014.
Clarke, Sathianathan. "World Christianity and Postcolonial Mission: A Path Forward for the Twenty-First Century." *ThTo* 71 (2014) 192–206.
Clayton, Philip. "Emergence, the Quest for Unity, and God: Toward a Constructive Christian Theology of the Person." In *The Depth of the Human Person: A Multidisciplinary Approach*, edited by Michael Welker, 58–76. Grand Rapids: Eerdmans, 2014.
Coakley, Sarah. *Powers and Submissions: Spirituality, Philosophy, and Gender*. Malden, MA: Blackwell, 2002.
Codina, Victor. "Analogía Sacramental: De la Eucaristía a la Solidaridad." *Estudios Eclesiásticos* 54.210 (1979) 335–62.
Collins, Paul M. *Partaking in Divine Nature: Deification and Communion*. New York: T&T Clark, 2012.
Comstock, Gary. "Truth or Meaning: Ricoeur Versus Frei on Biblical Narrative." *JR* 66 (1986) 117–40.
———. "Two Types of Narrative Theology." *JAAR* 55 (1987) 687–717.
Congdon, David W. "Dialectical Theology as Theology of Mission: Investigating the Origins of Karl Barth's Break with Liberalism." *IJST* 16 (2014) 390–413.
Conner, Benjamin. "For the Fitness of Their Witness: Missional Christian Practices." In *Converting Witness: The Future of Christian Mission in the New Millennium*, edited by John G. Flett and David W. Congdon, 123–37. Lanham, MD: Lexington, 2019.
Consejo Episcopal Latinoamericano, ed. "Discurso de S. S. Pablo VI en la apertura de la segunda conferencia." In *Las cinco conferencias generales del episcopado latinoamericano*, 63–81. Bogotá, Colombia: San Pablo, 2014.
———. "Medellín." In *Las cinco conferencias generales del episcopado latinoamericano*, 59–210. Bogotá, Colombia: San Pablo, 2014.
———. "Puebla." In *Las cinco conferencias generales del episcopado latinoamericano*, 211–469. Bogotá, Colombia: San Pablo, 2014.

Cooper, John W. "Scripture and Philosophy on the Unity of Body and Soul: An Integrative Method for Theological Anthropology." In *The Ashgate Research Companion to Theological Anthropology*, edited by Joshua R. Farris and Charles Taliaferro, 27–42. New York: Routledge, 2016.

Copeland, M. Shawn. *Enfleshing Freedom: Body, Race, and Being*. Innovations: African American Religious Thought. Minneapolis: Fortress, 2010.

Crisp, Oliver D. "A Christological Model of the *Imago Dei*." In *The Ashgate Research Companion to Theological Anthropology*, edited by Joshua R. Farris and Charles Taliaferro, 217–30. New York: Routledge, 2016.

———. "Problems with Perichoresis." *TynBul* 56 (2005) 119–40.

Crites, Stephen. "The Narrative Quality of Experience." In *Why Narrative: Readings in Narrative Theology*, edited by Stanley Hauerwas and L. Gregory Jones, 65–88. Grand Rapids: Eerdmans, 1989.

Davis, Ellen F. "Preserving Virtues: Renewing the Tradition of the Sages." In *Character and Scripture: Moral Formation, Community, and Biblical Interpretation*, edited by William P. Brown, 183–201. Grand Rapids: Eerdmans, 2002.

Day, Tammarie. *Constructing Solidarity for a Liberative Ethic: Anti-Racism, Action, and Justice*. New York: Palgrave Macmillan, 2012.

De Wit, Hans. *Empirical Hermeneutics, Interculturality, and Holy Scripture*. Intercultural Biblical Hermeneutics Series. Nappanee, IN: Evangel, 2012.

———. "Intercultural Bible Reading and Hermeneutics." In *Through the Eyes of Another: Intercultural Reading of the Bible*, edited by Hans de Wit et al., 477–92. Elkhart, IN: Institute of Mennonite Studies, 2004.

Dodds, Adam. *The Mission of the Triune God: Trinitarian Missiology in the Tradition of Lesslie Newbigin*. Eugene, OR: Wipf & Stock, 2017.

Dube, Musa W. *Postcolonial Feminist Interpretation of the Bible*. St. Louis: Chalice, 2000.

Dussel, Enrique. *Ethics and the Theology of Liberation*. Translated by Bernard F. McWilliams. Maryknoll, NY: Orbis, 1974.

Edgar, Brian. "The Consummate Trinity and Participation in the Life of God." *Evangelical Review of Theology* 38 (2014) 112–25.

Ellacuría, Ignacio. "The Crucified People." In *Mysterium Liberationis: Fundamental Concepts of Liberation Theology*, edited by Ignacio Ellacuría and Jon Sobrino, 580–603. Maryknoll, NY: Orbis, 1993.

———. *Freedom Made Flesh: The Mission of Christ and His Church*. Translated by John Drury. Maryknoll, NY: Orbis, 1976.

Fiddes, Paul S. *Participating in God: A Pastoral Doctrine of the Trinity*. Louisville: Westminster John Knox, 2000.

———. "Participating in the Trinity." *PRS* 33 (2006) 375–91.

———. *Past Event and Present Salvation: The Christian Idea of Atonement*. Louisville: Westminster John Knox, 1989.

Finlan, Stephen, and Vladimir Kharlamov. "Introduction." In *Theōsis: Deification in Christian Theology*, edited by Stephen Finlan and Vladimir Kharlamov, 1:1–8. Princeton Theological Monograph Series. Eugene, OR: Pickwick, 2006.

———, eds. *Theōsis: Deification in Christian Theology*. Princeton Theological Monograph Series. Eugene, OR: Pickwick, 2006.

Finn, Leonard G. "Reflections on the Rule of Faith." In *The Bible as Christian Scripture: The Work of Brevard S. Childs*, edited by Christopher R. Seitz and Kent Harold Richards, 221–42. Biblical Scholarship in North America. Atlanta: SBL, 2013.

Fitch, David E. "The Other Missional Conversation: Making Way for the Neo-Anabaptist Contribution to the Missional Movement in North America." *Miss* 44 (2016) 466–78.

Fitch, David E., and Geoffrey Holsclaw. "Mission amid Empire: Relating Trinity, Mission, and Political Formation." *Miss* 41 (2013) 389–401.

———. *Prodigal Christianity: 10 Signposts into the Missional Frontier*. San Francisco: Jossey-Bass, 2013.

Flett, John G. "*Missio Dei*: A Trinitarian Envisioning of a Non-Trinitarian Theme." *Miss* 37 (2009) 5–18.

———. *The Witness of God: The Trinity, Missio Dei, Karl Barth, and the Nature of Christian Community*. Grand Rapids: Eerdmans, 2010.

Foerst, Anne. *God in the Machine: What Robots Teach Us About Humanity and God*. New York: Plume, 2005.

Ford, David F. "The What, How, and Who of Humanity Before God: Theological Anthropology and the Bible in the Twenty-First Century." *MoTh* 27 (2011) 41–54.

Foucault, Michel. *Discipline and Punish: The Birth of the Prison*. Translated by Alan Sheridan. New York: Vintage, 1977.

Fowl, Stephen E. *Engaging Scripture: A Model for Theological Interpretation*. Eugene, OR: Wipf & Stock, 1998.

———. "The Role of Authorial Intention in the Theological Interpretation of Scripture." In *Between Two Horizons: Spanning New Testament Studies and Systematic Theology*, edited by Joel B. Green and Max Turner, 71–87. Grand Rapids: Eerdmans, 2000.

———. *Theological Interpretation of Scripture*. Cascade Companions 9. Eugene, OR: Cascade, 2009.

———. "Theological Interpretation of Scripture and Its Future." *Anglican Theological Review* 99 (2017) 680–82.

———. "Virtue." *DTIB* 837–39.

Fowl, Stephen E., and L. Gregory Jones. *Reading in Communion: Scripture and Ethics in Christian Life*. Grand Rapids: Eerdmans, 1991.

Franke, John R. "Contextual Mission: Bearing Witness to the Ends of the Earth." In *Four Views on the Church's Mission*, edited by Jason S. Sexton, 107–33. Counterpoints: Bible and Theology. Grand Rapids: Zondervan, 2017.

———. "God Is Love: The Social Trinity and the Mission of God." In *Trinitarian Theology for the Church: Scripture, Community, and Worship*, edited by Daniel J. Treier and David Lauber, 105–19. Downers Grove, IL: InterVarsity, 2009.

———. "Intercultural Hermeneutics and the Shape of Missional Theology." In *Reading the Bible Missionally*, edited by Michael W. Goheen, 86–103. Grand Rapids: Eerdmans, 2016.

———. *Missional Theology: An Introduction*. Grand Rapids: Baker Academic, 2020.

Frei, Hans W. *The Eclipse of Biblical Narrative: A Study in Eighteenth and Nineteenth Century Hermeneutics*. New Haven: Yale University Press, 1974.

———. *The Identity of Jesus Christ: The Hermeneutical Bases of Dogmatic Theology*. Updated and exp. ed. Eugene, OR: Cascade, 2013.

———. "The 'Literal Reading' of Biblical Narrative in the Christian Tradition: Does It Stretch or Will It Break?" In *Theology and Narrative: Selected Essays*, edited by George Hunsinger and William C. Placher, 117–52. New York: Oxford University Press, 1993.

———. "Response to 'Narrative Theology: An Evangelical Appraisal.'" In *Theology and Narrative: Selected Essays*, edited by George Hunsinger and William C. Placher, 117–52. New York: Oxford University Press, 1993.

Freire, Paulo. *Cultural Action for Freedom*. Cambridge: Harvard Educational Review, 1970.

———. *Pedagogy of the Oppressed*. 50th anniversary ed. New York: Bloomsbury Academic, 2018.

Frost, Michael. *Surprise the World: The Five Habits of Highly Missional People*. Colorado Springs: NavPress, 2016.

Frost, Michael, and Alan Hirsch. *The Shaping of Things to Come: Innovation and Mission for the 21st-Century*. Rev. ed. Grand Rapids: Baker, 2013.

Gavrilyuk, Paul L. "The Retrieval of Deification: How a Once-Despised Archaism Became an Ecumenical Desideratum." *MoTh* 25 (2009) 647–59.

Gilliland, Dean. "Contextualization." In *EDWM*, edited by A. Scott Moreau et al., 225–27. Grand Rapids: Baker, 2000.

Gittins, Anthony J. "Beyond Hospitality? The Missionary Status and Role Revisited." *CurTM* 21 (1994) 164–82.

Goetz, Stewart. "Substance Dualism." In *The Ashgate Research Companion to Theological Anthropology*, edited by Joshua R. Farris and Charles Taliaferro, 125–38. New York: Routledge, 2016.

Goheen, Michael W. "'As the Father Has Sent Me, I Am Sending You': J. E. Lesslie Newbigin's Missionary Ecclesiology." PhD diss., Utrecht University, 2000.

Gorman, Michael J. *Abide and Go: Missional Theosis in the Gospel of John*. The Didsbury Lectures 2016. Eugene, OR: Cascade, 2018.

———. *Becoming the Gospel: Paul, Participation, and Mission*. GOCS. Grand Rapids: Eerdmans, 2015.

———. *Cruciformity: Paul's Narrative Spirituality of the Cross*. Grand Rapids: Eerdmans, 2001.

———. *Elements of Biblical Exegesis: A Basic Guide for Students and Ministers*. Rev. ed. Grand Rapids: Eerdmans, 2009.

———. *Inhabiting the Cruciform God: Kenosis, Justification, and Theosis in Paul's Narrative Soteriology*. Grand Rapids: Eerdmans, 2009.

———. *Participating in Christ: Explorations in Paul's Theology and Spirituality*. Grand Rapids: Baker Academic, 2019.

Gottschall, Jonathan. *The Storytelling Animal: How Stories Make Us Human*. New York: Mariner, 2013.

Graham, Elaine. "Words Made Flesh: Women, Embodiment and Practical Theology." *FemTh* 7.21 (May 1999) 109–21.

Green, Joel B. *Body, Soul, and Human Life: The Nature of Humanity in the Bible*. STI. Grand Rapids: Baker Academic, 2008.

———, ed. *In Search of the Soul: Four Views of the Mind-Body Problem*. 2nd ed. Eugene, OR: Wipf & Stock, 2005.

———. "Narrative and New Testament Interpretation: Reflections on the State of the Art." *LTQ* 39 (2004) 153–66.

———. "Narrative Theology." *DTIB* 531–33.

———. "Practicing the Gospel in a Post-Critical World: The Promise of Theological Exegesis." *JETS* 47 (2004) 387–97.

———. *Practicing Theological Interpretation: Engaging Biblical Texts for Faith and Formation*. Theological Explorations for the Church Catholic. Grand Rapids: Baker Academic, 2011.

———. "Reading James Missionally." In *Reading the Bible Missionally*, edited by Michael W. Goheen, 194–212. Grand Rapids: Eerdmans, 2016.

———. "Rethinking 'History' for Theological Interpretation." *JTI* 5 (2011) 159–74.

———. "Scripture and Theology: Failed Experiments, Fresh Perspectives." *Int* 56 (2002) 5–20.

———, ed. *What About the Soul? Neuroscience and Christian Anthropology*. Nashville: Abingdon, 2004.

Grenz, Stanley J. *The Social God and the Relational Self: A Trinitarian Theology of the Imago Dei*. The Matrix of Christian Theology. Louisville: Westminster John Knox, 2001.

———. *Theology for the Community of God*. Grand Rapids: Eerdmans, 2000.

Grey, Mary. "'She Is a Great Man!' Missiology from a Christian Feminist Perspective." *IRM* 81.322 (1992) 201–11.

Grishakova, Marina, and Siim Sorokin. "Notes on Narrative, Cognition, and Cultural Evolution." *Sign Systems Studies* 44 (2016) 542–61.

Guder, Darrell L. *Called to Witness: Doing Missional Theology*. GOCS. Grand Rapids: Eerdmans, 2015.

———. *The Continuing Conversion of the Church*. GOCS. Grand Rapids: Eerdmans, 2000.

———. *Incarnation and the Church's Witness*. Eugene, OR: Wipf & Stock, 1999.

———, ed. *Missional Church: A Vision for the Sending of the Church in North America*. GOCS. Grand Rapids: Eerdmans, 1998.

———. "A Multicultural and Translational Approach." In *The Mission of the Church: Five Views in Conversation*, edited by Craig Ott, 21–39. Grand Rapids: Baker Academic, 2016.

Guitián, Gregorio. "El principio de solidaridad de la doctrina social de la iglesia: Fundamentación teológica." *Scripta Theologica* 52 (2020) 553–85.

Gunton, Colin E. *The One, the Three and the Many: God, Creation and the Culture of Modernity*. The 1992 Bampton Lectures. New York: Cambridge, 1993.

Gutiérrez, Gustavo. *The Power of the Poor in History*. Translated by Robert Barr. Eugene, OR: Wipf & Stock, 1983.

———. *A Theology of Liberation: History, Politics, and Salvation*. 15th anniversary ed. Maryknoll, NY: Orbis, 1988.

———. *We Drink from Our Own Wells: The Spiritual Journey of a People*. 20th anniversary ed. Translated by Matthew J. O'Connell. Maryknoll, NY: Orbis, 2003.

Habets, Myk. "Reforming Theōsis." In *Theōsis: Deification in Christian Theology*, edited by Stephen Finlan and Vladimir Kharlamov, 1:146–67. Princeton Theological Monograph Series. Eugene, OR: Pickwick, 2006.

Hallonsten, Gösta. "*Theosis* in Recent Research: A Renewal of Interest and a Need for Clarity." In *Partakers of the Divine Nature: The History and Development of Deification in the Christian Traditions*, edited by Michael J. Christensen and Jeffery A. Wittung, 281–93. Grand Rapids: Baker Academic, 2007.

Harrison, Verna. "Perichoresis in the Greek Fathers." *SVTQ* 35 (1991) 53–65.

Hartenstein, Karl. "Theologische Besinnung." In *Mission zwischen Gestern und Morgen: von Gestaltwandel der Weltmission der Christenheit im Licht der Konferenz des Internationalen Missionsrats in Willingen*, edited by Walter Freytag, 51–72. Stuttgart: Evagn. Missionsverlag, 1952.

Hastings, Ross. *Missional God, Missional Church: Hope for Re-Evangelizing the West.* Downers Grove, IL: InterVarsity, 2012.

Hauerwas, Stanley. *Performing the Faith: Bonhoeffer and the Practice of Nonviolence.* Eugene, OR: Wipf & Stock, 2015.

———. *Unleashing the Scripture: Freeing the Bible from Captivity to America.* Nashville: Abingdon, 1993.

———. *The Work of Theology.* Grand Rapids: Eerdmans, 2015.

Haydon, Ron. "A Survey and Analysis of Recent 'Canonical' Methods (2000–2015)." *JTI* 10 (2016) 145–55.

Hays, Richard B. "Reading the Bible with Eyes of Faith: The Practice of Theological Exegesis." *JTI* 1 (2007) 5–21.

———. "Salvation by Trust? Reading the Bible Faithfully." *Christian Century*, Feb. 26, 1997.

Heath, Elaine A., and Larry Duggins. *Missional, Monastic, Mainline: A Guide to Starting Micro-Communities in Historically Mainline Traditions.* Eugene, OR: Cascade, 2014.

Heidemanns, Katja. "Missiology of Risk? Explorations in Mission Theology from a German Feminist Perspective." *IRM* 93.368 (2004) 105–18.

Heo, Seong Sik. "Revisiting Newbigin's Ambivalence Toward Interreligious Dialogues: How Can We Reengage in Interreligious Dialogues in Asia?" In *Converting Witness: The Future of Christian Mission in the New Millennium*, edited by John G. Flett and David W. Congdon, 169–82. Lanham, MD: Lexington, 2019.

Heringer, Seth. "Worlds Colliding: A Theological Critique of the Historical Method." PhD diss., Fuller Theological Seminary, 2016.

Heuertz, Christopher L., and Christine D. Pohl. *Friendship at the Margins: Discovering Mutuality in Service and Mission.* Resources for Reconciliation. Downers Grove, IL: InterVarsity, 2010.

Hicks, John Mark. "Mediating the War Between Arminians and Calvinists on Election and Security: A Stone-Campbell Perspective." *Stone-Campbell Journal* 6 (2003) 163–84.

Hiebert, Paul G. "Critical Contextualization." *IBMR* 11 (1987) 104–12.

———. "Critical Contextualization." *Miss* 12 (1984) 287–96.

———. *Transforming Worldview: An Anthropological Understanding of How People Change.* Grand Rapids: Baker Academic, 2008.

Highfield, Ron. "Theological Anthropology in the Restoration Movement." *Leaven* 8 (2000) 139–43.

Hirsch, Alan, and Lance Ford. *Right Here, Right Now: Everyday Mission for Everyday People.* Grand Rapids: Baker, 2011.

Hoekendijk, J. C. "The Church in Missionary Thinking." *IRM* 41.163 (1952) 324–36.

———. *The Church Inside Out.* Edited by L. A. Hoedemaker and Pieter Tijmes. Translated by Isaac C. Rottenberg. Philadelphia: Westminster, 1966.

Holstein, James A., and Jaber F. Gubrium, eds. *Varieties of Narrative Analysis.* Los Angeles: Sage, 2011.

Horton, Michael S. *Covenant and Salvation: Union with Christ.* Louisville: Westminster John Knox, 2007.

Hoy, David Couzens. "Heidegger and the Hermeneutic Turn." In *The Cambridge Companion to Heidegger*, edited by Charles B. Guignon, 177–201. 2nd ed. New York: Cambridge University Press, 2006.

Hunsberger, George R. *Bearing the Witness of the Spirit: Lesslie Newbigin's Theology of Cultural Plurality.* GOCS. Grand Rapids: Eerdmans, 1998.

———. "Mapping the Missional Hermeneutics Conversation." In *Reading the Bible Missionally*, edited by Michael W. Goheen, 45-67. Grand Rapids: Eerdmans, 2016.

———. "The Newbigin Gauntlet: Developing a Domestic Missiology for North America." In *The Church Between Gospel and Culture: The Emerging Mission in North America*, edited by George R. Hunsberger and Craig Van Gelder, 3-25. Grand Rapids: Eerdmans, 1996.

———. "Proposals for a Missional Hermeneutic: Mapping a Conversation." *Miss* 39 (2011) 309-21.

Husbands, Mark. "The Trinity Is Not Our Social Program: Volf, Gregory of Nyssa, and Barth." In *Trinitarian Theology for the Church: Scripture, Community, and Worship*, edited by Daniel J. Treier and David Lauber, 120-41. Downers Grove, IL: InterVarsity, 2009.

Isasi-Díaz, Ada María. *Mujerista Theology: A Theology for the Twenty-First Century*. Maryknoll, NY: Orbis, 1996.

———. "Solidarity." *DFT* 266-67.

Isherwood, Lisa. "The Embodiment of Feminist Liberation Theology: The Spiralling of Incarnation." *FemTh* 12 (2004) 140-56.

Jenson, Robert W. *Canon and Creed*. Interpretation: Resources for the Use of Scripture in the Church. Louisville: Westminster John Knox, 2010.

———. "Hermeneutics and the Life of the Church." In *Reclaiming the Bible for the Church*, edited by Carl E. Braaten and Robert W. Jenson, 89-105. Grand Rapids: Eerdmans, 1995.

———. *Systematic Theology*. Vol. 2, *The Works of God*. New York: Oxford University Press, 1999.

Jiménez Limón, Javier. "Suffering, Death, Cross, and Martyrdom." In *Mysterium Liberationis: Fundamental Concepts of Liberation Theology*, edited by Ignacio Ellacuría and Jon Sobrino, 702-27. Maryknoll, NY: Orbis, 1993.

John Paul II. *Sollicitudo Rei Socialis*. Encyclical Letter. London: Catholic Truth Society, 1988.

Johnson, Adam J. *Atonement: A Guide for the Perplexed*. Guides for the Perplexed. New York: Bloomsbury T&T Clark, 2015.

Johnson, Keith L. "A Reappraisal of Karl Barth's Theological Development and His Dialogue with Catholicism." *IJST* 14 (2012) 3-25.

Johnson, Mark, and George Lakoff. "Why Cognitive Linguistics Requires Embodied Realism." *Cognitive Linguistics* 13 (2002) 245-64.

Johnson, William Stacy. "Reading the Scriptures Faithfully in a Postmodern Age." In *The Art of Reading Scripture*, edited by Ellen F. Davis and Richard B. Hays, 110-16. Grand Rapids: Eerdmans, 2003.

Jones, L. Gregory. "Embodying Scripture in the Community of Faith." In *The Art of Reading Scripture*, edited by Ellen F. Davis and Richard B. Hays, 143-160. Grand Rapids: Eerdmans, 2003.

———. "Formed and Transformed by Scripture: Character, Community, and Authority in Biblical Interpretation." In *Character and Scripture: Moral Formation, Community, and Biblical Interpretation*, edited by William P. Brown, 34-52. Grand Rapids: Eerdmans, 2002.

Kähler, Martin. *Schriften zur Christologie und Mission: Gesamtausgabe der Schriften zur Mission*. Theologische Bücherei 42. Munich: Chr. Kaiser Verlag, 1971.

BIBLIOGRAPHY

Kärkkäinen, Veli-Matti. *A Constructive Christian Theology for the Pluralistic World*. Vol. 3, *Creation and Humanity*. Grand Rapids: Eerdmans, 2015.

———. *A Constructive Christian Theology for the Pluralistic World*. Vol. 4, *Spirit and Salvation*. Grand Rapids: Eerdmans, 2016.

———. *One with God: Salvation as Deification and Justification*. Unitas Books. Collegeville, MN: Liturgical, 2004.

Kearney, Richard, ed. *Debates in Continental Philosophy: Conversations with Contemporary Thinkers*. PCP. New York: Fordham University Press, 2004.

———. "The Wager of Carnal Hermeneutics." In *Carnal Hermeneutics*, edited by Richard Kearney and Brian Treanor, 15–54, 317–29. PCP. New York: Fordham University Press, 2015.

———. "What Is Carnal Hermeneutics?" *New Literary History* 46 (2015) 99–124.

Keating, Daniel A. "Typologies of Deification: Typologies of Deification." *IJST* 17 (2015) 267–83.

Kelly, Conor M. "Everyday Solidarity: A Framework for Integrating Theological Ethics and Ordinary Life." *TS* 81 (2020) 414–37.

Kelsey, David H. *Eccentric Existence: A Theological Anthropology*. 2 vols. Louisville: Westminster John Knox, 2009.

Kharlamov, Vladimir. "Rhetorical Application of *Theosis* in Greek Patristic Theology." In *Partakers of the Divine Nature: The History and Development of Deification in the Christian Traditions*, edited by Michael J. Christensen and Jeffery A. Wittung, 115–31. Grand Rapids: Baker Academic, 2007.

———, ed. *Theōsis: Deification in Christian Theology*. Vol. 2. Princeton Theological Monograph Series. Eugene, OR: Pickwick, 2011.

Kilby, Karen. "The Trinity and Politics: An Apophatic Approach." In *Advancing Trinitarian Theology: Explorations in Constructive Dogmatics*, edited by Oliver D. Crisp and Fred Sanders, 75–94. Grand Rapids: Zondervan, 2014.

Kim, Kirsteen. *The Holy Spirit in the World*. Maryknoll, NY: Orbis, 2007.

———. *Joining in with the Spirit: Connecting the World Church and Local Mission*. London: SCM, 2012.

———. "Mission in Feminist Perspective." *Dharma Deepika* 5 (2001) 17–26.

Kirylo, James D., and Drick Boyd. *Paulo Freire: His Faith, Spirituality and Theology*. Boston: Sense, 2017.

Kline, Peter. "Participation in God and the Nature of Christian Community: Robert Jenson and Eberhard Jüngel." *IJST* 13 (2011) 38–61.

Kohák, Erazim V. "Translator's Introduction: The Philosophy of Paul Ricoeur." In *Freedom and Nature: The Voluntary and the Involuntary*, translated by Erazim V. Kohák, xi–xxxviii. NUSPEP. Evanston, IL: Northwestern University Press, 2007.

LaCugna, Catherine Mowry. *God for Us: The Trinity and Christian Life*. New York: HarperCollins, 1991.

Lang'at, Robert K. "Trinity and Missions." In *Trinitarian Theology for the Church: Scripture, Community, and Worship*, edited by Daniel J. Treier and David Lauber, 161–81. Downers Grove, IL: InterVarsity, 2009.

Lausanne Movement. "The Cape Town Commitment." https://www.lausanne.org/content/ctc/ctcommitment.

———. "The Lausanne Covenant." https://www.lausanne.org/content/covenant/lausanne-covenant.

Lawler, Michael G. "*Perichoresis*: New Theological Wine in an Old Theological Wineskin." *Horizons* 22 (1995) 49–66.

Leithart, Peter J. *Defending Constantine: The Twilight of an Empire and the Dawn of Christendom*. Downers Grove, IL: InterVarsity, 2010.

———. *Delivered from the Elements of the World: Atonement, Justification, Mission*. Downers Grove, IL: InterVarsity, 2016.

———. "Sacramental Mission: Ecumenical and Political Missiology." In *Four Views on the Church's Mission*, edited by Jason S. Sexton, 152–76. Counterpoints: Bible and Theology. Grand Rapids: Zondervan, 2017.

Letham, Robert. *Union with Christ: In Scripture, History, and Theology*. Phillipsburg, NJ: P&R, 2011.

Lett, Jonathan. "Narrative and Metaphysical Ambition: On Being 'in Christ.'" *MoTh* 33 (2017) 618–39.

Levenson, Jon D. *The Hebrew Bible, the Old Testament, and Historical Criticism: Jews and Christians in Biblical Studies*. Louisville: Westminster John Knox, 1993.

Lindbeck, George A. *The Nature of Doctrine: Religion and Theology in a Postliberal Age*. Louisville: Westminster John Knox, 1984.

Longkumer, Atola. "Not Without Women: Mission in the Third Millennium." *IRM* 100 (2011) 297–309.

Louw, D. J. "Beyond 'Gayism'? Towards a Theology of Sensual, Erotic Embodiment Within an Eschatological Approach to Human Sexuality." *JTSA* 132 (2008) 108–24.

Love, Mark. "Practices as Participation in the Life of God." *MDJ* 7 (2016). http://missiodeijournal.com/issues/md-7/authors/md-7-love.

Macaskill, Grant. *Living in Union with Christ: Paul's Gospel and Christian Moral Identity*. Grand Rapids: Baker Academic, 2019.

———. *Union with Christ in the New Testament*. Oxford: Oxford University Press, 2013.

MacIntyre, Alasdair. *After Virtue*. 3rd ed. Notre Dame: University of Notre Dame Press, 2007.

MacIntyre, Alasdair, and Paul Ricoeur. *The Religious Significance of Atheism*. New York: Columbia University Press, 1969.

Mackenzie, Catriona. "Embodied Agents, Narratives Selves." *Philosophical Explorations* 17 (2014) 154–71.

Mainwaring, Simon James. "Mutuality as a Postcolonial Praxis for Mission." *Ecclesiology* 10 (2014) 13–31.

Maluleke, Tinyiko Sam. "Postcolonial Mission: Oxymoron or New Paradigm?" *Svensk Missionstidskrift* 95 (2007) 503–27.

Mar, Raymond A. "The Neuropsychology of Narrative: Story Comprehension, Story Production and Their Interrelation." *Neuropsychologia* 42.10 (2004) 1414–34.

Marshall, Bruce D. "Absorbing the World: Christianity and the Universe of Truths." In *Theology and Dialogue: Essays in Conversation with George Lindbeck*, edited by Bruce D. Marshall, 69–102. Notre Dame: University of Notre Dame Press, 1990.

———. "Justification as Declaration and Deification." *IJST* 4 (2002) 3–28.

Maruggi, Matthew. "Disorienting Solidarity: Engaging Difference and Developing 'Fluidarity.'" *Journal of Interreligious Studies* 31 (2020) 37–47.

Matthey, Jacques, ed. "*Missio Dei* Today." *IRM* 92.367 (2003).

Maximos Confessor. *St. Maximos the Confessor on the Difficulties in Sacred Scripture: The Responses to Thalassios*. Translated by Maximos Constas. The Fathers of the Church. Washington, DC: The Catholic University of America Press, 2018.

Maynes, Mary Jo, Jennifer L. Pierce, and Barbara Laslett. *Telling Stories: The Use of Personal Narratives in the Social Sciences and History*. Ithaca, NY: Cornell University Press, 2008.
McClendon, James Wm., Jr. *Systematic Theology*. Vol. 1, *Ethics*. Rev. ed. Nashville: Abingdon, 2002.
———. *Systematic Theology*. Vol. 3, *Witness*. Nashville: Abingdon, 2000.
McCullough, Ross. "A Hermeneutic of Hope—and Faith and Love." *JTI* 12 (2018) 264–73.
McFague, Sallie. *Models of God: Theology for an Ecological, Nuclear Age*. Philadelphia: Fortress, 1987.
McGavran, Donald, ed. *The Conciliar-Evangelical Debate: The Crucial Documents, 1964–1976*. Pasadena, CA: William Carey Library, 1977.
McGuckin, J. A. "The Strategic Adaptation of Deification in the Cappadocians." In *Partakers of the Divine Nature: The History and Development of Deification in the Christian Traditions*, edited by Michael J. Christensen and Jeffery A. Wittung, 95–114. Grand Rapids: Baker Academic, 2007.
McKinzie, Greg. "Currents in Missional Hermeneutics." *MDJ* 5 (2014). http://missiodeijournal.com/issues/md-5-1/authors/md-5-1-mckinzie.
———. "Missional Hermeneutics as Theological Interpretation." *JTI* 11 (2017) 157–79.
———. "Perspectives on the Missio Ecclesiae: A Review Essay." *MDJ* 9 (2018). http://missiodeijournal.com/issues/md-9-2/authors/md-9-2-mckinzie.
McKinzie, Greg, et al. "Between Service and Scripture: A Qualitative Study of Missional Hermeneutics." *JTI* 15 (2021) 133–56.
McKnight, Scot. *A Community Called Atonement*. Living Theology. Nashville: Abingdon, 2007.
McLaren, Peter, and Petar Jandrić. "Paulo Freire and Liberation Theology: The Christian Consciousness of Critical Pedagogy." *Vierteljahrsschrift für wissenschaftliche Pädagogik* 94 (2018) 246–64.
McNeil, Lydia D. "Homo Inventans: The Evolution of Narrativity." *Language and Communication* 16 (1996) 331–60.
Medley, Mark S. "Participation in God: The Appropriation of Theosis by Contemporary Baptist Theologians." In *Theōsis: Deification in Christian Theology*, edited by Vladimir Kharlamov, 2:205–46. Princeton Theological Monograph Series. Eugene, OR: Pickwick, 2011.
Menary, Richard. "Embodied Narratives." *Journal of Consciousness Studies* 15 (2008) 63–84.
Merleau-Ponty, Maurice. *Phenomenology of Perception*. Translated by Donald A. Landes. New York: Routledge, 2012.
———. *The Visible and the Invisible: Followed by Working Notes*. Edited by Claude Lefort. Translated by Alphonso Lingis. NUSPEP. Evanston, IL: Northwestern University Press, 1968.
Mescher, Marcus. *The Ethics of Encounter: Christian Neighbor Love as a Practice of Solidarity*. Maryknoll, NY: Orbis, 2020.
Míguez Bonino, José. *Doing Theology in a Revolutionary Situation*. Philadelphia: Fortress, 1975.
———. *Toward a Christian Political Ethics*. Philadelphia: Fortress, 1983.
Milbank, John. *Being Reconciled: Ontology and Pardon, Radical Orthodoxy*. New York: Routledge, 2003.

Min, Anselm Kyongsuk. "Dialectical Pluralism and Solidarity of Others: Towards a New Paradigm." *JAAR* 65 (1997) 587–604.

———. *The Solidarity of Others in a Divided World: Postmodern Theology After Postmodernism.* New York: T&T Clark, 2004.

Mjaaland, Marius Timmann, et al. "Introduction." In *The Body Unbound: Philosophical Perspectives on Politics, Embodiment and Religion*, edited by Marius Timmann Mjaaland et al., 1–18. Newcastle-upon-Tyne: Cambridge Scholars, 2010.

Moberly, R. W. L. "'Interpret the Bible Like Any Other Book'? Requiem for an Axiom." *JTI* 4 (2010) 91–110.

Moltmann, Jürgen. *The Church in the Power of the Spirit: A Contribution to Messianic Ecclesiology.* Translated by Margaret Kohl. Minneapolis: Fortress, 1993.

———. *Experiences in Theology: Ways and Forms of Christian Theology.* Translated by Margaret Kohl. Minneapolis: Fortress, 2000.

———. *God in Creation: A New Theology of Creation and the Spirit of God.* Translated by Margaret Kohl. Minneapolis: Fortress, 1993.

———. "On Latin American Liberation Theology: An Open Letter to José Míguez Bonino." *Christianity and Crisis* 36 (1976) 57–63.

———. *The Trinity and the Kingdom: The Doctrine of God.* Translated by Margaret Kohl. Minneapolis: Fortress, 1993.

Moltmann-Wendel, Elisabeth. *I Am My Body: A Theology of Embodiment.* New York: Continuum, 1995.

Montero, Paula. "The Contribution of Post-Colonial Critique to an Anthropology of Missions." *RelSoc* 3 (2012) 115–29.

Moreau, A. Scott. *Contextualization in World Missions: Mapping and Assessing Evangelical Models.* Grand Rapids: Kregel Academic, 2012.

Myers, Benjamin. "The Patristic Model of the Atonement." In *Locating the Atonement: Explorations in Constructive Dogmatics*, edited by Oliver D. Crisp and Fred Sanders, 71–88. Grand Rapids: Zondervan, 2015.

Nelson, James B. *Body Theology.* Louisville: Westminster/John Knox, 1992.

———. *Embodiment: An Approach to Sexuality and Christian Theology.* Minneapolis: Augsburg, 1978.

Newbigin, Lesslie. *Foolishness to the Greeks: The Gospel and Western Culture.* Grand Rapids: Eerdmans, 1986.

———. *The Gospel in a Pluralist Society.* Grand Rapids: Eerdmans, 1989.

———. *The Household of God: Lectures on the Nature of the Church.* Eugene, OR: Wipf & Stock, 2008.

———. *The Open Secret: An Introduction to the Theology of Mission.* Rev. ed. Grand Rapids: Eerdmans, 1995.

———. *Trinitarian Doctrine for Today's Mission.* Eugene, OR: Wipf & Stock, 2006.

Noé, Keiichi. "'The Hermeneutic Turn' in Husserl's Phenomenology of Language." *Human Studies* 15 (1992) 117–28.

Norris, F. W. "Deification: Consensual and Cogent." *SJT* 49 (1996) 411–28.

Oduyoye, Mercy Amba. "The Church of the Future, Its Mission and Theology: A View from Africa." *ThTo* 52 (1996) 494–505.

Oh, Peter S. "Complementary Dialectics of Kierkegaard and Barth: Barth's Use of Kierkegaardian Diastasis Reassessed." *Neue Zeitschrift für Systematische Theologie und Religionsphilosophie* 48 (2007) 497–512.

BIBLIOGRAPHY

O'Keefe, John J., and R. R. Reno. *Sanctified Vision: An Introduction to Early Christian Interpretation of the Bible*. Baltimore: Johns Hopkins University Press, 2005.

Olson, Roger E. "Deification in Contemporary Theology." *ThTo* 64 (2007) 186–200.

Otto, Randall E. "The Use and Abuse of Perichoresis in Recent Theology." *SJT* 54 (2001) 366–84.

Owens, L. Roger. *The Shape of Participation: A Theology of Church Practices*. Eugene, OR: Cascade, 2010.

Padilla, C. René. "The Globalization of Solidarity." *Journal of Latin American Theology* 9 (2014) 69–90.

Pannenberg, Wolfhart. *Systematic Theology*. Vol. 2. Translated by Geoffrey W. Bromiley. Grand Rapids: Eerdmans, 1994.

Pardue, Stephen T. "Athens and Jerusalem Once More: What the Turn to Virtue Means for Theological Exegesis." *JTI* 4 (2010) 294–308.

Parsons, Susan. "Feminist Reflections on Embodiment and Sexuality." *Studies in Christian Ethics* 4 (1991) 16–28.

Paul VI. *Gaudium et spes*. http://www.vatican.va/archive/hist_councils/ii_vatican_council/documents/vat-ii_const_19651207_gaudium-et-spes_en.html.

———. *Populorum progressio*. http://www.vatican.va/content/paul-vi/en/encyclicals/documents/hf_p-vi_enc_26031967_populorum.html.

Peacore, Linda D. *The Role of Women's Experience in Feminist Theologies of Atonement*. Princeton Theological Monograph Series. Eugene, OR: Pickwick, 2010.

Peckham, John C. "The Rationale for Canonical Theology: An Approach to Systematic Theology After Modernism." *AUSS* 55 (2017) 83–105.

Pellauer, David. "Embodiment and Philosophical-Theological Reflection." *Di* 27 (1988) 174–77.

Perriman, Andrew. "The Pattern of Christ's Sufferings: Colossians 1:24 and Philippians 3:10–11." *TynBul* 42 (1991) 62–79.

Peters, Rebecca Todd. "Reflections on a Theology of Solidarity." *Ecumenical Review* 67 (2015) 222–33.

———. *Solidarity Ethics: Transformation in a Globalized World*. Minneapolis: Fortress, 2014.

Petrella, Ivan. *Beyond Liberation Theology: A Polemic*. Reclaiming Liberation Theology. London: SCM, 2008.

Pickstock, Catherine. "The One Story: A Critique of David Kelsey's Theological Robotics." *MoTh* 27 (2010) 26–40.

Pidel, Aaron. "Ricoeur and Ratzinger on Biblical History and Hermeneutics." *JTI* 8 (2014) 193–212.

Pinn, Anthony B. *Embodiment and the New Shape of Black Theological Thought*. New York: New York University Press, 2010.

Placher, William C. "Paul Ricoeur and Postliberal Theology: A Conflict of Interpretations?" *MoTh* 4 (1987) 35–52.

Pohl, Christine D. *Making Room: Recovering Hospitality as a Christian Tradition*. Grand Rapids: Eerdmans, 1999.

Polkinghorne, Donald E. *Narrative Knowing and the Human Sciences*. Albany: State University of New York, 1988.

Popova, Yanna B. "Narrativity and Enaction: The Social Nature of Literary Narrative Understanding." *Frontiers in Psychology* 5 (2014) 1–14.

Porpora, Douglas V. "Methodological Atheism, Methodological Agnosticism, and Religious Experience." *Journal for the Theory of Social Behavior* 36 (2006) 57–75.

Porter, Stanley E. "Biblical Hermeneutics and Theological Responsibility." In *The Future of Biblical Interpretation: Responsible Plurality in Biblical Hermeneutics*, edited by Stanley E. Porter and Matthew R. Malcolm, 29–69. Downers Grove, IL: IVP Academic, 2013.

———. "What Exactly Is Theological Interpretation of Scripture, and Is It Hermeneutically Robust Enough for the Task to Which It Has Been Appointed?" In *Horizons in Hermeneutics: A Festschrift in Honor of Anthony C. Thiselton*, edited by Stanley E. Porter and Matthew R. Malcolm, 234–67. Grand Rapids: Eerdmans, 2013.

Prokes, Mary Timothy. *Toward a Theology of the Body*. Grand Rapids: Eerdmans, 1996.

Proudfoot, C. M. "Imitation or Realistic Participation? A Study of Paul's Concept of 'Suffering with Christ.'" *Int* 17 (1963) 140–60.

Pui-lan, Kwok. "The Image of the 'White Lady': Gender and Race in Christian Mission." In *The Power of Naming: A Concilium Reader in Feminist Liberation Theology*, edited by Elisabeth Schüssler-Fiorenza, 250–58. Concilium Series. Maryknoll, NY: Orbis, 1996.

———. "Mission." *DFT* 186.

Rae, Murray A. *History and Hermeneutics*. New York: T&T Clark, 2005.

———. "Theological Interpretation and the Problem of Method." In *Ears That Hear: Explorations in Theological Interpretation of the Bible*, edited by Joel B. Green and Tim Meadowcroft, 11–25. Sheffield: Sheffield Phoenix, 2013.

Rahner, Karl. *The Trinity*. New York: Herder and Herder, 1970.

Rajendra, Tisha M. "Burdened Solidarity: The Virtue of Solidarity in Diaspora." *Journal of the Society of Christian Ethics* 39 (2019) 93–109.

Reichard, Joshua David. "Mutually Transformative Missions: A Postcolonial, Process-Relational Pentecostal Missiology." *Miss* 43 (2015) 245–57.

Reumann, John. "Colossians 1:24 ('What Is Lacking in the Afflictions of Christ'): History of Exegesis and Ecumenical Advance." *CurTM* 17 (1990) 454–61.

Reynolds, Thomas E. *The Broken Whole: Philosophical Steps Toward a Theology of Global Solidarity*. Albany: State University of New York Press, 2006.

Ricoeur, Paul. *The Conflict of Interpretations: Essays in Hermeneutics*. Edited by Don Ihde. NUSPEP. Evanston, IL: Northwestern University Press, 1974.

———. "Existence and Hermeneutics." In *The Conflict of Interpretations: Essays in Hermeneutics*, edited by Don Ihde, 3–24. NUSPEP. Evanston, IL: Northwestern University Press, 1974.

———. *Figuring the Sacred: Religion, Narrative, and Imagination*. Translated by David Pellauer. Edited by Mark I. Wallace. Minneapolis: Fortress, 1995.

———. *Freedom and Nature: The Voluntary and the Involuntary*. Translated by Erazim V. Kohák. NUSPEP. Evanston, IL: Northwestern University Press, 2007.

———. "The Hermeneutical Function of Distanciation." In *From Text to Action: Essays in Hermeneutics II*, translated by Kathleen Blamey and John B. Thompson, 144–67. NUSPEP. Evanston, IL: Northwestern University Press, 2007.

———. "Metaphor and the Central Problem of Hermeneutics." In *Hermeneutics and the Human Sciences*, edited and translated by John B. Thompson, 165–81. Cambridge: Cambridge University Press, 1981.

———. "The Model of the Text: Meaningful Action Considered as a Text." In *From Text to Action: Essays in Hermeneutics II*, translated by Kathleen Blamey and John B. Thompson, 144–67. NUSPEP. Evanston, IL: Northwestern University Press, 2007.

———. *Oneself as Another*. Translated by Kathleen Blamey. Chicago: University of Chicago Press, 1992.

———. "On Interpretation." In *From Text to Action: Essays in Hermeneutics II*, translated by Kathleen Blamey and John B. Thompson, 1–20. NUSPEP. Evanston, IL: Northwestern University Press, 2007.

———. "Philosophical Hermeneutics and Theological Hermeneutics." *Studies in Religion* 5 (1975) 14–33.

———. *The Symbolism of Evil*. Translated by Emerson Buchanan. Religious Perspectives 17. New York: Harper & Row, 1967.

———. "The Task of Hermeneutics." In *From Text to Action: Essays in Hermeneutics II*, translated by Kathleen Blamey and John B. Thompson, 53–74. NUSPEP. Evanston, IL: Northwestern University Press, 2007.

———. *Time and Narrative*. Vol. 1. Translated by Kathleen McLaughlin and David Pellauer. Chicago: University of Chicago Press, 1984.

———. *Time and Narrative*. Vol. 3. Translated by Kathleen Blamey and David Pellauer. Chicago: University of Chicago Press, 1988.

———. "Toward a Hermeneutic of the Idea of Revelation." *HTR* 70.1–2 (1977) 1–37.

———. "What Is a Text: Explanation and Understanding." In *From Text to Action: Essays in Hermeneutics II*, translated by Kathleen Blamey and John B. Thompson, 105–24. NUSPEP. Evanston, IL: Northwestern University Press, 2007.

Riessman, Catherine Kohler. *Narrative Methods for the Human Sciences*. Los Angeles: Sage, 2008.

Risser, James. "After the Hermeneutic Turn." *Research in Phenomenology* 30 (2000) 71–88.

Robert, Dana L. "Forty Years of the American Society of Missiology: Retrospect and Prospect." *Miss* 42 (2013) 6–25.

Rodrigues, Adriani Milli. "The Rule of Faith and Biblical Interpretation in Evangelical Theological Interpretation of Scripture." *Them* 43 (2018) 257–70.

Rogers, Andrew P. *Congregational Hermeneutics: How Do We Read? Explorations in Practical, Pastoral, and Empirical Theology*. New York: Routledge, 2015.

Rommen, Edward. "A Sacramental Vision Approach." In *The Mission of the Church: Five Views in Conversation*, edited by Craig Ott, 69–90. Grand Rapids: Baker Academic, 2016.

Rorty, Richard. *Contingency, Irony, and Solidarity*. New York: Cambridge University Press, 1989.

Rosin, H. H. *"Missio Dei": An Examination of the Origin, Contents and Function of the Term in Protestant Missiological Discussion*. Leiden: Interuniversity Institute for Missiological and Ecumenical Research, 1972.

Roxburgh, Alan J. *Missional Map-Making: Skills for Leading in Times of Transition*. San Francisco: Jossey-Bass, 2010.

Rudd, Anthony. "In Defence of Narrative." *European Journal of Philosophy* 17 (2007) 60–75.

Ruether, Rosemary Radford. *Sexism and God-Talk: Toward a Feminist Theology*. 2nd ed. Boston: Beacon, 1983.

Russell, Brian D. *(re)Aligning with God: Reading Scripture for Church and World*. Eugene, OR: Cascade, 2016.

Russell, Letty M. "Cultural Hermeneutics: A Postcolonial Look at Mission." *JFSR* 20 (2004) 23–40.

———. "God, Gold, Glory, and Gender: A Postcolonial View of Mission." *IRM* 93.368 (2004) 39–49.

BIBLIOGRAPHY

Russell, Norman. *The Doctrine of Deification in the Greek Patristic Tradition.* Oxford Early Christian Studies. New York: Oxford University Press, 2004.

Sanders, Fred. "Entangled in the Trinity: Economic and Immanent Trinity in Recent Theology." *Di* 40 (2001) 175–82.

Sanders, John. *Theology in the Flesh: How Embodiment and Culture Shape the Way We Think About Truth, Morality, and God.* Minneapolis: Fortress, 2016.

Santiago-Vendrell, Angel. "Not by Words Alone! Mujerista and Pentecostal Missiologies of Liberation from the Latina/o Margins." *JPT* 18 (2009) 285–300.

Sarisky, Darren. *Reading the Bible Theologically.* CIT. New York: Cambridge University Press, 2019.

Scalise, Brian T. "Perichoresis in Gregory Nazianzen and Maximus the Confessor." *Eleutheria* 2 (2012) 58–76.

Schaff, Philip, and Henry Wace, eds. *Nicene and Post-Nicene Fathers.* 2nd series. Vol. 2, *Cyril of Jerusalem, Gregory Nazianzen.* Peabody, MA: Hendrickson, 1994.

———. *Nicene and Post-Nicene Fathers.* 2nd series. Vol. 4, *Athanasius: Select Works and Letters.* Peabody, MA: Hendrickson, 1994.

Schaff, Philip, et al., eds. *Ante-Nicene Fathers.* Vol. 1, *Apostolic Fathers with Justin Martyr and Irenaeus.* Peabody, MA: Hendrickson, 1994.

Scherer, James A. *Gospel, Church, and Kingdom: Comparative Studies in World Mission Theology.* Minneapolis: Augsburg, 1987.

Schwarz, Gerold. "The Legacy of Karl Hartenstein." *IBMR* 8 (1984) 125–31.

The Scripture Project. "Nine Theses on the Interpretation of Scripture." In *The Art of Reading Scripture*, edited by Ellen F. Davis and Richard B. Hays, 1–5. Grand Rapids: Eerdmans, 2003.

Segundo, Juan Luis. *Liberation of Theology.* Translated by John Drury. Maryknoll, NY: Orbis, 1976.

Seitz, Christopher R. *The Character of Christian Scripture: The Significance of a Two-Testament Bible.* STI. Grand Rapids: Baker Academic, 2011.

Sexton, Jason S. "A Confessing Trinitarian Theology for Today's Mission." In *Advancing Trinitarian Theology: Explorations in Constructive Dogmatics*, edited by Oliver D. Crisp and Fred Sanders, 171–89. Grand Rapids: Zondervan, 2014.

Sigurdson, Ola. *Heavenly Bodies: Incarnation, the Gaze, and Embodiment in Christian Theology.* Grand Rapids: Eerdmans, 2016.

———. "How to Speak of the Body? Embodiment Between Phenomenology and Theology." *ST* 62 (2008) 25–43.

Smith, James K. A. *Imagining the Kingdom: How Worship Works.* Cultural Liturgies 2. Grand Rapids: Baker Academic, 2013.

———. "Will the Real Plato Please Stand Up?" In *Radical Orthodoxy and the Reformed Tradition: Creation, Covenant, and Participation*, edited by James K. A. Smith and James H. Olthius, 61–72. Grand Rapids: Baker Academic, 2005.

Smith, James K. A., and James H. Olthius, eds. *Radical Orthodoxy and the Reformed Tradition: Creation, Covenant, and Participation.* Grand Rapids: Baker Academic, 2005.

Sobrino, Jon. "Bearing with One Another in Faith." In *Theology of Christian Solidarity*, translated by Philip Berryman, 1–41. Maryknoll, NY: Orbis, 1985.

———. *Jesus the Liberator: A Historical-Theological Reading of Jesus of Nazareth.* Translated by Paul Burns and Francis McDonagh. Maryknoll, NY: Orbis, 1993.

BIBLIOGRAPHY

———. *Spirituality of Liberation: Toward Political Holiness*. Translated by Robert R. Barr. Maryknoll, NY: Orbis, 1988.

Spivey, Steven W. "Colossians 1:24 and the Suffering Church." *Journal of Spiritual Formation and Soul Care* 4 (2011) 43–62.

Stanglin, Keith D. "Arminius Reconsidered: Thoughts on Arminius and Contemporary Theological Discourse for the Church Today." In *Reconsidering Arminius: Beyond the Reformed and Wesleyan Divide*, edited by Keith D. Stanglin et al., 161–68. Nashville: Kingswood, 2014.

"A Statement on the Missionary Calling of the Church." In *Missions Under the Cross: Addresses Delivered at the Enlarged Meeting of the Committee of the International Missionary Council at Willingen, in Germany, 1952; with Statements Issued by the Meeting*, edited by Norman Goodall, 188–92. New York: Friendship, 1953.

Stetzer, Ed. "An Evangelical Kingdom Community Approach." In *The Mission of the Church: Five Views in Conversation*, edited by Craig Ott, 91–116. Grand Rapids: Baker Academic, 2016.

Stiver, Dan R. *Ricoeur and Theology*. Philosophy and Theology. New York: Bloomsbury T&T Clark, 2012.

———. *Theology After Ricoeur: New Direction in Hermeneutical Theology*. Louisville: Westminster John Knox, 2001.

Stott, John, and Christopher J. H. Wright. *Christian Mission in the Modern World*. Updated and exp. ed. Downers Grove, IL: InterVarsity, 2015.

Stramara, Daniel F., Jr. "Gregory of Nyssa's Terminology for Trinitarian Perichoresis." *VC* 52 (1998) 257–63.

Strawson, Galen. "Against Narrativity." *Ratio* 17 (2004) 428–52.

Sumney, Jerry L. "'I Fill Up What Is Lacking in the Afflictions of Christ': Paul's Vicarious Suffering in Colossians." *CBQ* 68 (2008) 664–80.

Swanson, David W. *Rediscipling the White Church: From Cheap Diversity to True Solidarity*. Downers Grove, IL: IVP Academic, 2020.

Swart, Jannie, et al. "Toward a Missional Theology of Participation: Ecumenical Reflections on Contributions to Trinity, Mission, and Church." *Miss* 37 (2009) 75–87.

Tanner, Kathryn. *Christ the Key*. CIT. Cambridge: Cambridge University Press, 2010.

———. "Trinity." In *The Blackwell Companion to Political Theology*, edited by Peter Scott and William T. Cavanaugh, 319–32. 2nd ed. Hoboken, NJ: John Wiley & Sons, 2019.

Taylor, Charles. *A Secular Age*. Cambridge: Belknap, 2007.

———. *Sources of the Self: The Making of the Modern Identity*. Cambridge: Harvard University Press, 1989.

Taylor, Derek W. *Reading Scripture as the Church: Dietrich Bonhoeffer's Hermeneutic of Discipleship*. Downers Grove, IL: InterVarsity, 2020.

Thiselton, Anthony C. *New Horizons in Hermeneutics: The Theory and Practice of Transforming Biblical Reading*. 20th anniversary ed. Grand Rapids: Zondervan, 2002.

Toffelmire, Colin M. "Scripture as Semiotic System: Theological Interpretation and the Multiple Senses of Scripture." *JTI* 5 (2011) 97–112.

Torrance, Alan J. *Persons in Communion: Trinitarian Description and Human Participation*. Edinburgh: T&T Clark, 1996.

Treier, Daniel J. *Introducing Theological Interpretation of Scripture*. Grand Rapids: Baker, 2008.

Turner, Léon. "Individuality in Theological Anthropology and Theories of Embodied Cognition." *Zygon* 48 (2013) 808–31.

Turner, Mark. *The Literary Mind: The Origins of Thought and Language*. New York: Oxford University Press, 1996.

Vähäkangas, Auli. "African Feminist Contributions to Missiological Anthropology." *Mission Studies* 28 (2011) 170–85.

Van Dyk, Leanne. "The Church's Proclamation as a Participation in God's Mission." In *Trinitarian Theology for the Church: Scripture, Community, and Worship*, edited by Daniel J. Treier and David Lauber, 225–36. Downers Grove, IL: InterVarsity, 2009.

Van Gelder, Craig. *The Ministry of the Missional Church: A Community Led by the Spirit*. Grand Rapids: Baker, 2007.

Van Gelder, Craig, and Dwight J. Zscheile. *The Missional Church in Perspective: Mapping Trends and Shaping the Conversation*. The Missional Network. Grand Rapids: Baker Academic, 2011.

———. *Participating in God's Mission: A Theological Missiology for the Church in America*. GOCS. Grand Rapids: Eerdmans, 2018.

Vanhoozer, Kevin J. *Biblical Narrative in the Philosophy of Paul Ricoeur: A Study in Hermeneutics and Theology*. New York: Cambridge University Press, 1990.

———. *The Drama of Doctrine: A Canonical Linguistic Approach to Christian Theology*. Louisville: Westminster John Knox, 2005.

———. "Introduction: What Is Theological Interpretation of the Bible?" *DTIB* 19–25.

———. *Is There a Meaning in This Text? The Bible, the Reader, and the Morality of Literary Knowledge*. Grand Rapids: Zondervan, 1998.

Vishnevskaya, Elena. "Divinization as Perichoretic Embrace in Maximus the Confessor." In *Partakers of the Divine Nature: The History and Development of Deification in the Christian Traditions*, edited by Michael J. Christensen and Jeffery A. Wittung, 132–45. Grand Rapids: Baker Academic, 2007.

Volf, Miroslav. *Exclusion and Embrace: A Theological Exploration of Identity, Otherness, and Reconciliation*. Nashville: Abingdon, 1996.

———. "'The Trinity Is Our Social Program': The Doctrine of the Trinity and the Shape of Social Engagement." *MoTh* 14 (1998) 403–23.

Wall, Robert W. "Reading the Bible from Within Our Traditions: The 'Rule of Faith' in Theological Hermeneutics." In *Between Two Horizons: Spanning New Testament Studies and Systematic Theology*, edited by Joel B. Green and Max Turner, 88–107. Grand Rapids: Eerdmans, 2000.

Wallace, Mark I. *The Second Naiveté: Barth, Ricoeur, and the New Yale Theology*. 2nd ed. Studies in American Biblical Hermeneutics 6. Macon, GA: Mercer University Press, 1995.

Watson, Francis. *Text, Church, and World: Biblical Interpretation in Theological Perspective*. Grand Rapids: Eerdmans, 1994.

Webster, John. *Holy Scripture: A Dogmatic Sketch*. CIT. New York: Cambridge University Press, 2003.

Welch, Sharon D. *Communities of Resistance and Solidarity: A Feminist Theology of Liberation*. Maryknoll, NY: Orbis, 1985.

Welker, Michael. Introduction to *The Depth of the Human Person: A Multidisciplinary Approach*, edited by Michael Welker, 1–4. Grand Rapids: Eerdmans, 2014.

Welton, Donn, ed. *Body and Flesh: A Philosophical Reader*. Malden, MA: Blackwell, 1998.

Wen, Clement Yung. "Maximus the Confessor and the Problem of Participation." *Heythrop Journal* 58 (2017) 3–16.

West, Gerald O. "Being Partially Constituted by Work with Others: Biblical Scholars Becoming Different." *JTSA* 104 (1999) 44–53.

———. "Constructing Critical and Contextual Readings with Ordinary Readers." *JTSA* 92 (1995) 60–69.

———. "Locating 'Contextual Bible Study' Within Biblical Liberation Hermeneutics and Intercultural Biblical Hermeneutics." *HvTSt* 70 (2014). http://dx.doi.org/10.4102/hts.v70i1.2641.

Westphal, Merold. *Whose Community? Which Interpretation? Philosophical Hermeneutics for the Church*. The Church and Postmodern Culture. Grand Rapids: Baker Academic, 2009.

Wierciński, Andrzej. *Hermeneutics Between Philosophy and Theology: The Imperative to Think the Incommensurable*. International Studies in Hermeneutics and Phenomenology 1. Piscataway, NJ: Transaction, 2010.

Williams, D. Newell, et al., eds. *The Stone-Campbell Movement: A Global History*. St. Louis: Chalice, 2013.

Womack, Deanna Ferree. "Converting Mission: Interfaith Engagement as Christian Witness." In *Converting Witness: The Future of Christian Mission in the New Millennium*, edited by John G. Flett and David W. Congdon, 183–98. Lanham, MD: Lexington, 2019.

Wright, Christopher J. H. *The Mission of God: Unlocking the Bible's Grand Narrative*. Downers Grove, IL: InterVarsity, 2006.

———. "Participatory Mission: The Mission of God's People Revealed in the Whole Bible Story." In *Four Views on the Church's Mission*, edited by Jason S. Sexton, 63–91. Counterpoints: Bible and Theology. Grand Rapids: Zondervan, 2017.

Wright, N. T. *The New Testament and the People of God*. Christian Origins and the Question of God 1. London: SPCK, 1992.

———. *Surprised by Hope: Rethinking Heaven, the Resurrection, and the Mission of the Church*. New York: HarperCollins, 2008.

Wrogemann, Henning. *Intercultural Theology*. Vol. 2, *Theologies of Mission*. Translated by Karl E. Böhmer. Downers Grove, IL: IVP Academic, 2018.

Yancy, George. *Black Bodies, White Gazes: The Continuing Significance of Race in America*. 2nd ed. New York: Rowman & Littlefield, 2017.

———. "Whiteness and the Return of the Black Body." *Journal of Speculative Philosophy* 19 (2005) 215–41.

Yong, Amos. *Beyond the Impasse: Toward a Pneumatological Theology of Religions*. Eugene, OR: Wipf & Stock, 2003.

———. *Hospitality and the Other: Pentecost, Christian Practices, and the Neighbor*. Faith Meets Faith. Maryknoll, NY: Orbis, 2008.

———. *The Missiological Spirit: Christian Mission Theology in the Third Millennium Global Context*. Eugene, OR: Cascade, 2014.

Young, Harvey. *Embodying Black Experience: Stillness, Critical Memory, and the Black Body*. Theater: Theory/Text/Performance. Ann Arbor: University of Michigan Press, 2010.

Young, Kay, and Jeffrey L. Saver. "The Neurology of Narrative." *SubStance* 30.1–2 (2001) 72–84.

Zizioulas, John D. *Being as Communion: Studies in Personhood and the Church*. Crestwood, NY: St. Vladimir's Seminary Press, 1985.

www.ingramcontent.com/pod-product-compliance
Lightning Source LLC
Chambersburg PA
CBHW030822230426
43667CB00008B/1338